VOYAGE TO NORTH AMERICA 1844–45

PRINCE CARL OF SOLMS'S TEXAS DIARY OF PEOPLE, PLACES, AND EVENTS

With best regards,
Wolfram M. Von-Maszewski

Prince Carl of Solms-Braunfels
Courtesy Sophienburg Museum & Archives

Voyage to North America 1844–45

Prince Carl of Solms's Texas Diary of People, Places, and Events

Translation from German and Notes
by Wolfram M. Von-Maszewski

Introduction
by Theodore Gish

German-Texan Heritage Society
and
University of North Texas Press
Denton, Texas

Printed in the United States of America

5 4 3 2 1

Permissions:
University of North Texas Press
PO Box 311336
Denton TX 76203-1336

The paper used in this book meets the minimum requirements of the American National Standard for Permanence of Paper for Printed Library Materials, z39.48.1984. Binding materials have been chosen for durability.

Library of Congress Cataloging-in-Publication Data

Solms-Braunfels, Carl, Prinz zu, 1812–1875.
[Tagebuch einer Amerikareise. English]
Voyage to North America, 1844–45 : Prince Carl of Solms's Texas diary of people, places, and events / translated from German and notes by Wolfram M. Von-Maszewski ; introduction by Theodore Gish.
p. cm.
Includes the author's Memoir on American affairs and the diary of Alexander Bourgeois d'Orvanne.
ISBN 1-57441-124-1 (alk. paper)
1. Texas—Description and travel. 2. Solms-Braunfels, Carl, Prinz zu, 1812–1875—Journeys—Texas. 3. Solms-Braunfels, Carl, Prinz zu, 1812–1875—Diaries. 4. Germans—Texas—Diaries. 5. Princes—Germany—Diaries. 6. Texas—Emigration and immigration—History—19th century. 7. Germany—Emigration and immigration—History—19th century. 8. Land settlement—Texas—History—19th century. 9. Texas—History—Republic, 1836–1846. 10. United States—Description and travel. I. Von-Maszewski, W. M. II. Solms-Braunfels, Carl, Prinz zu, 1812–1875. Memoir über Amerikanische Angelegenheiten. III. Bourgeois d'Orvanne, Alexander. Diary of the colonial director of the Society for the Protection of German immigrants in Texas. IV. Title.

F390.S69413 2000
976.4'04–dc21 00-064852
CIP

Design by Angela Schmitt

Contents

Illustrations

Acknowledgments

During the spring semester, 1988, I had the privilege of being a chaired faculty member of the American Studies program at the University of Mainz. During this academically and personally very rewarding semester, I taught a lecture course on the history of the German-Americans and conducted a seminar on German-Texan literature. I also advised the faculty members of the American Studies program on the current status of the research and educational programs in the area of German-American studies in the United States.

One of my own research tasks was to examine German state archives for material on the immigration of Germans to Texas during the nineteenth century. Before leaving Texas, I was able to make contact with Dr. Peter Brommer of the main Rheinland-Pfalz state archive in Koblenz. In a most friendly and collegial fashion, Dr. Brommer informed me of the relevant sources within his archive. Once I was in Germany, this information led me immediately to the material which included the Solms diary (which had been incorrectly attributed to a "Count Edmond von Hatzfeldt") and Solms's *Memoire* to Queen Victoria.

These documents are located in the archive of Prince Hartzfeldt at the Schönstein castle in Wissen. The Hartzfeldt-Wildenburg administrative office, in charge of the Prince Hartzfeldt archive, kindly granted me permission to use the two documents for the purposes of my research. To examine these manuscripts, it was necessary for them to be transmitted to the Rheinland-Pfalz archive where photocopies were made for my use.

The late Professor Günter Moltmann, a distinguished professor of History at the University of Hamburg, was an invaluable collaborator in the initial stages of this project, before he died tragically of cancer in 1994. But even in the last stages of his illness, one of Professor Moltmann's major research activities was the transcription of the Solms diary, which he completed shortly before his death.

This project also benefited from other individuals who assisted in one way or the other: Andreas Reichstein, Birgit and Walther Bayer, and Wilhelm Niermann, all of Germany; Donaly Brice, Archives and Information Services, Texas State Library; Bill Stein, Nesbitt Memorial Library, Columbus, Texas; Carol Johnson, Houston Public Library; Dorothy E. Justman, Houston; Ralph Elder and Stephanie Wittenbach, Center for American History, The University of Texas at Austin; Joyce Claypool Kennerly, Richmond, Texas; and Matthew E. Von-Maszewski, Westborough, Massachusetts. A heartfelt thanks to them and to others who may have been overlooked at this moment.

Acknowledgments are not normally accorded the author or editor of a book in question. But I believe it is fitting and certainly justified to acknowledge the tremendous amount of work done by Wolfram M. Von-Maszewski. Not only did Von translate the Solms and the Orvanne diaries, but he also compiled, often with tedious and time-consuming effort, the extensive and extremely illuminating endnotes for both documents. In the latter work, Von undertook trips both to Germany and to Yale University where the largest collection of *Adelsverein* material is housed. Von also created the maps for the Solms diary and secured all of the illustrations, itself not always an easy task. The hoped-for success of this publication, consequently, is due very largely to Von's tireless efforts over the last several years.

It is now exactly a decade since I first was able to identify the Solms's diary in the Rheinland-Pfalz state archive. It is our hope that this long overdue publication will provide both scholars and others interested in the history of Texas with a unique view of the major figure in the *Adelsverein* settlement in Texas.

Theodore Gish
Houston, Texas

Editor's note

I have adhered to the original in my translation where possible. In the original, for example, Prince Carl would often write the time of day in any of several different manners. I have retained these differences to reflect the way in which the text was written. It was my goal to have this translation presented in a readable style while retaining the flavor of the original words. Any changes were made for the sake of clarity. All endnotes are mine.

Wolfram M. Von-Maszewski

Introduction

The largest single immigration of Germans to the United States, and certainly the most unusual, occurred in Texas around the middle of the nineteenth century. With a sense of *noblesse oblige*, the organization formed to direct this German colonization of Texas entitled itself the *Gesellschaft zum Schutz deutscher Einwanderer in Texas* (*The Society for the Protection of the German Immigrants in Texas*). But since the twenty-one members who organized the Society in 1842 were of the nobility (including five sovereign princes), it has been more popularly known from its beginnings as the *Adelsverein* (*The Society of Noblemen*). The immigration sponsored by this body took place during the annexation period of the Republic of Texas, when French, Spanish, and especially British eyes saw Texas playing an important role in curtailing America's manifest destiny. The interplay of aristocrats, immigrants, and Anglo-Texans against this political background, as the Society attempted in vain to fulfill many of its ambitious plans for the colonization of Texas, seems to epitomize and symbolize much of what was taking place between Europe and America at the midpoint of the nineteenth century.

Because of organizational and logistical problems and particularly the lack of adequate financing, the *Adelsverein* fell far short of its elaborate colonization plans for Texas. On a strictly numerical basis, however, the Society's undertaking was quite successful. In the fall of 1844, several hundred Society immigrants came to Texas. By 1850, nearly 10,000 immigrants had arrived in Texas on ninety-three ships under the auspices of the *Adelsverein,* and another estimated 10,000 were attracted to the state by the *Adelsverein's* presence in Texas and by its publicity in Germany. But by 1847, the Society was bankrupt and its operations virtually collapsed within the next few years. In the decade of its existence, the Society founded the port of Carlshafen (which later became the short-lived coastal town of Indianola) and the cities of New Braunfels (once the fourth largest in the state) and Fredericksburg, and concluded purportedly the only successful peace treaty with the Comanches, thereby opening up West Texas to further settlement. Because of the *Adelsverein* settlement of Texas, the Texas Hill Country (including the cities of San Antonio and Austin) still retains today, as an anomalous and unusually large "folk island," an enduring and pervasive German quality. The colorful and dramatic history of the *Adelsverein* settlement also resides, in a variety of ways, as a collective memory in the minds of the German-Texans of the region.

The key figure in the *Adelsverein's* settlement of Texas was Carl, Prince of Solms-Braunfels (1812–76). Solms, the son of Queen Fredericke of Hannover, was a nephew (by marriage) of Queen Victoria and a student friend of Prince Albert at the University of Bonn. Presumably because of his military experience as an officer of the Imperial Austrian army and, more importantly, his own desire to play a role in this event, the *Adelsverein* appointed Solms Commissioner-General in 1843 to direct its colonization project in Texas. Solms left Germany in May 1844 and sailed to America via England, arriving in Boston on the first of June. Solms traveled overland by train and steamer through the United States and arrived in Galveston exactly one month later. He returned to Germany in June 1845. At the end of that year Solms married his fiancée, Princess Sophie von Salm-Salm. Before he left New Braunfels, Solms penned a lavish dedication of the Society's administration building, the *Sophienburg* to his beloved. (This act later gave rise to the popular myth that Prince Solms had planned to build a castle in New Braunfels for Sophie and only her unwillingness to come to America caused him to return to Germany and not complete these plans.) Once back in Germany, Solms resumed his military career before the exertions of this profession forced his retirement. He was sickly and feeble in his later years, and died in the family castle, *Rheingrafenstein*, in November 1876.

History and popular belief have not treated Solms with particular kindness. He has been viewed as a romantic, impractical, an old-worldly aristocrat, and one not up to the difficulty of the task given him. But, in reality, Solms did accomplish a great deal. During the year's time in Texas, he made the necessary arrangements with the officials of the Republic of Texas for the immigration, he secured several tracts of land for the settlement, made the logistical arrangements for the arriving immigrants, and established Carlshafen, the port of debarkation, and the colony of New Braunfels.

In 1988, while examining the archives of the state of Rheinland-Pfalz, I came upon two documents relating to the *Adelsverein*, both seemingly of considerable importance but without a clear indication of their authorship. I was soon able to confirm that Solms was the author of the anonymously listed *Memoir on American Affairs, Addressed to Queen Victoria, 1845* ("*Memoir über Amerikanische Angelegenheiten. Geschrieben zu Rheingrafenstein im December 1845. Abgesandt an S. M. die Königin Victoria durch den H. Fürsten Leiningen im Januar 1846*"). The second document was listed in the archive as the *Diary of a Trip to America 1844–45*, purportedly by a Count Edmond ("*Tagebuch [des Grafen Edmund?] einer Amerikareise [1844/45]*"). With the assistance of the late Professor Günter Moltmann of the University of Hamburg, Solms was soon confirmed as the author of this diary as well. In the original publication plans for these two documents, Professor Moltmann and I were collaborating on their editing and translation for a dual-language publication. Moltmann's death in the fall of 1994 curtailed this project for a time. Before he died, Moltmann did transcribe the diary as a preparation for its translation and publication. Soon, however, W. M. Von-Maszewski, Department Manager of Genealogy and Local History at George Memorial Library in Richmond, Texas, and the past President of German-Texan Heritage Society, agreed to translate and edit the diary itself. (*The Memoir* had been transcribed by Ute Ritzenhofen, a graduate student from the University of Mainz several years earlier.)

No other immigration in the history of the United States is as well documented as the *Adelsverein* colonization of Texas. The main body of material is the 45,000 page archives of the Society (now at the Beinecke Library at Yale) which has had, incidentally, a complicated and somewhat controversial depository history. The official reports, memoranda, and letters sent by Solms to the *Adelsverein* from Texas are all contained in these archives. Solms's eleven reports to the Society while in Texas have been published both in German and in English.[1] After returning to Germany, Solms authored in 1846 a somewhat quixotic guidebook on Texas, which appeared in an English translation in 1936 during the centennial anniversary of the Texas Republic.[2] Despite this abundance of material, the two Solms documents discovered in the Rheinland-Pfalz state archive, particularly the diary, contain additional and extremely important historical and personal data.

Solms's diary consists of eighty-eight transcribed pages. It begins with his departure from *Rheingrafenstein,* the family castle on the Rhine, on 13 May 1844, and breaks off on 30 June 1845, in New York, shortly before his return to Europe. Solms traveled from Germany to England and then by the steamer *Caledonia* to Boston. From Boston, he traveled by train and coastal steamer to New York then southwest across the United States both by train and riverboat through New York, Philadelphia, Baltimore, Pittsburgh, Cincinnati, Louisville, and Memphis to New Orleans and then to Texas.

During the same period of time covered by the diary, in addition to the eleven reports to the Society's directorate at Mainz, Solms wrote fourteen letters, semi-official in nature, to the business director of the Society, Count Castell. Within the dimensions of his role as the Commissioner-General of the *Adelsverein* Solms reveals himself politically and nationalistically in the eleven reports, (for example, in his opposition to the annexation of Texas and his anti-Americanism). In the letters to his friend Castell, Solms allowed himself a more personal rein, when he expressed, for example, his somewhat naive feelings of patriotism when he discussed what he considered to be the possibility of the German colonization of America. He also discussed personal matters, for instance, when he asked Castell to remind the Duke of Nassau, the Protectorate of the *Adelsverein,* not to forget to send to Texas his silver table service!

Solms's diary itself understandably contains a great deal of biographical data not found in these documents or elsewhere, for that matter. There are, for example, trivial but humanizing notations about his own person. Solms remarked, for example, that he did gymnastic exercises on the foredeck of the *Caledonia* (30 May, Thursday). When fearing an Indian attack in an encampment, Solms described sleeping on the ground in good western fashion, without taking off his vest and using his saddle and pistol case as a pillow. (Solms, incidentally, often slept much to his dislike in this fashion in Texas, and not only in the country but in the rustic villages and towns of Texas as well.). With respect to the Indian population of Texas, there are repeated vignettes of Solms able to exercise his role as a fearless military leader, mounting a defense against an Indian attack which, however, never came. Solms's reputation as a cultivated, if somewhat eccentric figure is also supported by the diary. Even in the midst of the preparations for the impending immigration, Solms took time out to read Goethe's *Faust* and Schiller's *Wallenstein* and the latter's unfinished novel *Geisterseher.* He also noted his writing of the poem "Deutschland Hoch!", a patriotic drinking song, celebrating and, in actuality, anticipating the arrival of the Germans in Texas and in Solms's poetic vision, their heroic confrontation with Indians. This extant work has particularly contributed to the view of Solms as an aristocrat of the old school who would take time out from the serious business at hand to exercise his skill in the arts. His diary is also a repository for his unabashedly romantic remarks about his fiancée, Princess Sophie Salm-Salm, whom Solms married shortly after his return to Germany. In New Orleans, for example, Solms could write: "At last! I received a letter from Sophie from the 15th to the 26th. Enclosed was a strand of her hair. The smell of the pomade delights me. What an angel my Sophie [is]!" (29 June, Saturday). Sophie's portrait and the perfumed locks often comforted Solms when he was camped out on the Texas prairie, mindful of the danger of Indians.

The personal nature of the diary allowed similar freedoms in the descriptions of people and places Solms encountered in America and in Texas. After arriving at Houston, he traveled immediately to the capital of the Texas Republic, Washington-on-the-Brazos, which he considered to be the "most miserable and unhealthy place in Texas" (7 July, Saturday). Solms had an audience with Dr. Anson Jones, the President of the Republic, whom Solms thought to be "a polite man with good manners but has cat eyes. I don't trust him" (7 July, Saturday). The decade old village of Houston which Solms visited frequently did not fare any better. He fell into a swamp one evening while he was returning to the town and he had to lodge in quarters he called (in English) "The Entertainment House" which he described as "dirty, bad, miserable. Children's screams during the night. Barking dogs and fleas" (3 November). Solms was not always so harsh on the people themselves he encountered. Given his ethnocentrism, it is quite natural that he always mentioned his encounters with Germans and he usually spoke of them in positive terms. He was also a lady's man and never failed to note the beauty of a woman he encountered.

While such biographical information about Solms in his diary is important, perhaps even more valuable is Solms's day-to-day account of the beginning *Adelsverein* settlement of Texas, not found elsewhere in such detail. There is, for example, the daily record of personal contacts with Texas officials and important citizens, numerous Germans of all stations already in Texas, and occasional Indian bands. He also described the extent and nature of his daily travels. When Solms felt it warranted, he also included a description of the region or the city or settlement. Solms particularly described the already existing German settlements in the area of central Texas as well as the Society's provisional plantation headquarters, "Nassau Farm," named after the Duchy of Hessen-Nassau where the *Adelsverein* was incorporated. The diary's day-to-day record of the initial stages of the immigration itself: the establishment of the port of Carlshafen, the arrival of the first immigrants, the numerous logistical and personnel difficulties Solms encountered, the purchase and exploration of the tract of land for the first colony, New Braunfels (named for the family estate at Braunfels on the Lahn River), and his residence in the settlement for nearly three months are particularly important.

As has already been mentioned, traditional historical accounts treat Solms as an idealistic, inexperienced member of the aristocracy, ill-suited to the enormity of his task in Texas. But the diary's seemingly unembellished record of Solms's time in Texas (aside from supporting the romantic cast to his personality) seems to present a somewhat more positive figure. Solms appeared, for the most part, to be very conscientious toward his mission of what he believed to be the foundation of the first German colony in the New World.

The diary seems, specifically, to controvert one of the primary items of the traditional historical account. In discussing Solms's lack of fiscal sense, historians have often cited the presumed fact that Baron Meusebach, his successor, had to rescue him financially in Galveston in late May, where the two men met for the first time.[3] In the diary, however, Solms wrote that he met Meusebach in San Marcos (near New Braunfels), in the middle of May, after looking for him for several days. After conferring with Meusebach for over two days (Solms only stated laconically, "long conversation," 18 May, Sunday), he returned to Galveston for the last time. During the four days in Galveston before leaving Texas, Solms mentioned neither Meusebach nor financial problems. There is no doubt that Meusebach did find the financial affairs of the *Adelsverein* in disarray and that he had to use most of the money he had brought to Texas to pay off the debts. But the Solms diary indicates here, as in other important historical matters, differing particulars.

The second of the two Solms's documents, the *Memoir* on American affairs, a "white paper" evaluating the political situation in America and written some months after Solms's return to Germany, consists of sixty transcribed pages. It warrants discussion here because of its connection to Solms's trip to America, chronicled by the diary. The document was transmitted to Queen Victoria by one of the several Count Leiningens who were members of the *Adelsverein.* This *Memoir* develops political and national views only touched upon elsewhere in Solms's writing, which were without doubt strongly influenced by his stay in America. Like many other Europeans, Solms was against the annexation of Texas, and he wrote this document on the eve of its enactment. In the *Memoir,* he expressed his concern about the developing maritime and political power of the United States, which he felt, would eventually eclipse the might of the British Empire. The heart of the document is Solms's detailed argument that German immigrants should be used to provide military bulwarks on the Canadian and the Mexican borders against American plans for expansion. For the border in the south, he believed that the English could become allied with the Mexicans as well as with the American Indians, particularly the

Comanches, since both groups considered Americans to be their archenemies. He believed fancifully that the *Adelsverein* lands might then become a military colony under the control of Mexico (which would then regain its monarchy) or Great Britain. As an extreme measure, Solms believed the English might also capture the southern ports and in doing so release the slaves. Such action would lead, however, he believed, to a severe decimation of the United States.

Solms couched these fanciful thoughts in a curious sort of anti-Americanism not seen this virulent in any of his other writings. The following remarks provide a good example of the harshness of Solms's views:

> *The so-called American nation is composed of the worst elements of all European nations, from the north to the south, from Sweden to Russia, down to Sicily, Spain, and Portugal. The immigrants from all of these nations have passed on part of their makeup to their descendants, so that one can easily say that the American nation possesses the vices of all of the European nations without having inherited any of their good qualities.*

Nearly every page of the body of the document contains remarks of this severity. The diary itself as well as Solms's official reports and letters home from America contain only a few anti-American remarks which are, moreover, much less critical in nature. Similar anti-American views are also prevalent in Solms's published travel guide to Texas, but on a much more subdued level, since the purpose of the travel guide was, after all, to encourage emigration to the *Adelsverein* colony. Solms's remarks in his *Memoir* to Queen Victoria likely represent the free rein of his true feelings, also elevated because of the *Memoir* diatribe in which he is engaged.

Because of the way in which Solms's *Memoir* departs from the political temperament of his other writings, it is difficult to evaluate its historical worth. Solms wrote a number of similar documents with similarly exaggerated views, some of them, in fact, addressed to the American president. These factors may diminish the historical value of the *Memoir* to Queen Victoria. On the other hand, it does provide a unique epilogue to the diary.

The diary of the colonial director of the *Adelsverein*, Alexander Bourgeois (translated from the German translation of the French original) is included in the appendix of this publication for several reasons. Since Bourgeois accompanied Solms until his dismissal by the latter in August 1844, his diary provides a unique counterpoint to Solms's own diary. Bourgeois's diary, however, was not compiled on a day-to-day basis, as was Solms's diary. Instead it seems to have been written during the time of his dismissal (in August 1844). Consequently, there is a strong likelihood that, in some respects at least, the diary is a "managed" version of the events covered by both diarists. Reading the Bourgeois diary on face value, for example, he demonstrates a greater grasp of the problems and possibilities of obtaining land for the immigrants, and he discussed these matters in much greater detail than Solms did in his diary. It is difficult, of course, to say to what extent this discussion, after the fact, was intended to shore up Bourgeois' problems with the Society. Also Solms's own diary style often tends to be much more elliptic (i.e. in the form of a kind of personal "notetaking"), particularly in his commentary on the acquisition of settlement land.

Very little is known about Alexander Bourgeois' life, prior to his association with the *Adelsverein*. According to a remark in the 1842 records of the French legation in Texas, Bourgeois had been a mayor of Clichy-la-Garenne and a prominent businessman.[4] Bourgeois or Bourgeois d'Orvanne (who seems to have made up the aristocratic surname, d'Orvanne, to appeal to the *Adelsverein*) has been viewed both by the participants of the settlement and later historians as a rather controversial figure. Already in 1843, Count Joseph von Boos-Waldeck, who had been sent to Texas by the *Adelsverein* to examine the settlement possibilities, warned Count Castell, the business director of the Society, in a letter that Bourgeois was a swindler.[5] The turn-of-the century historian, Moritz Tiling, in like manner, called him and Henry Francis Fischer the "evil spirits" of the Society and accused them of "scheming and misrepresentations."[6] While Tiling's remarks may be somewhat excessive, Bourgeois and his partner Armand Ducos have been generally criticized both by the members of the *Adelsverein* and subsequent historians. Bourgeois did obtain a colonization contract from the Republic of Texas on 3 June 1842.[7] Having learned about the *Adels-*

verein's intentions, Bourgeois then went to Germany and negotiated a partnership with the *Adelsverein.* On the basis of his colonization contract, which he turned over to the *Adelsverein,* he was made a member of the organization with the power of three votes in its General Assembly. Bourgeois would also receive forty-seven and one-half per cent of the sale of any of the land after the repayment of any debts. He was, furthermore, made the Colonial Director for the colonial establishment in Texas.

The focus of criticism of Bourgeois and Ducos is the purported misrepresentation of their contract. The contract expired in December 1843, without any immigrants having been settled on the land, and just a few months before Bourgeois entered into a partnership with the *Adelsverein* in September. Bourgeois did expect to get the contract renewed and the *Adelsverein* shared these expectations. But despite his considerable negotiation efforts in Texas, Bourgeois was unable to obtain the contract's renewal. On 24 August 1844, Solms wrote a letter to Bourgeois informing him that the contract between him and the *Adelsverein* was null and void. Solms offered Bourgeois the opportunity of being a *Beamter* (official) of the *Adelsverein,* receiving five per cent of the profits of the sale of lands, and the payment of his trip back to Europe and his expenses while in Texas. In December of the same year, the *Adelsverein* formally announced the severance of the relationship between itself and Bourgeois. Bourgeois, predictably, objected strenuously, returned to Europe, and prepared to initiate a lawsuit against the *Adelsverein.* But in August 1845, with a recompense of five thousand francs and the promise of a payment from an eventual sale of the Fisher-Miller grant, the *Adelsverein* could sever its relationship with Bourgeois.

The two diaries also amply point out the personality difficulties between Solms and Bourgeois, which no doubt complicated the problems of the eventual settlement of the land acquired in Texas. In Texas, Solms entered several disparaging remarks into his diary about Bourgeois, e.g. that he "played the hero" at one point (25 July 1844) and that he was "arrogant just like a Frenchman, knows everything" (3 August 1844). Characteristic of the frequent terseness of Solms's diary style, his only comments on Bourgeois' termination itself, however, are "Correspondence with Bourgeois" (24

August 1844) and "B. protests in writing" (25 August 1844). Throughout his diary, although in a more subdued and detailed fashion, Bourgeois also particularly criticized Solms's aristocratically cavalier handling of financial matters and his lack of organizational skills. This criticism reached a high point just before the Prince terminated him when Bourgeois wrote: "The Prince was not born to handle [business]. He is too supercilious" (20 August 1844). In the final paragraph of the diary Bourgeois summarized his concerns by saying, "Two heads with two different minds will not accomplish our goals" (22 August 1844). While these criticisms may be justified, their timing and the concluding format of the diary point out that Bourgeois was also directing these remarks now to the *Adelsverein* in Germany to whom he sent the diary as a report.

Thus, the diaries of Prince Solms, the Commissioner-General of the *Adelsverein's* settlement in Texas, and Alexander Bougeois d'Orvannne, the controversial Colonial Director of the settlement, provide a unique and perhaps, to some extent, compensatory portrait of the initial stages of this settlement. While Solms is, of course, the major figure in this undertaking, the plausibility of Bourgeois' remarks about the acquisition of the settlement land and, despite his reputation, perhaps also his criticism of Solms warrant the publication of his diary along with that of Solms. Despite the vicissitudes of their relationship and the problems that both men encountered in Texas, the resulting immigration of Germans to the Lone Star State is a singular fact in the history of Texas. These documents bring further illumination to that history. The mission of the German-Texan Heritage Society is the preservation of German heritage in Texas. This objective is also carried out in its publication program that brings to the English reader in translation relevant German writings about Texas. *Voyage to North America, 1844–45* is the third publication of historical material about Germans settling in Texas. The other two volumes are *A Sojourn in Texas, 1846–47, Alwin H. Sörgel's Texas Writings* (1992) and *The Diary of Hermann Seele & Seele's Sketches from Texas* (1995).

Theodore G. Gish
Houston, Texas

[1] Chester William and Ethel Hander Geue, eds., *A New Land Beckoned: German Immigration to Texas, 1844–47,* Waco, Texas: Texian Press, 1972.

[2] Carl, Prinz zu Solms-Braunfels, *Texas. Geschildert in Beziehung auf seine geographischen, socialen und übrigen Verhältnisse,* Frankfurt am Main, Germany: Sauerländer Verlag, 1846.

[3] Rudolph Leopold Biesele, *The History of the German Settlement in Texas,* reprint, San Marcos, Texas: German-Texan Heritage Society, 1987, p. 123.

[4] Bobby W. Weaver, *Castro's Colony: Empresario Development in Texas 1842–1865,* College Station, Texas: Texas A & M University Press, 1985, p. 18.

[5] Wolf-Heino Struck, "Die Auswanderung aus dem Herzogtum Nassau (1806–1866), in *Geschichtliche Landeskunde,* Wiesbaden, Germany: Franz Steiner Verlag, 1966, p. 54.

[6] Moritz Tiling, *German Element in Texas,* Houston, Texas: privately printed, 1913, p. 73.

[7] The account of Bourgeois' relationship with the *Adelsverein* is based on information in Biesele and the Solms-Braunfels *Archiv* (transcript prepared during 1934–35 by Biesele of *Adelsverein* material in the Library of Congress).

DIARY

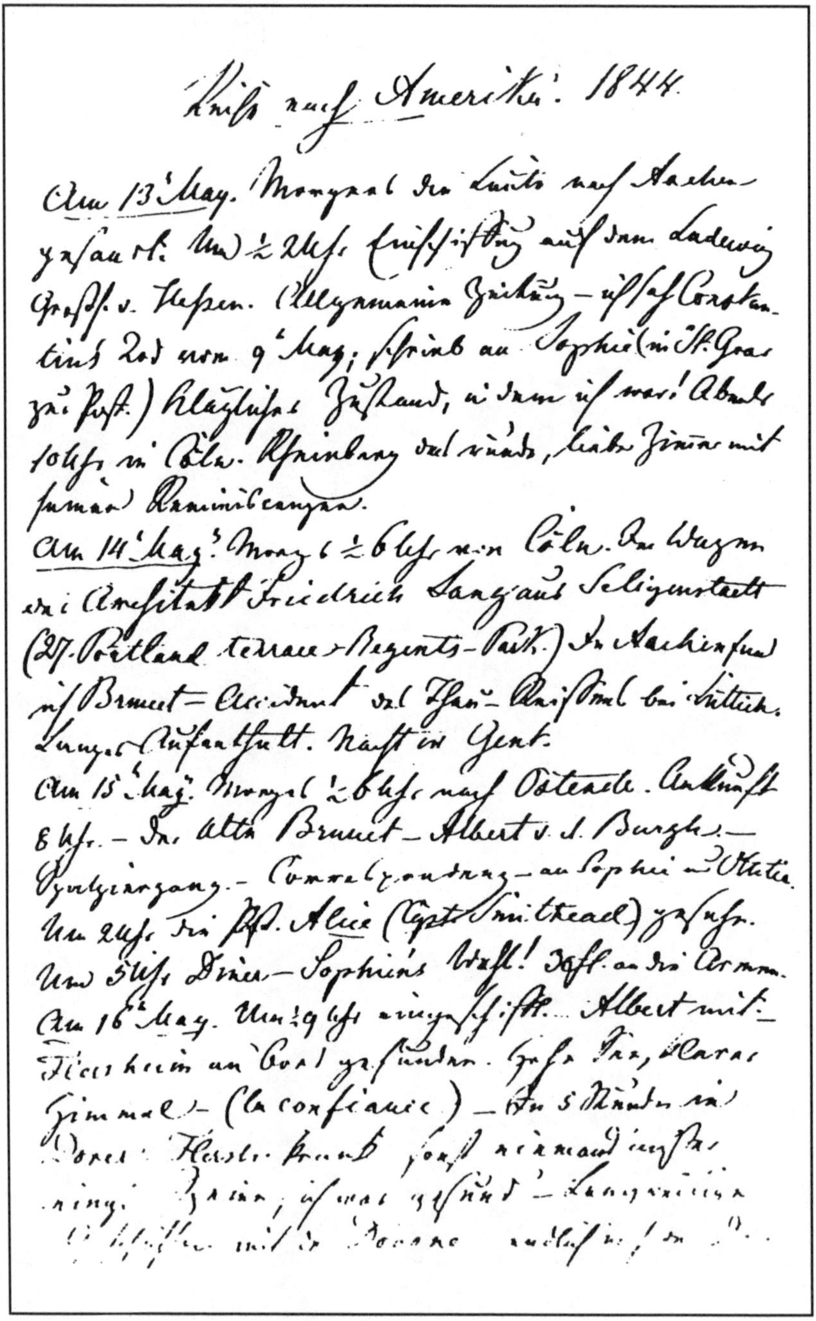
Reise nach Amerika: 1844.

Am 13t May. Morgens die Leute nach Aachen gesandt. Um ½ 2 Uhr Einschiffung auf dem Ludewig Großh. v. Hessen. Allgemeine Zeitung – ich las Constantins Tod vom 9t May; schrieb an Sophie (mit St. Goar zu Post.) Kläglicher Zustand, in dem ich war! Abends 10 Uhr in Cöln. [illegible] [illegible] [illegible] Reminiscenzen.

Am 14t May: Morgens ½ 6 Uhr von Cöln. Im Wagen [illegible] Friedrich Lang aus Seligenstadt (27 Portland terrace Regents Park.) In Aachen [illegible] Brunet – Accident [illegible] bei Lüttich. Langer Aufenthalt. Nacht in Gent.

Am 15t May. Morgens ½ 6 Uhr nach Ostende. Ankunft 8 Uhr. – Der alte Brunet – Albert v. d. Burgh. – Spaziergang. – Correspondenz an Sophie u. Ottilie. Um 2 Uhr die Sch. Alice (Capt. Smithead) gesehen. Um 5 Uhr Diner – Sophien's Wohl! 3 fl. an die Armen.

Am 16t May. Um ½ 9 Uhr eingeschifft. Albert mit. [illegible] an Bord gefunden. [illegible] (la confiance) – [illegible] 5 Stunden in Dover. [illegible] [illegible]

Diary entries for May 13–16, 1844

Chapter One

Voyage to [North] America [1844–45]

May 13th. In the morning the men were sent to Aachen. At 1:30 I boarded the *Ludewig Grossherzog von Hessen.* In the *Allgemeine Zeitung* I read of Constantin's death on 9 May; wrote Sophie (mailed at St. Goar). I was in pitiful circumstances! We arrived in Cologne at 10 P.M. Rheinberg, the round, wonderful room with its memories.[1]

May 14th. We departed Cologne at 5:30 A.M. In the coach was the architect Friedrich Land from Seligenstadt (27 Portland Terrace, Regents Park). I found Brunet in Aachen. In the vicinity of Lüttich the tearing of a rope caused an accident. A long delay. Spent the night in Gent.[2]

May 15th. At 5:30 A.M. on the way to Ostende. Arrived there at 8 o'clock. The old Brunet. Albert v. d. Burgh. Took a stroll. Correspondence to Sophie and Ottilie. The mail at 2 o'clock. Looked around the ship *Alice* (Capt. Smithhead). Dinner at 5 o'clock. Drank to Sophie's health! Gave 36 florins for the poor.[3]

May 16th. I boarded the ship at 8:30. Albert was along. Found Flersheim on board. High seas and clear sky. (Confidence!). Arrived in Dover in five hours. Flersheim became seasick as well as a few others. I felt well. Boring business with customs. Finally, after dinner, on the ship *Hotel* to London. A beautiful landscape, what contrast to Ostende and Dover. We departed at 6:30 and arrived at Bricklayer's Arm by 10:30. By omnibus and two-horse coach to Minart's Hotel where we arrived at 11 o'clock. d'Orvanne was waiting outside the building. Tea-beer.[4]

May 17th. In the company of Albert and Flersheim. I conducted business in the city proper, etc. The park. At 7 o'clock dinner with the two and d'Orvanne; accompanied the latter home.

May 18th. I bathed; later wrote to Sophie (letter will be finished in Liverpool), Ottilie, Castell, Radowitz, and Herding. Strolled with Albert through the streets (the lady with the marabou-feather). Dined at 6 o'clock. Left at 7:30 and departed by train at 8:30.[5]

The 19th [May]. Rode the train through the night. In Birmingham one sees nothing but the fire of blast furnaces. Arrived in Liverpool at 5:15. Checked into the Adelphi Hotel. Wrote only to Sophie, just two lines to Castell in regard to money. Sophie's letter will be completed on the *Caledonia*. Boarded the ship at 9 o'clock. We were underway by 10 o'clock. Flersheim who saw us on board took Sophie's letter with him. Wonderful weather until 3 o'clock when I went to bed. I slept rather well.[6]

Monday, [May] the 20th. I was up at 8 o'clock. The weather was beautiful. First we saw the coast of the Isle of Man, then the coast of Ireland; yesterday the coast of Wales was to our left. The travelers are about eighty passengers. Among them two Americans with wives and a child, a cute blond girl of one and one-half years. Another family with a grown daughter. Mr. Serurier, secretary at the French Embassy in Washington, a charming individual. A captain C. F. Hartwig from Stettin and his helmsman C. Krog who will go on a Prussian brig from New Bedford to the South Sea on a whaling expedition. The English Captain Hamilton who has traveled throughout the Orient. I eat with appetite, that is, breakfast at 8:30; lunch at 12; dinner at 4:30; tea at 7 o'clock. At 9 o'clock we left Cape Clear, Ireland, behind us. I became sick and went to bed.[7]

Tuesday, May 21. I got up in the morning but was sick all day; was helped to the deck; threw up; rested in the captain's cabin; didn't eat a thing; went to bed at 7 o'clock. At noon we were at 14° 19' longitude, 51° 8' latitude. Most of the time we traveled at 10 knots or 10 miles an hour.

Wednesday, May 22. The night, with some interruption, was good. I was lucky in my dreams, for I dreamt of Sophie and Ellichen. God be praised! The waves are running quite high. I can't walk but I can write lying down. At noon we were at: 20° 55' longitude, 50° 54' latitude. Since noon yesterday we have traveled 251 miles. Our course is WNW to W. I rested in the salon the entire day.[8]

Thursday, [May] the 23rd. I had a bad night. The weather is calm, the day beautiful. The wind comes out of SW. At noon we were at: 26° 55' longitude, 49° 50' latitude. During the past 24 hours we covered 236 miles. I spent all day on deck and smoked. Everyone strolled around the deck.

Friday, May the 24th. Wonderful weather in the morning, strong winds around noon, I had to lie down. Yesterday, at 4 P.M., we caught up, or actually passed, a French fishing brig from St. Malo on its way to fish on the Banks of Newfoundland. This morning we passed two [boats] and another at noon. The first one we passed at the distance of a rifle shot, and we gave them the longitude and latitude. Today at noon we were at: 32° 57' longitude, 48° 42' latitude. Since yesterday we put 234 miles behind us. (Capt. Hamilton, the Viennese Razim, von der Stratten de Ponthoze).[9]

Saturday, May 25th. Last night the wind and the rolling of the ship were so strong that I couldn't sleep. I didn't feel well in the morning in spite of the bitter ale with the breakfast. Felt better toward noon. At the sound of the polka and the Tirolienee from our quadrille which the Viennese merchant sang, I jumped up and was able to dance. Went to bed early. Latitude 47° 33'; longitude 38° 5'; distance covered 230 miles.[10]

Sunday, May 26th. Whitsunday. In the morning on deck I noticed far off the first iceberg, around 11 o'clock the second. It was closer, circa 50' tall and very expansive. At 11 o'clock a clergyman read the prayers. During the night it became noticeably colder and increased so during the day. My turn at the machine, conversed with the French wine merchant whose destination is Canada. He is a Carlist. Latitude 46° 26', longitude 43° 27'. Distance covered since yesterday 228 miles. In the afternoon icebergs with glaciers all around. Danger. High seas. Fog. Strong wind.[11]

May 27th. Stayed in bed all day. I didn't close an eye all night because the ship rolled so badly. Latitude 45° 59', longitude 47° 34'; distance covered 175 miles. Tremendously cold.

Tuesday, May the 28th. The weather improved. I wrote sitting up. We are at the Banks of Newfoundland. The engineer shot ducks. Flat sea. Latitude 45° 45', longitude 53° 6'. Distance covered 233 miles.

Wednesday, May the 29th. Latitude 45° 45', longitude 59° 32'; distance covered 274 miles. The weather is quite good.

Thursday, May 30th. Reached Halifax at 6 A.M. Nice bay, a harbor and anchorage for an entire fleet. The bay is surrounded with fortifications. Fort Camperdown and York Redoubt. The town presents a miserable sight. The dwellings as well as the barracks are built of wood. I went immediately ashore with letters to Sophie, Ottilie, Castell. Strolled over to the Citadel which is still under construction. We departed at 9 o'clock on the dot. A wonderful day; calisthenics on deck. Saw 10–12 whales. Spectacular moonlight! Oh, the memories! Where was I at the last full moon? At Sophie's heart! And today on the cold ocean.[12]

Friday, May the 31st. Fog all day, the despair of all the passengers. The anchor was put out at 6 o'clock because of the rock outcroppings close to the harbor.

The morning of June 1st. We entered Boston harbor. Outstanding weather, a beautiful sight. I disembarked for Hotel Tremont. Boston is a port and commercial city with a population of about 100,000. The State House monument is on Bunker Hill. Climbed the hill, my poor legs! Took a walk with Hamilton before the meal. The dinner was good. Goodbyes to the Commodore-Capt. Lott and Hamilton. At 4 o'clock on the train via Worcester to Norwich. Attractive countryside, little cultivation but heavily populated. As one travels there is one community after another. Everything is painted neatly in white. In each community there are 2 or 3, sometimes even more churches. In Boston the houses are mostly of brick, not many of granite. Many are also of wood. Church towers are all of wood. Churches are of a poor gothic style, that is, heavy or Greek temples. Everything is a mixture and next to each other. In the country there are nothing but wooden structures, very little brick. Manufacturing and factory buildings are of brick. The trees are German and American oak, sycamore, maple, much is coniferous wood and everything is green wood. The area abounds with water, there are many creeks, ponds, lakes and delightful vistas in the area. There is nothing remarkable about the construction of the railroad itself. The engines burn wood. It is terrible the way sparks fly everywhere. There are no train guards, everything is left to luck. Arrived in Norwich by 9 o'clock. Went immediately on board the large steamer *Worcester.* It is of unbelievable size. It has 500 beds. Marvelous moonlit night. Homesick![13]

Sunday, June 2nd. Arrived in New York at 6:30 A.M. The city and its shore offer a beautiful sight. Splendid location. Same latitude as Naples but poor climate. To the north, light blue sky. I went to the Astor House. It is colossal but very eerie. Sunday in New York is much worse compared to London. (Broadway). The town has a population of 500,000. After dinner Baron de Pontoze, the Viennese gentleman and I strolled to Hoboken. It is quite nice on the Hudson (North River). Met Germans, a woman from *Khyrn*! and two men from Trier. In the evening walked around the harbor, ran into Capt. Hartwig. There are mostly Germans and Irishmen there. In the evening at Serurier's. Slept badly. A thunderstorm at night.[14]

Monday, June 3rd. Enormous activity on Broadway. Called on Schmidt, the Prussian Consul, at 34 Broad Street, an impressive individual, a true German; also on Brower, Texan consul, an American. Did correspondence. Dinner, at my place. Called on Mad. Schmidt who acted rather stiff; has four to six daughters, of passable beauty.[15]

Tuesday, June 4th. Did correspondence; later went to the Bishop of New York who was not at home. Dinner. At 4 o'clock departed by train for Philadelphia. Razim accompanied us. (The fare from Boston to New York is $5 per person, from New York to Philadelphia it is $6.) Arrived at 10 P.M. Checked into the Mansion House, it is excellent.

Wednesday, June 5th. Departed 7 A.M. We ran into Serurier at breakfast, he accompanied us to Baltimore. By steamboat on the Delaware to Wilmington, then by train. Arrived [in Baltimore] at 3:30 P.M. The dinner at the Exchange Hotel was poor. Afterward I strolled through the city; many German names, even a German beer hall. Washington's monument (leaves something to be desired), a similar one for the heroes of the American Revolution. The archbishop's cathedral, a massive granite building. A German Catholic church, rather attractive gothic style (the architect is Long, an American); German workers, one from Mainau by Aschaffenburg, showed me the way to the Redemptionists (German Catholic) missionaries. Father Alexander, the superior, was out-of-town. Father Joseph Veit from Aachen. (Aisquith-Street). It was Corpus Christi Day, the small church of the statue of [?] was decorated with greenery; a pleasant small church. I took a walk to the harbor (on Chesapeake Bay).[16]

Thursday, June 6th. Departed by train at 7:15 A.M. (From Philadelphia to Wheeling or Pittsburgh the fare is $13 per person). Beautiful valley of the Patapasko, then on the Potomac in the Allegheny Hills (forerunners of the Allegheny). Poor dinner at Harper's Ferry. Arrived in Cumberland around 5:30. Departed by coach at 6:30. Just us and Mr. Gardener, a rather decent man. Beautiful country, the beginning of the Allegheny Mountains; temperature of the past two days 28° R[eaumur]. Supper in Frostberg awfully bad and watery. Sky was threatening when we departed. Soon there was a thunderstorm. It poured. There were precipices, primeval forest, sky-high trees, all this during lightening and thunder, the air filled with electricity, the road was awfully bad as was the coach. It was not an enviable night, the worst that I have yet encountered; the danger was rather great.[17]

Friday, June 7th. Breakfast in Uniontown at 8 A.M. German waitress from Bayreuth, her parents are in Cumberland where many Germans live. At 10:30 in Brownsville. On the steamer *Clayton* traveled the Monongahela River, in the past a popular place frequented by the Indians. It is a small river with lush woods along the shore. On both sides are located coal mines (train from the top come down to the river). Much farming; homes of poor quality. One lock, to carry water to the river. Finally, at 9:45 I arrived in Pittsburgh; iron and glass works with blast furnaces on both sides, a beautiful view. (The Jochgahela is a tributary of the Monongahela.) Hotel of the same name at the dock site.[18]

Saturday, June 8th. I slept splendidly. At 9 o'clock visited a glass factory, no work was going on, only the smelting. Then across to Sligo; an iron factory; the foreman a German from the Lahr area in the uplands of Baden. He had forgotten the name of his birthplace, has been in America for 27 years. (There were two Germans on the boat yesterday; one was a former slave trader whose facial features were terrible. The other was an innkeeper in Allegheny City who smelled of whiskey and was overbearing.) At 12:30 I came on board of the *Majestic* where I am writing this. It has rather poor accommodations and even worse company, all with a hang-dog look with the exception of a Quaker couple. The confluence of the Monongahela and Allegheny make up the Ohio River on which we are traveling. It has not much water so that we constantly scrape bottom. The boat jerks terribly; we sit on the gallery in front of the stateroom and write on our knees. Now I will write to my angel Sophie. God never fails he who is courageous. He will also look after us and protect us. Unbelievable heat, reached 30° R.[19]

Sunday, June 9th. Had a good night's sleep. Life is boring on board among the awful company. Wrote to Sophie in spite of the engine's pounding; whether or not she will be able to read it, only God knows. There are two pleasant old people from Pennsylvania and an Indian who was educated in government schools. He is studying medicine and wants to go to Paris and Germany; I promised him letters [of introduction]. He is the son of a Frenchman and an Indian squaw, nephew of a chief. His non-Indian name is J. W. Barrow. He is from the tribe of the Pottawatomie, the territory of Missouri. Heavy thunderstorm in the afternoon. The boat stops constantly to take on coal, passengers, and freight. The night was very dark, the shore illuminated by fire-flies. I was in bed at 10 o'clock.[20]

Monday, June 10th. Still no prospect for an early arrival. There is talk of our arrival between 3 and 4 o'clock. Too much travel is horrible, one can only tolerate it when the goal is in sight. What illusions that I have. The Ohio River is monotonous, the shore is wooded but sparsely settled. There are also a few coal mines here.

Remarks: Distances which I covered and those ahead of me before I reach New Orleans.

By boat: Bingen to Cologne, 17 German or	85	English	miles
train: Cologne to Ostende, 40 German or	200	"	"
steamboat: Ostende to Dover,	80	"	"
train: Dover to London,	90	"	"
train: London to Liverpool,	244	"	"
Europe	699	"	"
steamer: Liverpool to Boston,	2,764	"	"
train: to Worcester,	43	"	"
train: to Norwich,	70	"	"
steamer: to New York,	135	"	"
train: to Philadelphia,	88	"	"
steamer: to Wilmington,	25	"	"
train: to Baltimore,	70	"	"
train: to Cumberland,	149	"	"
stage coach: to Brownsville,	80	"	"
steamer: to Pittsburgh,	54	"	"
steamer: to Cincinnati,	456	"	"
steamer: to the Mississippi,	509	"	"
steamer: to Natchez,	738	"	"
steamer: to New Orleans,	1,300	"	"
Total:	6,481	"	"

Finally arrived [in Cincinnati] at 4:30; to the Broadway Hotel. The old lawyer from Pennsylvania and the merchant from Wheeling came with us. Changed garments. Strolled through the streets to Augustus Rentz for whom I had a letter from Schmidt. He praised Rentz very much. I found a little Swabian with glasses and stained teeth who spoke half Swabian, half English. He had a commission business, like most Germans around here. Strolled on the hill that offers a view over the town that has a population of 70,000. Of those, 20,000 are Germans who occupy the part of town along the hill. On the way back had white Ohio wine at Mohn's who is from Langenselbold. Mailed a letter (which will leave on the 11th). Wrote to Castell via Schmidt; via the latter because of von Raumer. After a walk along the Miami Canal, early to bed. Slept well. The town was founded by General Harrison in 1792. At night a storm, very beautiful.[21]

Tuesday, June 11th. Went with Rentz to the market. He brought Mohn along who told me the story of his trial with Wolf Ysenburg and the Hessian courts. I boarded the *Pike* at 10 o'clock. The lawyer stayed with us until Madison, the merchant until Louisville. The shoreline was monotonous, forest and not much cultivation. The journey was slow because of the frequent stops to load and unload. A young man spoke to me about the works by Countess Ida Hahn-Hahn (*Sigismund Forster*). The *Daily Enquiries & Messages*, Cincinnati, has the following article: "A live Prince. There is at the Broadway Hotel—so Johnson says—a bona fide live Prince, who lords it over a principality in Germany called Salms or Solms. He is making the tour of the United States and is now on his way to N. Orleans. He is tall and rather good looking, dresses fashionably, wears red hair and mustachios much of the same color—and it is said that he has the strange peculiarity of eating, when he is hungry. Queer, isn't it ladies?" Clipped the article to mail to Sophie. Arrived in Louisville at 12 o'clock. To the Hotel Galthouse, which is dirty and terrible. The *Memphis* is scheduled to depart at 4 o'clock on Wednesday. (Cincinnati has four German newspapers, New York six).[22]

Wednesday, June 12th. Before breakfast at 10 o'clock I experienced the date change to Thursday the 13th. Coach ride to Portland (five miles) where the *Memphis* was docked. It looks good. The captain's parents are Germans from the Rhine area. He promised the sky, that the trip would take 3 and one-half to 5 days, the speed would be 16 to 20 miles an hour, and we would not get stuck. I took several strolls through the streets; they are all terrible. The heat was oppressing. Met a German by the name of Wenzel, a short, fat man with a sly face. Like others here he has done well in land speculation but business has slowed down now. Asked about Max Wied. (Read on a door the names Dr. and Mrs. von Dönhof.) Started a letter to Sophie. Chatted with Wenzel in the evening. He described von Dönhof as a young man trained in the sciences.[23]

Thursday, [June] the 13th. Accompanied by Wenzel visited the justice building. Very splendorous stonework but poor arches and a meaningless design. Called on von Dönhoff [*sic*], found only his wife who looks like a house maid from Berlin, but conversed rather well. Apparently they are not doing well. Left my calling card. Boarded the *Memphis* at 11:30. At 3:00 o'clock there was no sign of departure. A few ladies on board. Food is horrible. The captain is a drunkard. What prospects! I regret not spending 48 hours instead in the stagecoach. On deck in the evening made the acquaintance of a young Creole and his wife from New Orleans. They are decent folks. Mr. Urquhart.[24]

Friday, June 14th. Had a terrible night; the heat, mosquitoes, roaches. A boring day.

Saturday, June 15th. The days that followed were just like before and the nights were the same. Heat and mosquitoes, fleas and roaches; lice. At 6:00 o'clock in the evening took on wood at Rucker's Point, Tenn. Mr. Louis, a backwoodsman who fought against the Spanish in 1814, has a bullet in the right wrist and two in the hip. Had a good education, knows all the English and French classics, talked of *La Martine.* His nephew boarded later as a passenger. He is a misanthrope however. The next plantation to him is one-half mile. Even this is too close for him and for this reason he wants to resettle in the west. Was married, had children; every one is dead. Now he loves his bloodhounds, horses, cattle, etc. like he did his children. Despises mankind. Stays poor because he gives to anyone who asks for help.[25]

Sunday, June 16th. Arrived in Memphis at 5 o'clock. Took on freight for three hours. At night a thunderstorm, terribly dark. Had the Almighty not guided us where would we be? Very likely on the bottom of the Mississippi. Yesterday, at 8:30 in the morning, we reached Cairo at the mouth of the Mississippi. At noon we passed New Madrid, formerly an important town, but totally destroyed by the earthquake of 1811. Today there are only a few buildings standing. Flooding on both sides of the river, large number of logs (trunks) in the river. Eight miles below Memphis stopped for several hours to take on wood. Plantation of maize, cotton, fruit. His residence and wife. The slave dwellings. Cotton gin, a simple method. First it is pressed and then it goes through a simple machine (that costs $175, three wheels for $170, belt(s) for $15 and a brassport for $10, for a total of $370 which does not include the wood and construction cost).[26]

Monday, June 17th. Today it has been five weeks since I have been separated from Sophie! There was a thunderstorm last evening but the night was still hot. At 9 o'clock today arrived at Egg's Point. A German lives here, left Germany 25 years ago. He had gone to Kentucky, has a nice home.[27]

Tuesday, [June] 18th. Boredom as usual, no bread, no milk. I told the captain and some others what I thought.

Wednesday, June 19th. Arrived in New Orleans at 7:30 A.M. Bathed in the St. Charles Hotel. Visited Lanfear and Schmidt. Took letters for Sophie, Ottilie, Castell as well as daughter Marie to the post office. Dinner, a lady's ordinary at 4 o'clock. Mailed letters to Schmidt. Lanfear and Ward called on me. Dr. Labatut and Ducos.[28]

Thursday, June 20th. Correspondence in the morning. Visits by Vogel; Major Möllhausen who had been a lieutenant in the 7th Artillery of the Prussian army, following that in Texan-Mexican service, and is now a civil engineer in New Orleans; in the afternoon he brought a beautifully executed map of St. Louis in Texas. Goldenbow from Rostock, recipient of the Knight of the Red Eagle, 4th Class, for his work that he wrote on the Indian tribes and sent a copy to F. W. IV. He knew my mother. Ducos dined with us. Afterward took a walk to the *Neptun* (steamer between New Orleans and Galveston) which took my letters, one to Castell that I wrote today (instructions regarding my talk with Ducos) and one to Sophie with only a few lines. Unbelievable heat. The *Neptune* is scheduled to depart for New York in seven days.[29]

Friday, June 21st. Ducos & Barttezz, the latter has very interesting details about Texas which makes it fascinating. Vogel; both Urquharts. Hunt arranged for Sunday. In the evening on board the *Chateaubriand*. Tasted and bought wine. Visited Schmidt & Vogel to purchase various items.[30]

Saturday, June 22nd. Put the bills in order. The painter William Frei (from Eger). Visit from Vogel. Hammocks. Urquhart & Labatut. In the afternoon to the slave market. On board the *New York* which finally arrived today; then on board the *Chateaubriand*, it leaves for Havre tomorrow.[31]

June 23rd. Mr. Urquhart (Robert) picked us up at 6 A.M. Crossed the river accompanied by Dr. Labatut. Through forest and prairie to Concepcion previously a Jesuit monastery exquisitely arranged. Breakfast on the Canal which the owners extended to the Bayou. On board; fishing in the bayou; alligators. I shot three, one was 8 feet long, with the Altenburger rifle; James Urq. killed three; Dr. L. one which regained consciousness in the boat. I hit it on the head and the throat. Afterwards dinner; prior to that we viewed the slave quarters and the residence of the overseer. Mons. Villeut father-in-law of J. Urq. Returned home.[32]

Monday, the 24th. Made purchases. Supper at Vogel's from 4:30 to 9:30; unbearable heat. He has a beautiful wife. In the evening smoked with Dr. Labatut.

Tuesday, the 25th. Made additional purchases in the morning. Ate at home. In the evening at Dr. Labatut's.

Wednesday, June 26th. Had supper at Lanfear's from 4:30 to 7 o'clock. Castro. Carriage ride by moonlight to the Canal. In the evening at Labatut's.[33]

Thursday, June 27th. Visited the Mint. The treasurer is a polite individual, he took us around. The person in charge of the mint is familiar with Texas. He spoke of the San Saba mine which was productive until 1764. He traveled there in 1842 accompanied by 100 men, because of skirmishes with Indians, they could not reach the mine. Rare Prussian coin that depicts Friedr. I (1 Frd'or) but shows no year. I dined at home. Spent the evening at Dr. Labatut's.[34]

Friday, June 28th. With the arrival of the mail from Europe (via the *Acadia*) there was hope for letters. But no such luck. Only despair and hope for tomorrow! Conversation with Dr. Jones.[35]

Saturday, June 29th. The mail arrived at 9 o'clock! At last! I received a letter from Sophie from the 15th to the 26th. Enclosed was a strand of her hair. The smell of the pomade delights me. What an angel my Sophie [is]! Received also letters from Ottilie, Castell, Flersheim. Finished my letters in haste on account of my departure. At 1 o'clock on board the *New York*. Very crowded, hot and terrible conditions. Around 11 o'clock passed the Balize. What a horrible night! The bugs and the heat![36]

Sunday, June 30th. Unbelievable heat, poor food, very crowded; poor company, as always. Spent the night in the open, slept on top of beer and whiskey kegs. Bearable, spent the whole day there also.

---

[1] Aachen: historic city in the state of Nordrhein-Westfalen (coronation place of thirty-seven German kings; burial place of Charlemagne). Solms's entry for 12 May 1845 indicates that he boarded at Bingen on the Rhine. *Allgemeine Zeitung*: possibly the widely respected newspaper which

was published in Augsburg, 1798–1910. Constantin's relationship to Solms is unknown. Princess Sophie of Salm-Salm (9 August 1814–9 January 1876), former Princess of Löwenstein-Wertheim-Rosenberg, was Solms's fiancee. Her first marriage (24 March 1841) was to Prince Franz of Salm-Salm (? –31 December 1842). She married Prince Carl of Solms-Braunfels on 3 December 1845. One child was born to this union, Prince Alexander Friedrich Karl Maria (4 November 1855–3 June 1926) (Hans Friedrich v. Ehrenkrook, ed., *Genealogisches Handbuch der fürstlichen Häuser* [*Genealogical Handbook of Princely Households*], Limburg a. d. Lahn, Germany: C. A. Starke Verlag, 1961, Vol. VI, pp. 306–307). St. Goar: town on the middle Rhine, located between the cities of Bingen and Koblenz. Cologne: major city on the Rhine. Rheinberg: lodging place in Cologne.

[2] Seligenstadt: located approximately twelve miles southeast from Frankfurt-on-the-Main. Portland Terrace, London: presumably Land's London address. Brunet: acquaintance of Solms, further identity unknown. Lüttich: Liege, Belgium.

[3] Ostende: seaport on the Belgian coast. Albert v. d. Burgh: identity unknown. Ottilie: in a letter written from London on 18 May 1844, Solms refers to an Ottilie at Braunfels but her relationship to him is unknown (*Archiv des Vereins zum Schutz deutscher Einwanderer in Texas* [*Archive of the Society for the Protection of German Immigrants in Texas*], Beinecke Rare Book and Manuscript Library, Yale University, New Haven, Connecticut; Box 12, Folder 77). Florin: a European gold coin patterned after the Florentine florin. Solms presumably made the donation to assure a safe voyage.

[4] Albert: acquaintance of Solms. L. H. Flersheim: the Society's banker from Frankfurt-on-the-Main who saw Solms off in Liverpool. Dover: English harbor and stopping point for ferry boats from Ostende, Belgium. Alexander Bourgeois d'Orvanne: secured colonization contracts from the Republic of Texas which, in 1844, he hoped to fulfill by attracting the Society and their colonists (Ron Tyler, et al., editors, *The New Handbook of Texas,* Austin: Texas State Historical Association, 1996, Vol. I, p. 662; see also "Introduction").

[5] Carl Graf zu Castell: vice-president and member of the Society's executive committee as well as the Society's business director. Radowitz: identity unknown. Herding: identity unknown. Marabou-feathers: the soft feathers covering the bases of the larger feathers of the marabou stork's wing and tail; used in millinery.

[6] Birmingham: industrial city in England's Midland. Liverpool: major seaport on the Irish Sea. *Caledonia* of the British & North American Royal Mail Steamship Company, later renamed the Cunard Steamship Company, was one of four ships of similar design ordered by the com-

pany expressly for monthly service between England and North America. The *Caledonia* was a sidewheel-propelled steamer of 1,134 gross tons, 207 ft in length and 34 ft in breadth with one smoke stack and three masts. Constructed of wood, the ship had a speed of nine knots and carried 115 first class passengers (Eugene W. Smith, *Passenger Ships of the World: Past and Present.* 2nd edition. Boston, Massachusetts: George H. Dean Co., 1978; Electronic Web Site: England. Liverpool. University of Liverpool. Cunard Archives. Online <http:// www. Liv.ac. uk/~archives/ cunard/ship/ colum.htm>).

[7] For a complete list of the passengers on the *Caledonia*, Edward G. Lott, master, see a transcription in Appendix. Stettin: former German port on the Baltic Sea; after World War II it received the Polish name Szczecin. New Bedford: harbor town in Massachusetts.

[8] Ellichen: relationship unknown.

[9] St. Malo: harbor on the northwest coast of France. The Viennese Carl Razim. Auguste van der Straten-Ponthoz: first secretary at the Belgian embassy in Washington, D. C. He authored *Forschungen über die Lage der Auswanderer in den Vereinigten Staaten von Nordamerika [Inquiries into the State of Emigrants in the United States of America].* Translated from French into German by H. Fr. Oswald. German edition: Augsburg, Germany: K. Kollmann, 1846.

[10] Tirolienee: also spelled Tyrolienee, a round dance from Tyrol. Quadrille: a square dance performed by four couples.

[11] The statement "My turn on the machine": may imply that Solms took a turn at the ship's wheel. The passenger list shows a "Quelton St. Georges, twenty-four year old male, proprietor, from France, going to Canada." Carlist: supporter of Don Carlos (1788–1855), Spanish pretender to the throne, during the Carlist War in Spain (1833–39).

[12] Citadel: the historic hilltop fort that dominates Halifax.

[13] Worcester and Norwich: towns in the state of Massachusetts. Steamer *Worcester*: a side-wheeler, 605 tons, built in New York, NY; in 1841, first home port New London, Connecticut, sold to the U.S. War Department in 1861 (William M. Lytle, compiler, *Merchant Steam Vessels of the United States, 1807–1868*, Mystic, Connecticut: The Steamship Historical Society of America, 1952, p. 206).

[14] Solms lodged at the Astor House (*[New Orleans] Daily Picayune*, 13 June 1844, p. 2, col. 1). Hoboken: town in New Jersey, across the Hudson River from New York. Khyrn: spelled Kirn today, the town is located in the state of Rheinland-Pfalz. Solms underlined the name because the castle of Kyrburg was in the vicinity and it apparently had sentimental meaning to him. See entry for 10 May 1845. Trier: town in the state of Rheinland-Pfalz.

[15] John H. Brower: New York merchant, served as consul for the Republic of Texas from 1841 to 1846. It was not uncommon for a nation to appoint as consul an influential individual who was not a citizen of that country but sympathetic to its cause. The position carried no salary. The prestige of office was considered a sufficient reward (*The New Handbook of Texas,* Vol. I, p. 758; Alma Howell Brown, "The Consular Service of the Republic of Texas," *Southwestern Historical Quarterly,* Vol. 33, p. 185; Franz Josef Pitsch, *Die wirtschaftlichen Bezieh-ungen Bremens zu den Vereinigten Staaten von Amerika bis zur Mitte des 19. Jahrhunderts* [*Bremen's Economic Relationship with the United States of America until the mid-1800s*], Bremen, Germany: Staatsarchiv der Freien Hansestadt Bremen, 1974, p. 81). Mad. Schmidt: presumably the Prussian consul's wife.

[16] Aschaffenburg: town east from Frankfurt-on-the-Main. Redemptorists: Order of the Roman Catholic Congregation of the Most Holy Redeemer founded in 1732 and devoted to preaching to the poor. In Baltimore the order was located on Aisquith Street. The purpose of Solms's visit is revealed in the *Sixth Report* where he states that he requested from Father Alexander a priest for the colony in Texas (Chester W. and Ethel H. Geue. *A New Land Beckoned,* Waco, Texas: Texian Press, 1972, p. 50).

[17] Wheeling: At the time Solms passed through Wheeling the town was in Virginia. During the Civil War this area was organized as West Virginia as was also the region of Harper's Ferry. Patapasko: presumably the Patuxent River. Cumberland: in Virginia. Solms refers to the Reaumur temperature scale, once widespread, which began to disappear in the 20th century. On this scale, under standard atmospheric pressure, the freezing point of water is at zero degree and the boiling point at 80 degrees. The temperature quoted here, 28° R, corresponds to 95° F; Frostburg, in Virginia.

[18] Brownsville in Pennsylvania. Steamer *Clayton*: no information available. Jochgahela: Solms could be referring to the Youghiogeny River.

[19] Sligo: into the early 19th century, Pittsburgh's population was composed chiefly of Irish and Scottish settlers. Possibly Irish immigrants named the place for Sligo County, Ireland ("Pittsburgh" in *Encyclopedia Americana,* Danbury, Connecticut: Grolier, Inc., 1996. Vol. XXII, p. 154). Lahr: town in the southwest of the present state of Baden-Württemberg. Allegheny City, today Allegheny, in Pennsylvania. Ship *Majestic*: side-wheeler, 238 tons, built in Pittsburgh, Pennsylvania, in 1843; first home port Pittsburgh, abandoned in 1852 (Lytle, *Merchant Steam Vessels,* p. 119). 30° R temperature corresponds to 100° F.

[20] Pottawatomie: Potawatomie.

[21] Schmidt: Johann W. Schmidt, Prussian consul in New York (*The American Almanac and Repository of Useful Knowledge for theYear 1845*, Boston: James Munroe & Co., 1844, p. 116). Swabian: a person from Swabia, a duchy in medieval Germany, today the general area is known as the Black Forest. Solms may be referring to a section of town known as "Over-the-Rhine," an area predominantly settled by Germans in the nineteenth century (Don H. Tolzmann, *Cincinnati's German Heritage*, Bowie, Maryland: Heritage Books, 1994, p. 7). von Raumer: identity unknown. Miami Canal, like other canals built in the U.S. beginning in the 1820s, was an important economic asset to this region. This artificial waterway not only accelerated the settlement of the interior lands, it also stimulated commerce between regions and, in turn, the growth of the nation. William Henry Harrison (1773–1841), became the ninth president of the United States.

[22] Court trial of Wolf Ysenburg: meaning unknown. Ship *Pike*: side-wheeler, 294 tons, built in Jeffersonville, Indiana, in 1838; first home port Cincinnati, Ohio, abandoned in 1845 (Lytle, *Merchant Steam Vessels*, p. 152). Madison: on the Ohio River, in Indiana. Countess Ida Hahn-Hahn (1805–1880), prolific and widely read German novelist of the nineteenth century, *Sigismund Forster* (1843) is the title of one of her works. The correct title of the newspaper is *Daily Enquirer and Message*. The article, a direct and complete quote, appeared on 11 June 1844, p. 3, col. 1. Ship *Memphis*: side-wheeler, 462 tons, built in New Albany, Indiana in 1843, first home port Memphis, Tenn., lost in 1847 (Lytle, *Merchant Steam Vessels*, p. 126).

[23] Navigation on the Ohio River was interrupted at Louisville, Kentucky, by the Falls of the Ohio below town. These were long rapids created by a twenty-four-foot drop of the river over a two-mile-long series of limestone ledges. Boats were off-loaded, the cargo hauled overland past the falls, reloaded on different boats and the journey continued (Samuel Cummings, *The Western Pilot*, Cincinnati, Ohio: George Condin, 1847, reprint: Cincinnati, Ohio: Young Klein, 1978, p. 50). Max Wied: possibly Prince Maximilian of Wied (1782–1867) who, accompanied by the Swiss artist Karl Bodmer (1809–1893), explored the upper reaches of the Missouri River in 1833/34 and conducted ethnographic studies among the Mandan Indians. Dönhof: a young German physician in Louisville whom Solms wanted to hire for the colony in Texas, except that a physician was already on his way from Germany (*Solms-Braunfels Archives*, Center for American History, The University of Texas at Austin; Vol. XLIX, p. 140).

[24] *Memphis*: Fritz, master (*[New Orleans] Daily Picayune*, 20 July 1844, p. 3, col. 6).

[25] Louis' statement that he fought against the Spanish in 1814 is open to question. It can be assumed that he fought against the Creek Indians in Florida, which was a Spanish possession until 1819. (Spain's military presence in the War of 1812, which lasted from 1812 to 1815, was insignificant and was no threat to the United States). *La Martine*: presumably Alphonse de Lamartine (1790–1869), French politician and early Romantic writer.

[26] Cairo: town in southern Illinois. New Madrid: town in Missouri. The earthquake in 1811 destroyed thousands of acres of land making them unusable for farming and, in turn, spelled the doom for the once flourishing town. When Solms wrote that "first it [the cotton] is pressed and then it goes through a simple machine," he shows his unfamiliarity with ginning. The procedure is just the reverse. The parts mentioned by him used in this machine, three wheels, a belt and a brassport, were some of the workings of a gin. One wheel, up to ten feet in diameter, was mounted horizontally and kept in motion by horses or mules. This power was transferred by cogs to a vertical and slightly smaller wheel which by a belt drove the wheel on the gin stand. Here the cotton fiber was separated from the seed. The important part in this equipment was the "breastwork," Solms referred to it as "brassport." The breastwork was a thick piece of brass, notched not unlike a comb. As the cotton was passed through the gin stand the breastwork let the lint (fibers) through but held back the seed.

[27] Egg's Point: On the left side of the Mississippi River, below Greenville, Mississippi.

[28] Ambrose Lanfear: merchant and Society's banker in New Orleans. Schmidt: of Schmidt & Vogel, merchant and banker as well as Prussian consul in New Orleans (*Solms-Braunfels Archives*, Vol. XLIX, p. 135). "daughter Marie," identity unknown. "a lady's ordinary," meaning unknown. Ward: possibly Ambrose Lanfear's business partner. Dr. Labatut of New Orleans: identity unknown. Armand Ducos, former subprefect of Civray, France, in partnership with Alexander Bourgeois d'Orvanne received a land grant from the Mexican government. The passenger list of the *Caledonia* does not contain Ducos' name. He probably joined Solms and d'Orvanne in New Orleans (Nancy Nichols Barker, editor, *The French Legation in Texas*, Austin: Texas State Historical Association, 1971, p. 336; see also note 4 this chapter and note 5 in Chapter II).

[29] Wilhelm Vogel, partner of Schmidt & Co. in New Orleans as well as Consul for Prussia and Hamburg (*[New Orleans] Daily Picayune*, 22 June 1844, p. 1, col. 6). Möllhausen: former artillery officer in the Prussian army who had lived in Austin, Texas, in 1840. Möllhausen tried to secure

a contract from the Republic of Texas for making three large maps of Texas. He did not want to establish a colony in Texas but was confident that he could induce Germans emigrants to go to Texas (Rudolph L. Biesele, *The History of the German Settlements in Texas 1831–1861*, Southwest Texas State University, San Marcos, Texas: German-Texan Heritage Society, 1987, p. 39). Goldenbow: identity unknown. Rostock: German city on the Baltic coast. Knight of the Red Eagle, 4th class: medal. F. W. IV: Friedrich Wilhem IV, King of Prussia who ruled 1840 to 1861. While the steamship *Neptun*, Wright master, traveled between New Orleans and Galveston, the steamship *Neptune*, William Rollins, master, traveled between New Orleans and New York.

[30] Barttezz or Barthez: Frenchman who formerly served in the navy; further identity unknown (*Solms-Braunfels Archives*, Vol. XLIX, pp. 140 and 149). Robert and James Urquhart: identity unknown.

[31] William Frei: identity unknown. Eger: possibly Egern in Bavaria.

[32] Concepcion: identity unknown. Villeut: identity unknown.

[33] Henri Castro (1786–1865), a native of France, was partner in a banking house in France negotiating a loan for the Republic of Texas when he became interested in the republic. He traveled there in 1842 and eventually entered into a contract with the Texas government to settle a colony on the Medina River. Although this is the first mention of Castro in the diary, in a letter of May 30 mailed from Halifax to the Society Solms states that the two crossed the Atlantic together. "*. . . de Castro ist am Board, er ist ein wahrer Paria schon dem Aeusseren nach - seit 10 Tagen sprach niemand ein Wort mit ihm . . .*" (. . . de Castro is on board, he is an outcast just by his outward appearance. During our 10 days at sea no one spoke a word with him . . .). They also traveled on the same ship from New Orleans to Galveston (*Verein Papers*, Yale University, Box 12, Folder 77; *The New Handbook of Texas*, Vol. I, p. 1022; *The Civilian and Galveston Gazette*, 6 July 1844, p. 1, col. 2).

[34] San Saba mine, called La Mina de Los Almagres by the Spanish, is an enigma in Texas history. Shortly after its opening in the 1700s, Indian hostilities forced its abandonment. With time the location was forgotten. Although it is doubtful that the mine was productive, its purported riches had expeditions looking for its location. Fredr. I: King Frederick I. Frd'or: Friedrichs d'or: gold coin, at the time it had a value of about $4.00 (Biesele, *German Settlements in Texas*, p. 82).

[35] The New Orleans *Daily Picayune* reported that "the steamship *Acadia*, Capt. Ryle, arrived at Boston at one o'clock on the afternoon of the 19th, with London and Liverpool intelligence to the 4th June" (29 June 1844, p. 1, col. 6). The *Acadia*, with the *Britannia*, *Caledonia* and *Columbia* were

sisterships that belonged to the British & North American Royal Mail Steamship Company and were utilized in the North Atlantic service. (See note 6 this chapter.) Dr. Jones: In another source Solms identifies this individual. "*. . . gestern suchte ein Dr. Jones, Mitglied des Texan. Congresses mich auf, ließ sich mir vorstellen und ich hatte eine lange und weitläufige Conversation mit ihm.*" [Yesterday a Dr. Jones, member of the Congress of Texas, looked me up, was introduced and we had a lengthy and wide-ranging conversation]. Levi Jones (1786–1879), a physician by profession, represented Galveston County in the House of the Eighth Congress (1843–44) (*Solms-Braunfels Archives,* Vol. XLIX, p. 142; *Biographic Directory of the Texan Conventions and Congresses, 1832–1845.* Austin, Texas: Book Exchange, Inc., ca. 1941, p. 116).

[36] *New York,* regular packet, John T. Wright, master. Balize: a series of channel markers and lighthouses set out to mark the mouth of the Mississippi River below New Orleans.

Chapter Two

Monday, July 1st. At 11 o'clock we noticed land, I arrived in Galveston at 4 o'clock. Low coast line with dunes. The entire island is flat, intersected by bayous. Mons. Cobb and Mons. Arcieri welcomed us, as did Maas. Mons. A., a charming, short man, is secretary at the French legation. He dined with me at the Tremont Hotel (Capt. Seymor, owner). After the meal I went horseback riding along the beach to the Point or Fort. There are six 24-pounders, six 12-pounders, all in fixed position except for the two 12-pounders which are on wheels. None of them have any breastwork. Ducos fell but did not hurt himself. In the evening visit by Mons. Arc[ieri]. I didn't go to sleep until 3 A.M., chased roaches and in the morning ants.[1]

Tuesday, July 2nd. Did correspondence in the morning afterward visits from Colonel Hockley, Kennedy and Cobb. Later visited Kennedy, arrival of Greeve and his accounts of the Indians. At 5 o'clock supper at Arcieri's. The night was tolerable.[2]

Wednesday, July 3rd. Departed at 9:30 by steamboat for Houston. On board a German woman, Mad. Schneider from LaGrange. Greeve's companion is the Englishman Stevenson; Miller is the president's secretary. Arrived at 6:30. Called on Bishop Odin. Abbé Auzier traveled with us from Galveston. Bad quarters at the Old-Capitol and even worse supper and a dirty bed.[3]

Thursday, July 4th. I had a good night's sleep. Did correspondence in the morning. Looked at horses and went riding. (21 cannon salute) The Bishop and Abbé Auzier came over for lunch. In the afternoon saw a panther, a bear and the cats. Later visited the Bishop who wrote to Sophie. In the evening, during supper, arrived the Polish officer.[4]

Friday, July 5th. Purchased horses, a dapple-gray horse for me at $100, three others, an Indian pony, a roan and a pinto at $25 each, for a total of $75. Stephenson left for Galveston, I gave him letters to mail. Ran around and made purchases. We left Houston at 7 o'clock in the evening. Ducos left [for Nassau Farm] with Anton, Pierre and the cook at the same time. What a procession of riders. In the lead, Hunt, land surveyor on the Red River, on a small mule which kept an unbelievable pace! Wangen on the Indian pony, Tory on the roan and I. What a sight. Through woods and prairie (pine forest). Crossed Buffalo Bayou near Houston. Arrived at Tuckham's at 9 o'clock.[5]

Saturday, July 6th. A night without comparison, mosquitoes, fleas, lice. In the saddle at 5:30. At 9 o'clock on the open prairie. In shooting at chicken, my horse went crazy. In the heat I walked five English miles to Big Cypress Creek. Everyone looked for things and by two o'clock everything was accounted for but for a pistol which is broken. Tory rode hard and made funny faces. By 5 o'clock we were again on the way through the never-ending prairie. At 10 o'clock we arrived at Stephenson's on Fish Pond Creek where we found the group that had left Houston on Thursday evening except Castro. I slept on the ground, gave Tory and Wangen my cot.[6]

Sunday, July 7th. Mr. Hunt left us and I led through the prairie and the bottom lands of the Brazos. We crossed the river on a ferry. A mile from it we found a marvelous well, 65 feet deep. Two miles from the Brazos we passed Castro and Miller. At 10:30, and after a detour of a few miles, we arrived in Washington. We put up at Norward's. I sent immediately a message by courier to Dr. Jones because the president was still on the Trinity River. Washington must be the most miserable and unhealthy place in Texas. Thorough clean-up which was much needed. Visit in Dr. Anson Jones' office. He is a polite man with good manners but has cat eyes. I don't trust him. Castro also arrived. In the evening a large number of individuals were introduced. General Sherman, Major Webstern, many colonels, Commodore Moore, etc., etc. Went to bed at 9:30. Slept on the floor in the parlor; Wangen on the sofa.[7]

Monday, the 8th. I slept wonderfully. At 10 conference with Dr. Jones; he offers the most wonderful promises of congress. We have to wait for the president's letter concerning my business. (Temperature 30° R). Dr. [Anson] Jones dined with me. We departed on horseback at 6:30. On the road we met an Irishman, Campbell, carpenter by trade. Stayed overnight at Forke's, a distance of 4 miles from Washington. A beautiful night, the starry sky formed the canopy.[8]

Tuesday, July 9th. Broke camp at 5:30; went by way of Independence to Mount Vernon (Capt. Fuller); over rolling land and undulating prairie, alternated by meadows and woods. Arrived at 11 o'clock. Mrs. Fuller, Col. Bell. James Madison, son from the first marriage, were present. (Madison [Sr.] was murdered. The murderer lives on New Years Creek, eight miles from Mount Vernon. His deed could not be proven.) On the way again at 4 o'clock. By way of Round Top House to Nassau. They expected my arrival. Ducos' group had not arrived. Took care of my affairs. Wonderful night's rest.[9]

Wednesday, July 10th. In the morning, Massy, a Negro girl, came with the message that the party had spent the night at Fortrand's. At 10 o'clock the girl guided them all in. Dr. Meyer was with them. In the evening Willke arrived with his brother-in-law.[10]

Thursday, July 11th. Fortrand returned. The young Saulter became sick with bilious fever. Meyer took care of him. In the evening I took a walk with the Abbé who had also arrived.[11]

Friday, July 12th. At 7 o'clock rode to Fordtran's *Castle of Indolence* with the Abbé and Dr. Meyer. His wife speaks German and French. They have 5 children who are not baptized. The Abbé brought up the subject of religion and things got heated up. At 2 o'clock we were off to Ernst in Industry. There we found Ernst, his wife, Lindheimer who is a botanist from Frankfurt, Ervendberg, a Protestant minister who in payment of one cow and a calf will baptize

F.'s children. He is the teacher to the Ernst children, candidate and demagogue of the Frankfurt Revolution. Departed at 5 o'clock, arrived home at 7 o'clock.[12]

Saturday, July 13th. Willke and his brother-in-law left this morning. Jordt brought a letter from Ernst.

Remarks. Distances in Texas

Galveston to Houston (8 hours by steamer):	70 miles
Houston to Tuckham's:	9 miles
to Hamblin (Big Cypress Creek):	15 miles
to Stephenson (Fish Pond Creek):	22 miles
to Washington:	19 miles
Total:	65 miles

Washington to Independence:	14 miles
to Mount Vernon (Capt. Fuller):	16 miles
to Round Top House:	13 miles
to Nassau:	3 miles
Total:	46 miles

I hired Jordt. In the evening, at sundown, the hunt for chickens without dogs. It was a failure.[13]

Sunday, July 14th. Correspondence in the morning, in between visits by Honnen and von Röder, I like the former but the latter is very much like a vagabond. At noon Fordtran and the doctor arrived, in the evening the Abbé. Strolled around the plantation.[14]

Monday, July 15th. Correspondence. In the evening the news that the mules and horses had disappeared. Set out guards for the night. I took the first shift. Pulled the guards off at 5 A.M.

Tuesday, July 16th. The mules suddenly showed up. Did correspondence and financial matters. We are supposed to leave in the evening. Finally at 4 o'clock we got on the way. (Gave Ducos $35.) Fordtran accompanied us [as a guide]. A difficult creek, otherwise a good trail, beautiful area. Broke the wagon shaft crossing the last creek before Rutersville. Dr. Manley's oxen pulled us out. He is a Methodist. At 9 o'clock we covered 12 miles. Camped in front of Dr. M.'s house.[15]

Wednesday, July 17th. Worked on the wagon in the morning. The Dr. and Fordtran also repaired it. Departed at 7 o'clock, arrived in LaGrange at 10 o'clock. Mad. Schneider. Rohde. Because the cook was sick the meal was bad. Continued at 3 o'clock. In crossing the Colorado [River] had difficulty with loading and unloading. Camped at Brookfield's who talks constantly.[16]

Thursday, July 18th. At 6 o'clock on the way to the Navidad River. Rested there, ate and bathed. Schadouen attempted to overcharge us when we showed interest in a horse. Three miles past him the Dr. killed a deer. I sent the wagon ahead while the deer was dressed. When I caught up with the wagon I found it in a deep creek. It overturned going down to the creek. It was B.'s fault. At the same moment the rest of the party arrived with long faces. They saw three Indians. The Dr. and I made up the rear guard. The others unloaded the wagon, righted and reloaded it. We continued. A thousand feet from there the wagon got stuck in the mud of Mixon Creek. It was 3 miles from Schadouen and 3 miles from Mitchell. After I reconnoitered, we made camp at 6 o'clock. Yordt [*sic*] left to procure oxen. Our party consisted of myself, B. d'O., Ducos, Dr. Meyer, Abbé Auzier, Tory, Anton, Pierre. The cook does not count, he is like a clown on an express train. When wolves howl he shouts, holding a spoon in his hand, "Those are Indians for sure!" The guard was set up at two hour shifts. I patrolled every 15 or 20 minutes; everyone was up at 3 o'clock. You call out "Halt!" If there is no answer, shoot. Throughout it all, I didn't sleep an hour but I did not forget to kiss Sophie's picture and her locks or to say my prayer. The saddle and pistol case served as a pillow. Didn't take off my jacket.[17]

Friday, July 19th. We rode off at 6 o'clock. We were hardly an English mile past the camp when Indians charged across the creek to recover the deer carcass, proof that possibly they were no more than 100 paces from us. We met Jordt with the oxen. Crossed the LaBacca, from there it was another 2.5 miles to Clarke's. Saw the bishop again. Cleaned up, it was badly needed. Found three red bugs.[18]

Saturday, July 20th. Day of rest. Wagon was repaired and weapons were cleaned. Yordt was discharged. $8.[19]

Sunday, July 21st. 6 A.M. service in a pitiful church which serves also as school, living quarters and whatever. The bishop in his vestment conducted the service. Outside one saw the pleasant bivouac area. What a unique picture. I gave Ducos $10 in LaBacca, the bishop $5. A mule was purchased for $35. In the saddle at 7 o'clock, through wide and hot prairie, lots of wildlife and mustangs, herds of 20 to 30 of every kind. Rested for an hour beside a creek; then to Brockhaus (he is from the area between Langenfeldt & Vorst). Obtained meat, milk & butter, but the water was salty.[20]

Monday, [July] the 22nd. After Smith caught both mules which he had let escape we were on the way to Gonzales at 6 o'clock. A dangerous creek. In Gonzales at noon. Mr. Smith got drunk. On the way again at 3 o'clock. The bishop, Dr. Meyer and I rode in the lead. A curious fellow with cocked pistols in his waistband rode with us and made suspicious motions. We were very careful, he soon departed. Crossed the San Marcos on a ferry assisted by Mathieu's oxen which swam across. On the way again at 4 o'clock and at King's at 6 o'clock. Camped in the horse pasture.[21]

Tuesday, July 23rd. Paid King $8, gave Ducos $10 more. On the way at 6 o'clock. Rested beside Mill Creek. Gave the mail rider whom I met a couple of penciled lines for Dr. Jones. Gerwin, a young Westphalian farmer, lives in Gonzales. In Seguin at 3:30. Johnstone takes us across the Guadalupe to Señor Flores' place. Magnificent countryside and a beautiful river with the water emerald-green and clear. Labored crossing over. Bathed in the evening, followed by supper and bed. First night since Nassau that there was no need for guards.[22]

Wednesday, July 24th. Day of rest. Bathed and washed then wrote in my diary; at 11 o'clock to Johnstone, ate there. Wonderful clear and cold spring. Returned [to Flores] in the afternoon. In the evening Señor Navarro brought the news of a Mexican invasion. We talked about it.[23]

Thursday, July 25th. Left at 5 A.M. Before that d'O. played the hero; I was very firm and repeated how we were to conduct ourselves on the trail. The Dr. and I with a Mexican were in the lead. We crossed the following creeks: Santa Clara, Cibolo and Salado. Between the Cibolo and Santa Clara we rested for an hour. Cold breakfast with wine for the people. The Germans built a bridge from oaks. From the last high ground the Dr. and I spotted the tower of San Fernando, we shouted "Hurrah." At 3:30 we arrived at the Alamo. The entrance to the church has columns similar to the entrance at Dhaun. I failed to mention that between the Santa Clara and Cibolo we spotted the smoke of an Indian camp to our right. As we pointed that way, B. came asking what the matter was. Pointing behind me I said, "Nothing, just an Indian camp." He was startled. Across the Cibolo we noticed another encampment on the left side of the trail. The Mexican looked around suspiciously and said "los Indios." B. turned white. The Dr. called for his companion Schmidt and we rode toward the camp. They were Hays' people. Rahm, a Swiss from the canton of Schafhausen. At 4 o'clock we were in town, the bishop offered us wine. We leased a house from Cassiano. It was full of trash. We slept in the yard close to our horses. Ate at Guilbeau's. In bed at 10 o'clock. All of Bexar is in ruins.[24]

Distances:

Nassau to Rutersville:	12 mi.
to LaGrange:	7 mi.
to Mr. Brookfield:	7 mi.
to Mrs. Lyons (prairie):[25]	12 mi.
to Schadouens (Navidad):	5 mi.
to Mixon Creek:	3 mi.
to Mr. Mitchell:	3 mi.
to La Bacca:	2.5 mi.
to Mr. Clarke:	2.5 mi.
to Brockhaus:	25 mi.
to Gonzales:	15 mi.
to Mr. King:	12 mi.

to Mill Creek:	16 mi.
to Seguin:	8 mi.
to Señor Flores:	2 mi.
to San Antonio de Bexar:	35 mi.
	Total: 167 miles

Friday, July 26th. Wrote Sophie and my sister Auguste. Drank to their health. In the evening went with the bishop to the Alamo. The Alsatian families are left by Castro in deplorable conditions. Became acquainted with Major Howard, Capt. Hays, and Rahm, savior of the unfortunate. The Dr. helps where he can. So much misery and ruin everywhere spoil everything for me.[26]

Saturday, July 27th. At 7 o'clock, with the bishop [Odin] and Major Howard to San Jose which is in relatively good shape. It is 5 miles outside San Antonio. Then to San Juan before which we had breakfast at the mill. Two miles from the former; two miles further is La Espada and two miles back is La Concepción. It is three miles to San Antonio. Started back at 2 o'clock. Letter to Sophie. Idle talk with Torzinsky. At night I had wine dispensed to the people.[27]

Sunday, July 28th. Sunday mass at 10 o'clock; sermon in Spanish; at five in the afternoon sermon by Abbé Auzier. He did quite well. The gunsmith Goodman fatally shot an Irishman and wounded a German. The Alsatians flock around me. To my joy Germans are seen in the church.[28]

Monday, July 29th. Everyone went to mass to pray for the July heroes, but neither I nor the Dr. In the evening a dance took place at Guilbeau's. Demoiselle Mendjak. Mlle. Seguin danced the bolero without music. Indians came to town in the afternoon. Mr. Elliot cheats them, an American roughed them up; we took them under our protection. In the morning Chief Oketown disturbed my sleep. I responded likewise.[29]

Tuesday, July 30th. Chiefs Roon & Ltzeti had breakfast with me. It is awfully hot. In the evening conference with McMullen at the bishop's place. Castro returned from his journey.[30]

Wednesday, July 31st. Introduced to Cassiano. McMullen becomes difficult on account of Castro's proposal. Talked with Glewin.[31]

Thursday, August 1st. I did not feel well and rested on my bed all day. In the evening went on a short horseback ride. We met four Lipan Indian chiefs.

Friday, August 2nd. Festive reception at the armory, weapons were displayed also the saddles and bits. The bishop was in his vestments accompanied by both priests. All my people wore belts without side-arm. I wore all my medals. They [Lipan Indians] promise peace and friendship. They want to tell the Comanches that the great prince has arrived. I had to kiss them. They bored me throughout the day with their constant begging. Anton took sick at 9 o'clock. Blood letting by moonlight and with a lantern.[32]

Saturday, August 3rd. Anton felt better in the morning. The decision was made that we leave Sunday after mass. Bourg. wanted to know why so late; because Hays' people cannot make it sooner. He is of the opinion that we do not need them. Arrogant just like a Frenchman, knows everything.[33]

Sunday, August 4th. Mass in the morning, preceded by the bishop's sermon in English about the mysteries. After church B. and Ducos came to say that we cannot travel without a guard of 20 men. Visited by Deputy Surveyor James; next came Hays. The dinner at 2 o'clock was very bad. We departed with Rilcipi, Tom Lyons and Walker. The direction taken is WSW. Camped at Leon Creek.[34]

Monday, August 5th. We went west across the Aroyo [sic] Medio and then the Medina below the presidio. At Lucky Spring at noon. Thunderstorms; Rahm joined us. I ate squirrel, a tolerable meal. Continued upriver along the Medina, magnificent bottom lands. Encampment with the Medina to our back, hills to our front, and to the right and to the left dry, deep gullies. The night was very dark.[35]

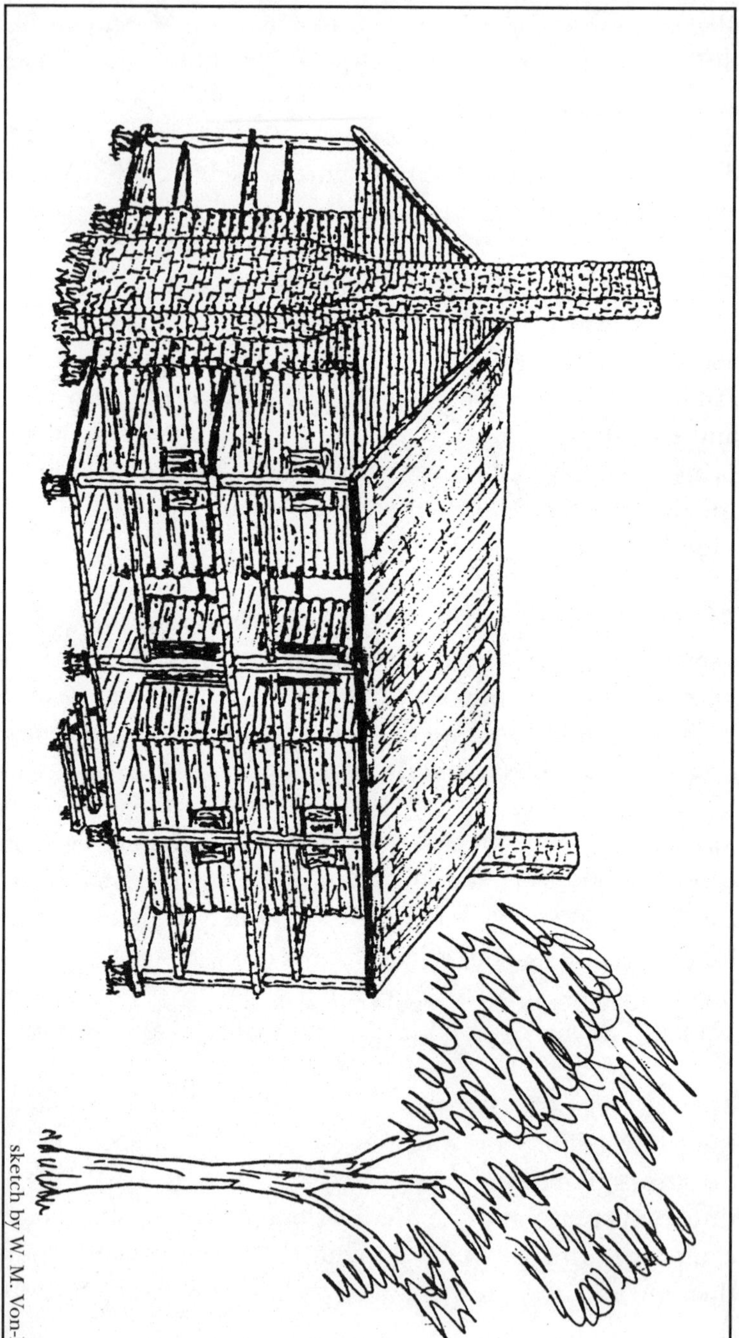

sketch by W. M. Von-Maszewski

Conceptual view of the Manor House at Nassau Farm
Based on observations by Amanda F. von Rosenberg and Ferdinand Roemer

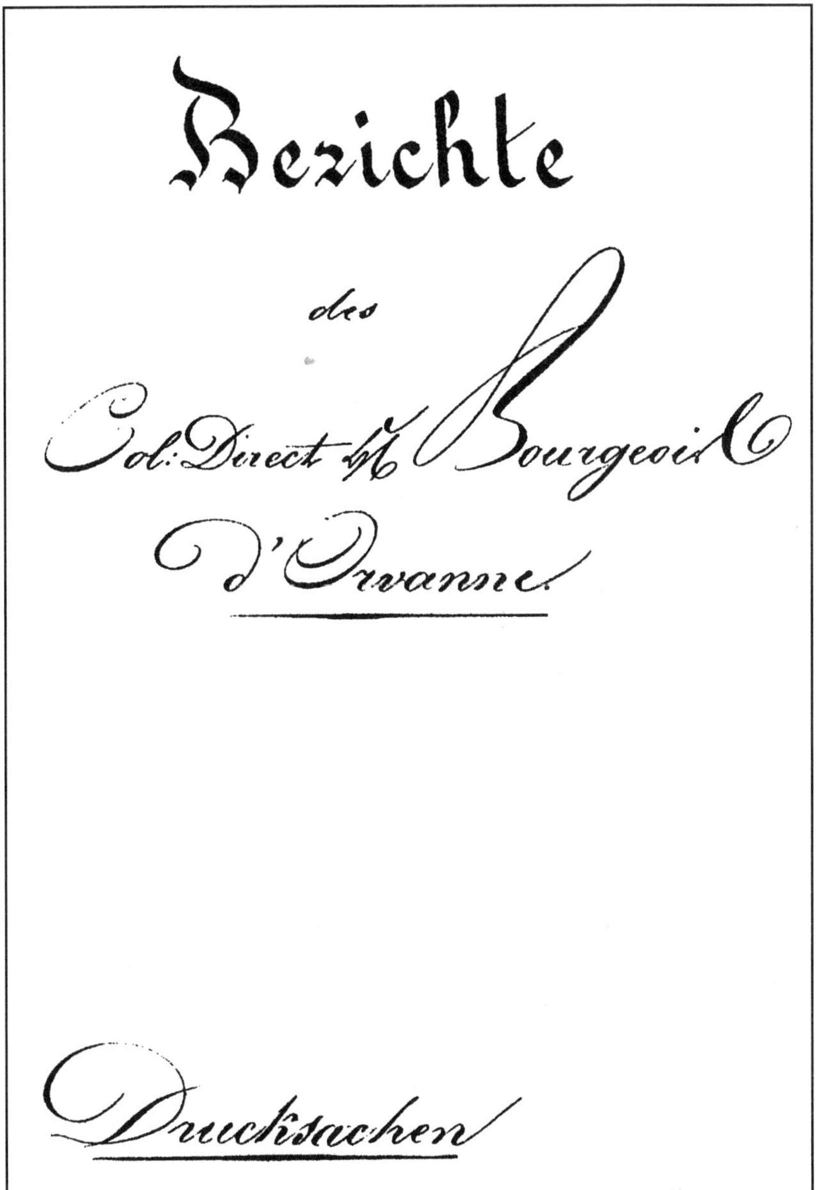

Berichte

des

Col: Direct. H. Bourgeois

d'Orvanne

Drucksachen

Bourgeois d'Orvanne's Nassau Farm Inventory
(and following pages)
Yale Collection of Western Americana,
Beinecke Rare Book and Manuscript Library

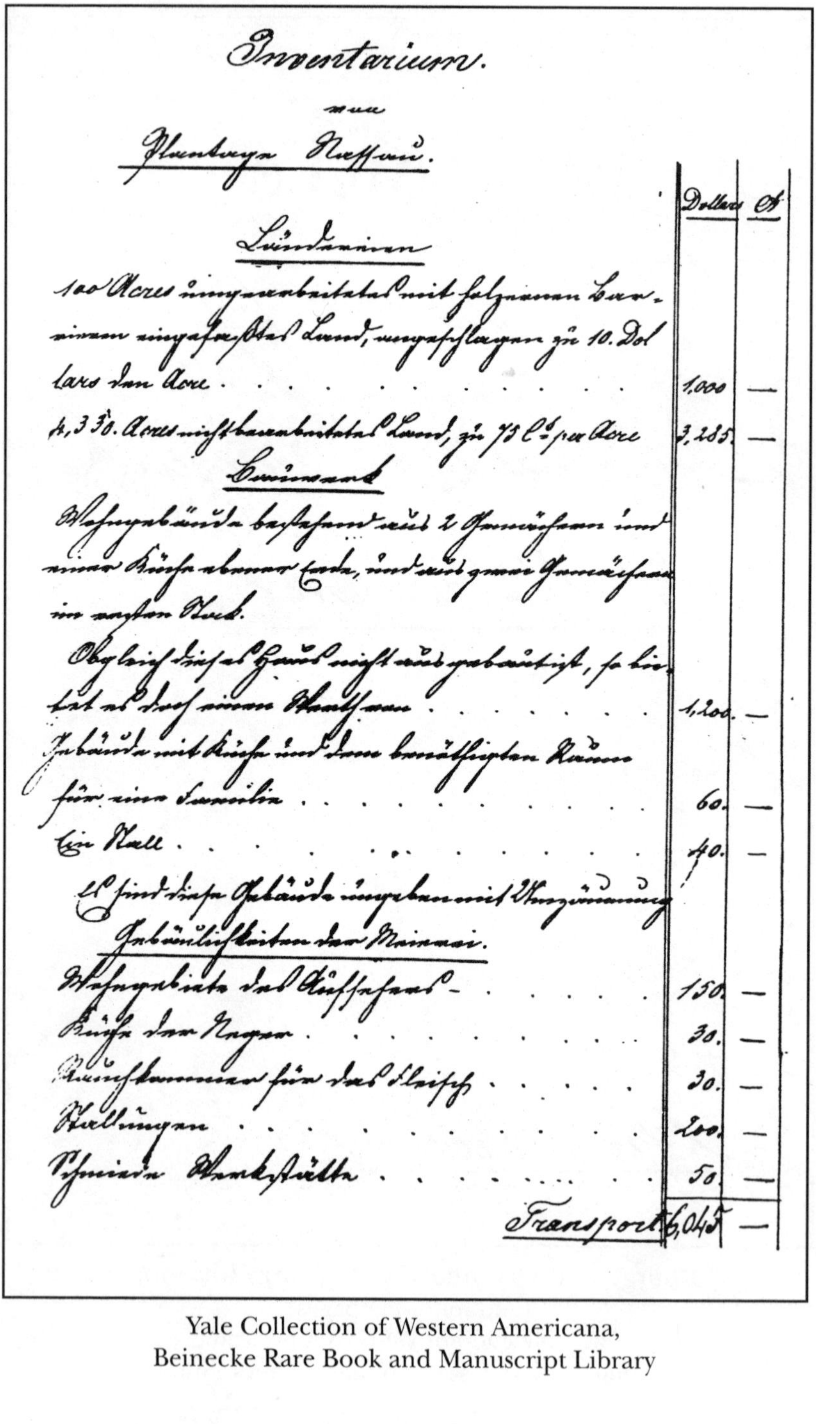

Inventarium.

von

Plantage Nassau.

	Dollars	Ct
Ländereien		
100 Acres umgearbeitetes mit hölzernen Barrièren eingefriedetes Land, angeschlagen zu 10. Dollars den Acre	1,000	—
4,380. Acres nicht bearbeitetes Land, zu 75 Cts per Acre	3,285.	—
Gebäude		
Wohngebäude bestehend aus 2 Gemächern und einer Küche unten Erde, und aus zwei Gemächern im zweiten Stock.		
Obgleich dieses Haus nicht ausgebaut ist, so bietet es doch einen Werth von	1,200.	—
Gebäude mit Küche und den benöthigten Räumen für eine Familie	60.	—
Ein Stall	40.	—
Es sind diese Gebäude umgeben mit Umzäunung		
Gebäulichkeiten der Meierei.		
Wohngebäude des Aufsehers	150.	—
Küche der Neger	30.	—
Räucherkammer für das Fleisch	30.	—
Stallungen	200.	—
Schmiede Werkstätte	50.	—
Transport	6,045	—

Yale Collection of Western Americana,
Beinecke Rare Book and Manuscript Library

	Dollars	Ct.
Transport	6,045	—
Kohlenbehälter	10.	—
Sechs Negerhütten à 20 Dollars	120.	—
Umzäunung dieser Gebäude	100.	—
Namen der Neger		
Georg Buttler	600.	—
Henry Carvan	650.	—
Hark Bedford	650.	—
Charlotte Valley	500.	—
Hanna Hurley	500.	—
Rachael Titus	500	—
Elisa Allen	500.	—
James (Black Smith)	1,300	—
Patience	400	—
Marthea	300	—
Anna Amanda	225.	—
Richard	250	—
Emily	1500	—
Mary	500	—
Margarethea	500.	—
Vieh = Stamm		
Pferde:		
Ein gut beschaffenes Amerikanisches Pferd	100.	—
Zwei Amerikanische Pferde, in übler Beschaffenheit	70.	—
Latus	14,320	

Yale Collection of Western Americana,
Beinecke Rare Book and Manuscript Library

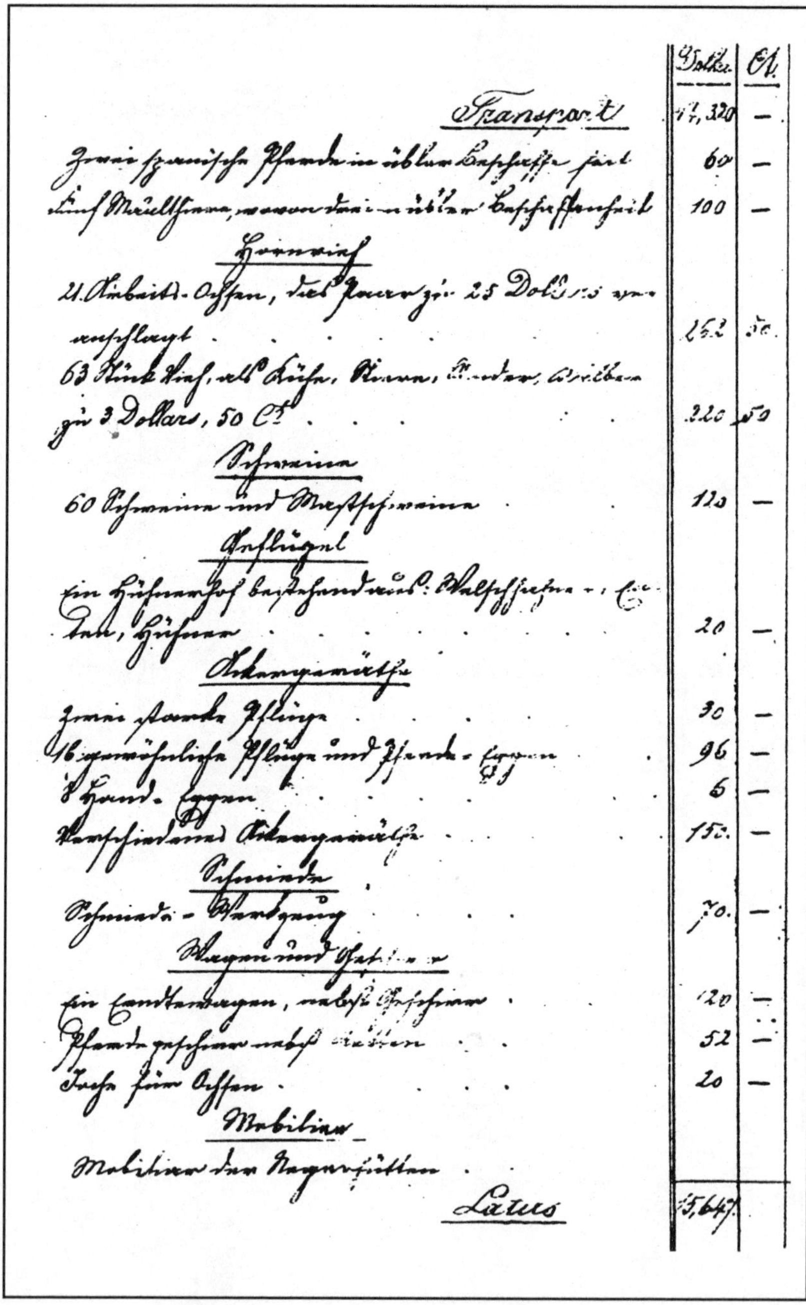

	Dollar	Ct.
Transport	17,320	—
Zwei spanische Pferde in übler Beschaffenheit	60	—
Fünf Maulthiere, wovon drei in übler Beschaffenheit	100	—
Hornvieh		
21 Arbeits-Ochsen, das Paar zu 25 Dollars veranschlagt	262	50
63 Stück Vieh, als Kühe, Rinder, R[illegible], Kälber zu 3 Dollars, 50 Ct.	220	50
Schweine		
60 Schweine und Mastschweine	120	—
Geflügel		
ein Hühnerhof bestehend aus Welschhühner, Enten, Hühner	20	—
Ackergeräthe		
zwei starke Pflüge	30	—
16 gewöhnliche Pflüge und Pferde-Eggen	96	—
8 Hand-Eggen	6	—
Verschiedene Ackergeräthe	150	—
Schmiede		
Schmiede-Werkzeug	70	—
Wagen und Geschirr		
ein Landwagen, nebst Geschirr	120	—
Pferdegeschirr nebst Ketten	52	—
Joche für Ochsen	20	—
Mobilien		
Mobilien der Negerhütten		
Latus	15,647	

Yale Collection of Western Americana,
Beinecke Rare Book and Manuscript Library

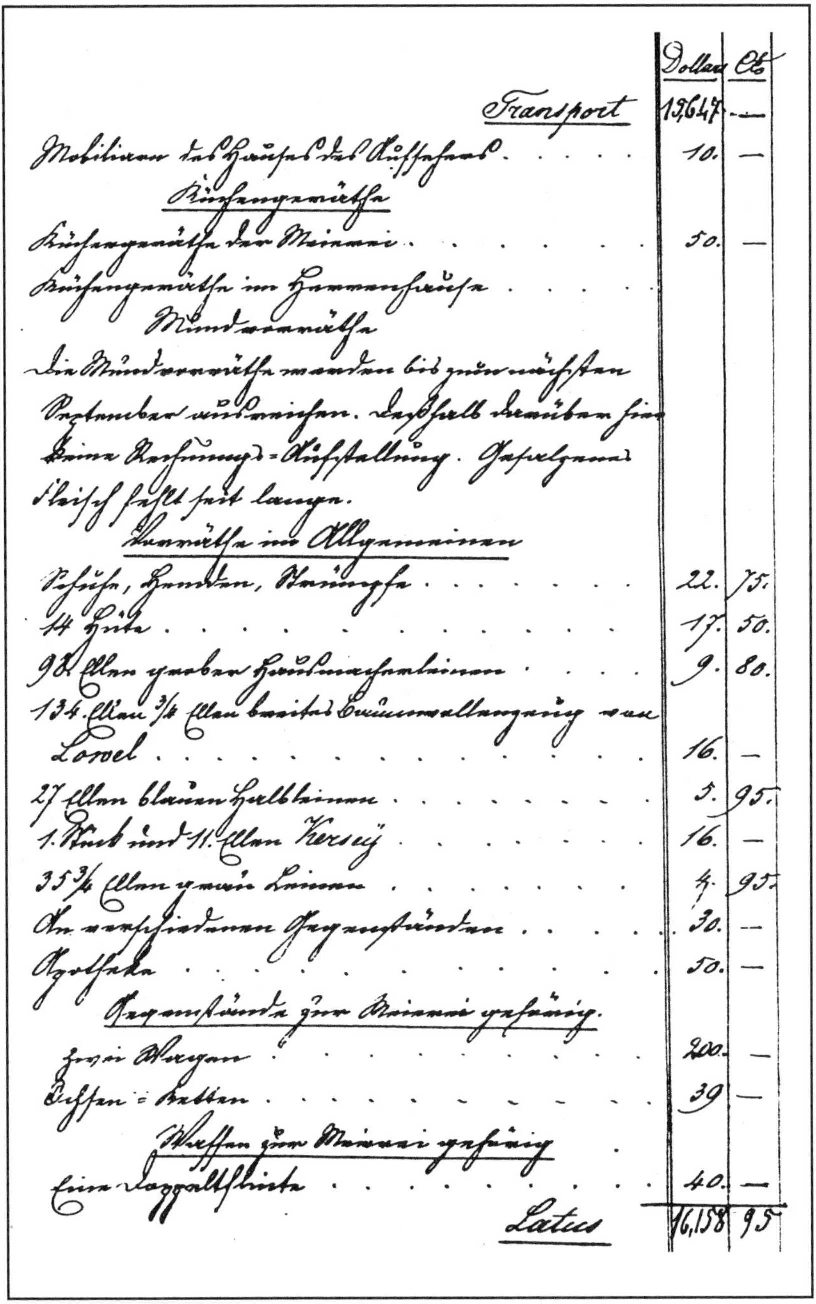

	Dollar	Cts
Transport	15,647	—
Mobiliar des Hauses des Aufsehers	10.	—
Küchengeräthe		
Küchengeräthe der Meierei	50.	—
Küchengeräthe im Herrenhause		
Mundvorräthe		
Die Mundvorräthe werden bis zum nächsten September ausreichen. deshalb bleiben sie beim Rechnungs-Aufstellung. Gesalzenes Fleisch fehlt seit lange.		
Geräthe im Allgemeinen		
Schuhe, Hemden, Strümpfe	22.	75.
14 Hüte	17.	50.
98 Ellen grober Hausmacherleinen	9.	80.
134 Ellen 3/4 Ellen breites Baumwollenzeug von Lowel	16.	—
27 Ellen blauen Halbleinen	5.	95.
1 Tuch und 11 Ellen Kersey	16.	—
35 3/4 Ellen grobes Leinen	4.	95.
An verschiedenen Gegenständen	30.	—
Apotheke	50.	—
Gegenstände zur Meierei gehörig		
Zwei Wagen	200.	—
Ochsen-Ketten	39	—
Waffen zur Meierei gehörig		
Eine Doppeltflinte	40.	—
Latus	16,158	95

Yale Collection of Western Americana,
Beinecke Rare Book and Manuscript Library

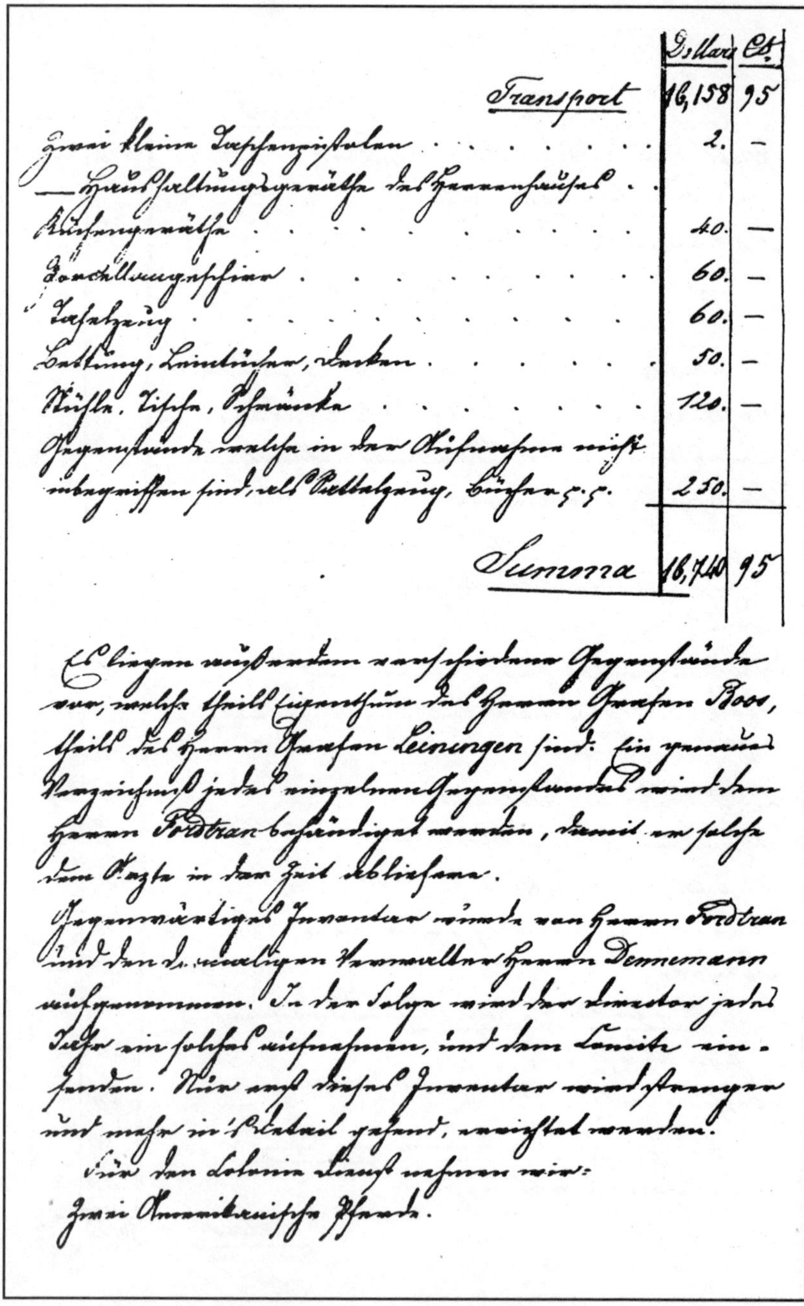

	Dollars	Cts.
Transport	16,158	95
Zwei kleine Taschenpistolen	2.	–
Haushaltungsgeräthe des Herrenhauses:		
Küchengeräthe	40.	–
Porcellaingeschirr	60.	–
Tafelzeug	60.	–
Bettung, Leintücher, Decken	50.	–
Stühle, Tische, Schränke	120.	–
Gegenstände welche in der Aufnahme nicht inbegriffen sind, als Bettzeug, Bücher p.p.	250.	–
Summa	16,740	95

Es liegen außerdem verschiedene Gegenstände vor, welche theils Eigenthum des Herrn Grafen Roos, theils des Herrn Grafen Leiningen sind: ein genaues Verzeichniß jedes einzelnen Gegenstandes wird dem Herrn Fordtran behändigt werden, damit er solche den Rechte in der Zeit abliefere.
Gegenwärtiges Inventar wurde von Herrn Fordtran und dem derzeitigen Verwalter Herrn Dennemann aufgenommen. In der Folge wird der Director jedes Jahr ein solches aufnehmen, und dem Comite einsenden. Nur muß dieses Inventar weit strenger und mehr in's Detail gehend, verfertigt werden.
Für den Colonie Dienst nehmen wir:
Zwei Amerikanische Pferde.

Yale Collection of Western Americana,
Beinecke Rare Book and Manuscript Library

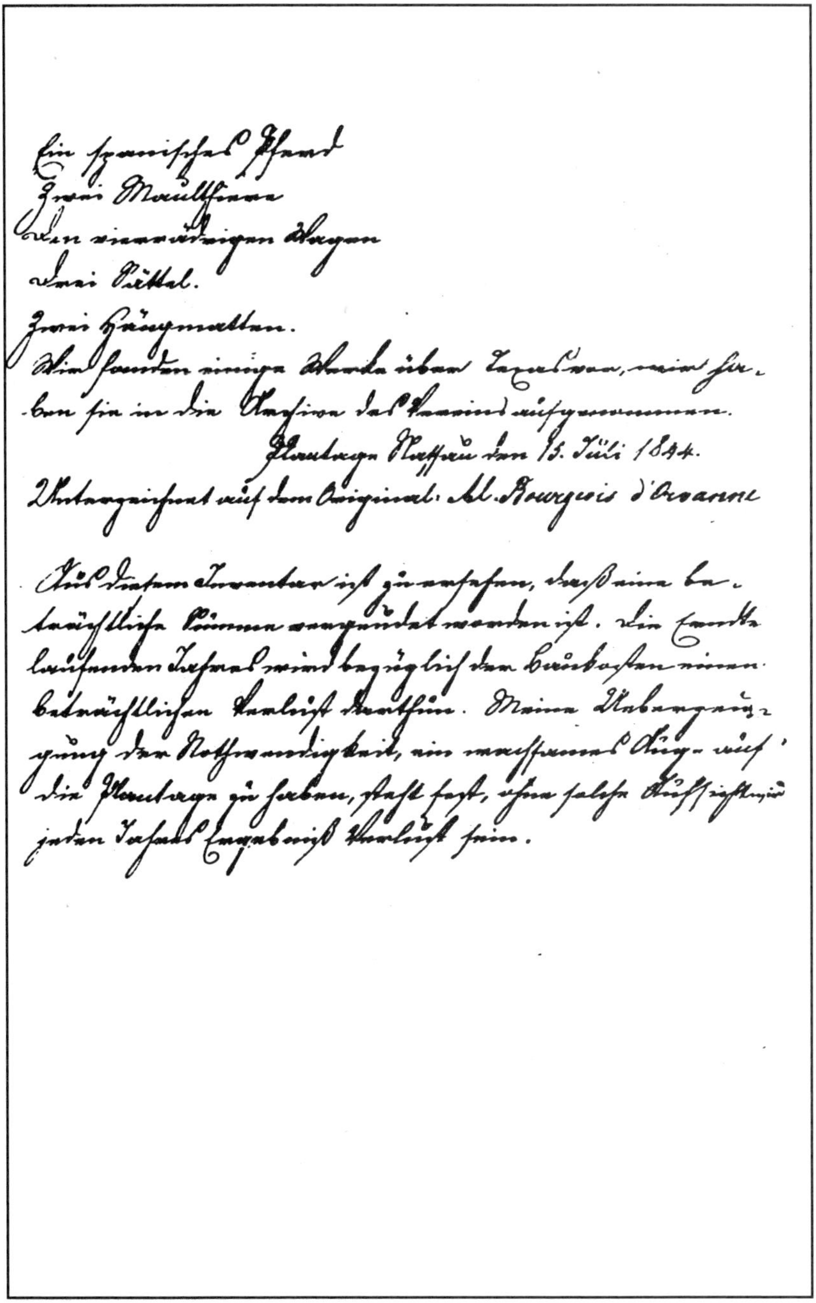

Ein spanisches Pferd
Zwei Maulthiere
Ein vierrädrigen Wagen
Drei Sattel.
Zwei Hängmatten.
Wir fanden einige Werke über [illegible], wir haben sie in die [illegible] das [illegible] aufgenommen.
Plantage Nassau den 15. Juli 1844.
Unterzeichnet auf dem Original: M. Bourgeois d'Orvanne

Aus diesem Inventar ist zu ersehen, daß eine beträchtliche Summe verwendet worden ist. Die Ernte laufenden Jahres wird bezüglich der Baukosten einen beträchtlichen Verlust darthun. Meine Ueberzeugung der Nothwendigkeit, ein wachsames Auge auf die Plantage zu haben, steht fest, ohne solche Aufsichtsmüh jeden Jahres Ergebniß Verlust sein.

Yale Collection of Western Americana,
Beinecke Rare Book and Manuscript Library

Tuesday, August 6th. Fog in the morning. I didn't feel well because of the rancid bacon. Rode along the line of hills on the Medina to a point where it is closest to the Quihe. B. said that there were "wonderful lakes." That is water holes without water, therefore we went back to the Medina where the Canyon road crosses it. Arrived at 2. Camped above, where below there was a splendid spring, bathed twice. Red bugs en masse, orphans, invalids and a supply depot for the red bugs. At night we noticed an Indian signal fire. Fell out of the hammock when a dry branch broke.[36]

Wednesday, August 7th. Day-break found us riding due east. Crossed many small creeks, 10 miles to the Potruaka Creek that held not even a drop of water, on to the San Lucas Springs with good water, after 10 miles crossed the Aroyo Medio to the Leon. Rested there during noon. Rifle practice. Frenchmen who worked in the fields came thinking there was a gun fight. Walker told them, "If you really believed it, you would not be here." Started out again at 3 o'clock. Another 10 miles and we arrived in Bexar at 5:45. Ate. Visited the bishop. Later came Hays. Latest news about the Mexicans.[37]

Thursday, August 8th. Slept until 8:30. Then there was a visit by Major Howard and Capt. Mendjak. The former ate with me. Expressed his idea how to defend Bexar. In the afternoon we, that is he, the Dr., Hill and I, rode out to prove to him the impossibility of doing this. Walked in the evening.[38]

Friday, August 9th. Today is Sophie's birthday. I wrote to the dear angel. Called on the bishop. At supper made a toast. Cannon fired in her celebration, the Germans cheered. Everyone thought those were the Mexicans, a few swam across the river, others came running out of their houses with their pistols. Things calmed down. Gave $30 to the poor.[39]

Saturday, August 10th. The Mexicans are expected. Had a discussion with Bourgeois about yesterday's celebration. I told him candidly my opinion. Everything is in motion. We changed our quarters.[40]

Sunday, August 11th. Slept wonderfully in my new quarters. The Dr. spent the night with Tuwig who shot himself in the thigh. Wanted him held down during the surgery. They said: "No, we cannot do it, he is a free Texian." Last night there came a letter from Sam Houston. I answered it today. News and mail arrived from New Orleans, no letters for me. This makes me despair. Mass was interrupted by a haystack on fire. In the evening news arrived from the Rio Grande that an invasion is anticipated.[41]

Monday, August 12th. A Mexican merchant's wagon train arrived. Went riding in the evening.

Tuesday, August 13th. Corresponded yesterday and today. Preparation were made for the journey which was postponed on Tuwig's account.

Wednesday, August 14th. On the trail at 5 A.M. with Cassiano, Rahm and Lyons. Philippi the mule. At 11 o'clock we covered over 24 miles to Cassiano's ranch. In the evening 10 miles to Seguin's ranch. Camped there. Chief Chiquito appeared unexpectedly with his wife and daughter and a Lipan Indian who is very wild and has no manners whatsoever.[42]

Thursday[August] the 15th. Broke camp at 5 A.M. It was 12 miles to the Marcellino, than another 3 miles to Cassiano's ranch on the Cibolo. We stopped there for lunch. Continued at 4 o'clock. We wanted to reach the Passo del Capote. Cassiano and Mons. Bourgeois talk big. I was angered and demanded that they ride with me. We divided into three groups. With me were the Dr. and Anton. Cassiano's directions were wrong. I took a southerly course but found no trail or pass. Then I turned west. In the evening we camped along the San Antonio. There was nothing to eat. Only warm water to drink. We started a prairie fire. It burnt all around. We had to put out the fire. A panther cried close to us. We had no gunpowder. I had only two bullets in my pistols.[43]

Friday,[August] the 16th. (St. Rochus Day) I recall the times a year ago! If I could only see Sophie at the Rochus Chapel again! In the saddle at 4 A.M. We rode in a southeasterly direction to the confluence of the Cibolo and the San Antonio. Couldn't find a trail. Why? Because there is none. Passed the Capote by about 1,000 paces. Took a northwesterly course and arrived back at our camp. Nothing to eat, everything is withered. "Pelikan" is like a piece of leather. Ate two pieces, each about 12 inches long. Water was quite warm, I bathed. And the sun! It was hot! At 2 P.M. back in the saddle. Went in a west north west direction. My calculation was correct, we reached the trail at Marcellino. From there it was 12 miles to Seguin's ranch. I put lead bullets in my mouth. Passed through a Lipan encampment, one of them led us to the camp. Bourgeois and Cassiano arrived there first, followed by Rahm, Lyons, Tory and the cook. When they didn't find me there, they thought I was lost and had the entire Lipan camp searching for me. Tory was glad to see me. Since I had not eaten for the past 36 hours, I devoured the food. Twelve Indians around me by the campfire. I slept poorly. Bourgeois and Cassiano. What will become of me?[44]

Saturday, [August] the 17th. Seguin was the first to appear in the morning , a cultured man. At 6 o'clock rode to the Salado, 25 miles. Rested there; from there 9 miles to San Antonio. Arrived there at 5 o'clock. I had a headache and a rash on the leg which is swollen. Supper prepared by Mr. Jack's cook. Slept well.[45]

Sunday, [August] the 18th. It's been a year since I was in the company of Sophie at *Rheingrafenstein* where she presented me with the cigar case. My headache is terrible and the old rheumatism is creeping up again. Went to mass in the morning, then called on Mrs. Jack. Didn't feel well all day and rested. In the evening Maroma showed up, the soldier thought to be dead. Traveled 120 miles on foot; six and a half days without food. Has three arrow wounds.[46]

Monday, [August] the 19th. Other than rheumatism and weakness I am somewhat better. [?] makes building plans.

Tuesday, [August] the 20th. Wrote the entire day. Went horseback riding in the evening.[47]

Wednesday, [August] the 21st. The same. Aklin, the last believed to be dead, arrived. He has five wounds. In the evening the Dr. cut the arrow from his jaw bone.[48]

Thursday, [August] the 22nd. The Dr. departed at 3 A.M. Conversation with Bourg. In the evening argument with him at the bishop's place.[49]

Friday, [August] the 23rd. Cassiano doesn't want to be a part. The Dr. returns. Wrede arrived with him and brought letters from Castell, dated 28 June, as well as from Ottilie, none from Sophie! In the evening I went horseback riding.[50]

Saturday, [August] the 24th. Correspondence with Bourgeois. In the evening to the Powder House and past it. The evening mail brings letters dated June 19th, one from Flersheim and none from Sophie! Only my belief in God keeps me going. He never lies.[51]

Sunday, [August] the 25th. B. protests in writing. Wrote to him. In the evening went horseback riding.

Monday, [August] the 26th. Correspondence. Prepared for the departure. Visited the bishop in the evening. Had supper at Mrs. Jack's. A courier arrived from Castro with news that Indians set a wagon on fire, Gilbeau's belongings among them (wines & cigars). They scalped an Alsatian.[52]

Tuesday, [August] the 27th. Wrote in the morning, later packed. At noon lunch at Mrs. Jack's. Departed for the Cibolo at 5 o'clock. Camped there until 3 A.M. Ridel and Erskine (of Capote) accompanied us. The latter delights going through mud puddles, he is a flying Dutchman. He asked where I carried my money. What childish simplicity, what naiveté.[53]

Wednesday, [August] the 28th. Arrived at Mrs. Johnstone's in Seguin in the coolness of the morning. Good hospitality, good bed. The day was pleasantly cool, some rain and thunderstorms. Surveyor of Bastrop County was at Johnstone's.

Thursday, [August] the 29th. Departed at exactly 4 A.M. It was 24 miles to King where we arrived at 10 o'clock. I slept and ate. At 4 o'clock we traveled an additional 8 miles to Gonzales. I learned that the mail courier had German newspapers for me. I noticed also that I left my gold chain with key at King's. Wrede & Anton rode all night; carried with them a letter for the mail courier to take to the postmaster in San Antonio. They returned with the chain which luckily King had not yet found. We rested in the inn devoid of other people. Hardtack and bad schnapps were our sustenance.

Friday, [August] the 30th. Wrede and Anton returned at 6 A.M. Their horses needed rest. I shot a goat and with a young rabbit and two chickens it made a fine meal. At 4 o'clock we continued ten miles to Brockhaus.

Saturday, August 31st. Left at 3 A.M. It was 32 miles to Cristwell where we arrived at 10 o'clock. Unbearable heat. Poor bed as it has also been the previous night. Off again at 4 o'clock, eight miles to Brookfield, who wanted his leg amputated. A sparse supper and a fair camp. Today was Dr. Meyer's birthday.[54]

Sunday, September 1st. In the saddle at 6 A.M.; eight miles to LaGrange. The ferryman was drunk and asleep. A small boy took us across. Arrived in LaGrange at 7:30 where we made purchases. Wrede stayed behind to look after the freighting. From here it was 14 miles to Nassau. Arrived there at noon. Awful heat. Etzel deserted, took half of the things. One Negress is dead, another ran off. Denman had just arrived. Finished and sealed letters in the evening.[55]

Monday, September 2nd. Dr. Meyer left at 5 A.M. I was alone with Wrede the whole day. In the evening rode to the farm. James rode on a mule to LaGrange.[56]

Tuesday, [September] the 3rd. James returned with flour, wine, etc. Fordtran rode up at 11 o'clock, he was pale from fear. [?] he fell. In the evening I accompanied him for a mile. The well on the farm has no more water. Richard brought brackish water from the creek.[57]

Wednesday, [September] the 4th. We fetched water from Capt. Sutton's farm. In the evening rode leisurely to Keseirer for eggs, about one mile from Shelby. Made a good jump on the white horse.[58]

Thursday, [September] the 5th. At six in the morning I rode the horse with only the halter and bit which gave me a roaring headache; slept some; then washed myself thoroughly. A well is started on the hill. Tuesday night I dreamt of Sophie and this morning again. Oh, when will I hear from her. Life here is terrible, no pleasures, only tribulations.

Friday, [September] the 6th. Awoke without a headache. Wrede went to LaGrange, returned with small items but no letters! Wilke came during the day; Fordtran came in the evening, his horse and mule ran off.

Saturday, [September] the 7th. Poem: *Deutschland hoch!* [Hail, Germany!] Preparations were made for the trip to Washington. We departed at 5 o'clock. At 7 o'clock in the evening arrived at Capt. Fuller's, excellent supper. Gobbled it up in a Texas manner, naturally. I had a bad night, couldn't fall asleep on account of my headache.[59]

---

[1] Henry Adolph Cobb: merchant and French vice-consul in Galveston (Nancy Nichols Barker, *The French Legation in Texas*, Austin, Texas: Texas State Historical Association, 1971, pp. 339, 452, and 491). Flavio Arcieri: secretary of the Legation, later French consular agent at Galveston (*Ibid.*, p. 312). Samuel Maas: the 1850 census gives the following information: thirty-eight years old, merchant, born in Germany, his wife Isabella, thirty years, also born in Germany (*1850 U.S. Census, Galveston County, Texas*, p. 241, National Archives Microfilm M432, Roll 910). Mons. A.: Mons. Arcieri. The Tremont Hotel stood on the southwest corner of Tremont and Post Office Streets. It opened to the public in September 1839 and for a long time it was the largest and most elegantly furnished hotel in Texas. At the time of Solms's visit James M. Seymour was the proprietor. This building was destroyed by fire in 1867 (Charles W. Hayes, *Galveston, History of the Island and the City*, Austin, Texas: Jenkins Garrett Press, 1974, pp. 293 and

393). Following the victory at San Jacinto, Fort Point was established on the eastern end of the island to protect the entrance to Galveston Bay against possible attacks by Mexico. Victim to the frequent storms in the Gulf of Mexico it was given up after its last calamity in 1843 (Gerald S. Pierce, *Texas Under Arms,* Austin, Texas: The Encino Press, 1969, pp. 49 and 56).

[2] Colonel Hockley: George Washington Hockley (1802–1854), colonel of ordnance, in charge of Galveston Island's fortification. Kennedy: William Kennedy (1799–1871), British consul in Galveston and author of *The Rise, Progress, and Prospect of Texas* (London: R. Hastings, 1841). Greeve: James H. Grieve and William Bollaert just returned to Galveston from an inspection trip to western Texas. Grieve and William Pringle received a colonization contract from the Republic of Texas in 1843 for land located between the Nueces and Frio Rivers with the stipulation that within three years from the issuance of the contract they settle six hundred families on this tract of land (Eugene W. Hollon and Ruth L. Butler, eds., *William Bollaert's Texas,* Norman: Oklahoma University Press, 1956, pp. 331, 332–359 and 380–384).

[3] Mad. Schneider, LaGrange, Texas: identity unknown. Stevenson: Henry Stephenson. Miller: Washington D. Miller (1814–1866): President Sam Houston's private secretary. Bishop Odin: Jean Marie Odin (1801–1871): Catholic bishop and Vicar Apostolic to Texas. Texas' independence from Mexico severed the political ties as well as the ties with the Bishop of Monterrey. Finding themselves without any religious guidance the Catholics in Texas petitioned the archbishop of New Orleans for help. Odin was sent to the newly declared apostolic prefecture. He worked in Texas for twenty-one years and established the Diocese of Texas (1847) with its base in Galveston. As the state's population increased new dioceses were carved out of the sprawling Galveston Diocese: Diocese of San Antonio (1874), Diocese of Dallas (1890), Diocese of Corpus Christi (1912) (James T. Moore, *Through Fire and Flood: The Catholic Church in Frontier Texas 1836–1900,* College Station, Texas: Texas A&M University Press, 1992). Abbé Auzier: Names unfamiliar to Solms are written phonetically in his diary. The spelling of Ogé for Auzier is one example. Bishop Odin in his journal, entry for 4 July 1844, states: "Prince Charles of Solms and Messrs. Bourgeois d'Orvanne & Ducos with Mr. Ogé arrived at Houston." The Abbé's full name was Jean Pierre Ogé (Jean Marie Odin's *Daily Journal,* photostatic copy, Austin, Texas: Catholic Archives of Texas, p. 57; Ralph Bayard, *Lone-Star Vanguard: The Catholic Re-Occupation of Texas 1838–1848.* St. Louis, Missouri: The Vincentian Press, 1945, p. 338n). Old Capitol Hotel: After the capitol of the Republic was relocated from Houston to

Austin, the structure previously used by congress was converted into Houston's chief hotel. It was a rather commodious frame building two-stories in height and stood on the present-day corner of Main and Texas (*Telegraph & Texas Register*, 8 May 1844, p. 3, col. 3; Dr. S. O. Young, *A Thumb-Nail History of the City of Houston, Texas,* Houston: Rein & Sons, Co., 1912, p. 50).

[4] Solms, a Roman Catholic himself, asked the bishop to write to Sophie.

[5] The journey by Solms and Alexander Bourgeois d'Orvanne to Washington-on-the-Brazos, seat of government of the Republic, was one of necessity, to confirm that the Bourgeois-Ducos land grant was still a viable issue. Bourgeois d'Orvanne obtained a colonization contract from the Republic in June 1842 with the stipulation that one third of twelve hundred families be settled on the land by the end of eighteen months or the contract would be forfeited. The grant, located west of San Antonio, was quoted to have the boundaries as follows: "Commencing at the junction of the Rio Potranca with the Rio Medina, thence extending up the Potranca to its source, thence due North to the Sabinas [Creek, Kendall County], thence extending along the Sabinas to the source of that Stream, thence in a direct line to the source of the Arroyo de Ubalde [Sabinal River?], thence in a direct line to the source of the southern branch of the of the Rio Frio, thence extending down the said stream to the junction of the Rio Frio with the Arroyo de Ubalde, thence extending along

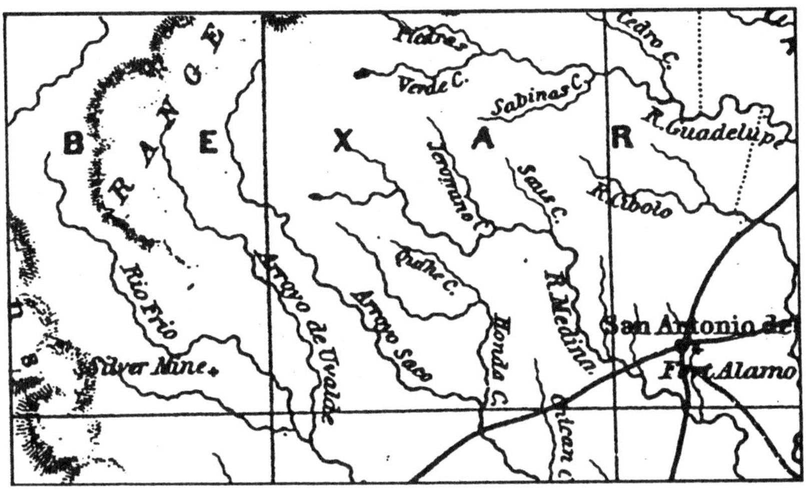

Area of the Bourgeois-Ducos land grant
MAP OF TEXAS, C. S. Williams, Publisher, Philadelphia, 1845
Courtesy Texas General Land Office (GLO K-4-43A)

the line of the grant made to Henri Castro & John Jaussand to the northeastern Corner of said grant, thence in a direct line to the place of beginning." The grant included areas in the present-day counties of Medina, Uvalde, Real, and Bandera. An attempt to plot the boundaries of the Bourgeois-Ducos grant on a modern map proves to be a challenge. The reference points in the description of the grant were based on the perception of the lay of the land at that time. Superimposing this information on today's map results in boundaries of questionable configurations. Only the boundary along the Frio River can be drawn with any assurance. When d'Orvanne learned of the Society's colonization plan in Texas, he traveled to Germany in 1843 and gained the directors' interest in his contract. That the terms of the contract could not be met in time he explained to be only a minor point, fully confident that the officials of the Republic would readily extend it once they learned of the Society's settlement plans. The Texas Congress, however, in 1843 repealed all colonization contracts where the terms had not been fulfilled at that time (Biesele, *German Settlements in Texas*, pp. 70–73; Bobby D. Weaver, *Castro's Colony, Empresario Development in Texas, 1842–1865*, College Station, Texas: Texas A&M University Press, 1985, pp. 82, 110n; H. P. N. Gammel, *The Laws of Texas, 1822–1897*, Austin, Texas: C. W. Raines, 1898, Vol. II, pp. 958–959; see also "Introduction" and map on page 59). Stephenson: very likely the same person mentioned in the previous entry. Anton, Pierre and the cook: employed by Solms; Anton was a guide (*Solms-Braunfels Archives*, Vol. XLVIIIa, p. 172); Wangen and Tory: apparently Solms's man servants. Although he makes frequent mention of all these individuals in his diary, he does not identify them by their full names. Ducos, Anton, and Pierre left for Nassau Farm (*Ibid.*, p. 153). Tuckham (Harris County): identity unknown. A regular passenger service existed between Houston and Washington-on-the-Brazos. The following advertisement, for example, appeared in the *Telegraph & Texas Register* for 29 May 1844:

REGULAR LINE OF STAGES FROM HOUSTON TO WASHINGTON

The subscriber having the contract for carrying the mail,
will run regular with a carriage to accommodate passengers.
Leave Washington every Monday at 6 A.M.
Leave Houston every Thursday at 6 A.M.—through each way in 30 hours.
All Packages for Washington must be left at the Houston House the morning previous to the departure of the Stage, and charges paid, or they will not be taken.

Agents.
H. BALDWIN, Houston House, Houston
W. MASSIE, Washington

Solms departed Houston, crossing Buffalo Bayou in its proximity, and after two hours his party reached Tuckham's place in present northwest Houston, presumably the area where Highway 290 splits off from Highway 610. Solms quotes a distance of nine miles (see Solms's entry for 13 July).

[6] Chicken: very likely, wild turkeys. Big Cypress Creek: it coursed through William K. Hamblin's land, located where today Highway 290 crosses over the creek in western Harris County. Fish Pond Creek, also known as Clear Creek, rises in northern Waller County and flows south about fourteen miles into the Brazos River. Stephenson: unable to identify. A three hours' ride from Tuckham's place brought Solms and his party to the open prairie around present-day Jersey Village. Near where Highways 6 and 290 cross, Solms's horse spooked and he had to continue on foot. He walked five miles to W. K. Hamblin's place on Cypress Creek. After a rest and the passage of the day's intense heat the party continued to Stephenson's at Clear Creek (Fish Pond Creek), east of Hempstead.

[7] Washington: Washington-on-the-Brazos, capital of the Republic of Texas from 1842 to 1845. Norward: identity unknown. Dr. Anson Jones (1798–1858): Secretary of State (1841–1844), President (1845), by profession a physician. President: Sam Houston (1793–1863), third president of the Republic of Texas (1841–1844). The President was still on the Trinity River due to illness. General Sidney Sherman (1805–1873): major general of the militia, Republic of Texas. Webstern: Major Thomas G. Western (ca. 1792–1847), at this time superintendent of Indian Affairs, Republic of Texas. Edwin Ward Moore (1810–1865), commodore of the Texian Navy. On a course of NWN the trail led through the Clark Bottom to the Rock Island ferry on the Brazos River. On the other side it continued in a northerly course and after an unplanned detour Solms arrived in Washington-on-the-Brazos (see *J. deCordova's Map of the State of Texas.* Houston, 1849).

[8] Secretary of State Anson Jones could not extend the Bourgeois-Ducos colonization grant without the consent of Congress. Solms asked to be notified on the outcome of this question as well as about President Houston's return to Washington (*Solms-Braunfels Archives*, Vol. XLVIIIa, p. 155). 30° R equals 100° F. Forke: it very likely that this is a phonetic rendition of what Solms thought he heard. The person in question is possibly James L. Farquhar who lived on a tract of land on the Andrew Miller grant located about four miles from Washington. The 1850 census

shows Farquhar as a substantial landholder with 6,000 acres (*Washington County [Texas] Deed Records,* Vol. F, p. 69; *1850 U.S. Census, Washington County, Texas,* p. 319A, National Archives Microfilm M432, Roll 916). With business completed and the heat subsided by the late afternoon Solms departed from Washington. He followed the La Bahia Road, a trail from the Spanish Colonial period that linked Goliad and Nacogdoches. Four miles down the trail about where Highway 105 crosses Doe Run Creek he stopped for the night at Farquhar's.

[9] Independence, Washington County: described as a village with approximately fifty inhabitants (Richard S. Hunt & Jesse F. Randel, *A New Guide to Texas,* New York, 1845, reprint: Austin, Texas: Jenkins Publishing Company, 1970, p. 56). Mount Vernon, Washington County: six miles northwest of Brenham, laid out in 1841 by John Stamps, and briefly the county seat. The Census of 1850 shows that Capt. Samuel Fuller, born in Massachusetts, was sixty-three years of age, farmer by occupation with a real estate value of $25,000. The facts related to the murder are these. Richard Matson Sr., Solms calls him Madison, brought his family to Washington County from Ralls County, Missouri, in 1831. They settled near Burton on land purchased from Asa Mitchell in December 1838 who shortly thereafter killed Matson. His widow married Samuel Fuller on January 1, 1840 (Joyce M. Murray, compiler, *Washington County, Texas, Deed Abstracts 1834–1841,* Dallas, Texas: privately published, 1985, pp. 66, 103; Lois W. Burkhalter, *Gideon Lincecum, 1793–1874, A Biography,* Austin, Texas: The University of Texas Press, 1965, pp. 76, 79; *1850 U.S. Census, Washington County, Texas,* p. 287A, National Archives Microfilm M432, Roll 916; Frances Terry Ingmire, compiler, *Washington County, Texas, Marriage Records 1837–1870,* St. Louis, Missouri: Ingmire Publishers, 1980, p. 3). Col. Bell: identity unknown. Round Top, northern Fayette County. Nassau Farm: located a short distance to the southeast from Round Top. The plantation property on the William H. Jack league had been bought by the Society in 1843 and named in honor of Duke Adolf of Nassau, protector of the Society. It was a working plantation with a blacksmith shop, smokehouse, barns and stables, slave quarters and a house for the overseer. On a rise one-quarter mile to the south was the manor house. A two-story log structure, it had a fireplace at each end and glass panes in the downstairs windows. This land, however, served no purpose in the forthcoming settlement of German immigrants in Texas. Solms, disliking the property's proximity to Anglo settlements, began looking for more isolated large tracts of land. A conceptional view of the Manor House found on page 44 is based on contemporary observations by Amanda Fallier von Rosenberg and Ferdinand Roemer (*The New Handbook of Texas,* Vol.

IV, p. 939; Ferdinand Roemer, *Texas*, translation by Oswald Mueller, Southwest Texas State University, San Marcos: German-Texan Heritage Society, 1983, pp. 162–164; Crystal Sasse Ragsdale, editor, "Letters of Amanda Fallier von Rosenberg," *The Golden Free Land*, Austin: Landmark Press, 1976, pp. 122–123). The route then followed the county road to the community of William Penn and on FM 390 to Independence. Here the trail split, to the right continued La Bahia Road, to the left an alternate route led through Mount Vernon (see map in *Roemer's Texas*, San Antonio, Texas: Standard Printing Company, 1935). This settlement vied with Brenham, six miles to the east, to become the county seat. After it lost the contest it quickly faded away. Beyond Mount Vernon the trail rejoined La Bahia Road in the vicinity of Burton and followed Highways 290 and 237 to Round Top. From here Nassau Farm was three miles to the southeast.

[10] Fortrand: Karl or Charles Fordtran (1801–1900), tanner by training, was born in Minden, Westphalia, the son of Johannes H. Fordtran, soapmaker. He emigrated to New York in 1830. The following year he joined Friedrich Ernst in their move to the west. They arrived in Texas in 1831 and each obtained land grants from the Mexican government in present Austin County. In 1834 Fordtran married Almeda Brookfield, daughter of William Brookfield (see note 16 this chapter); in 1835–36 Fordtran served in Captain Bird's Ranger company (Kurt Klotzbach, "Ernst Kapp, der Gründer der 'Lateinischen Kolonie' Sisterdale" in *Mitteilungen des Mindener Geschichtsvereins* ["Ernst Kapp, founder of the Latin settlement Sisterdale," in *Proceedings of the Minden Historical Society*], Minden, Germany, 1982, Vol. LIV, p. 22; *The New Handbook of Texas*, Vol. II, p. 1076). Friedrich Ernst (1796–1848), who came with Fordtran to Texas, was attracted by the liberal land grants offered by Mexico. Ernst and his family obtained one league of land (4,428 acres) and Charles Fordtran as a single man received one-quarter of a league. Ernst extolled Texas in a letter which was widely circulated and reprinted in a local newspaper. His account convinced people, such as Kleberg, von Roeder, Fuchs, to try their future in Texas. Because of this Ernst is referred to as the "father of German immigration to Texas" and Industry, the settlement he founded, "the cradle of German settlement in Texas." Dr. Emil Meyer lived in Texas before Solms's arrival. Ferdinand Lindheimer commented that Dr. Meyer had married in 1844 and was a practicing physician. Solms hired him on the strength of his familiarity with tropical diseases, a knowledge he thought valuable to the arriving German immigrants. Bourgeois d'Orvanne considered Solms's decision premature. Other than appearing intelligent and well-educated, being by nationality a Swiss, having

served in the Dutch army and a recent arrival in Texas not much more was known about Dr. Meyer. This caution was justified. Before Solms reached his own conclusion, a contemporary observer described Dr. Meyer as a liar, slanderer, gossip, and loafer (Minetta Altgelt Goyne, *A Life Among The Texas Flora: Ferdinand Lindheimer's Letters To George Engelmann*, College Station, Texas: Texas A&M University Press, 1991, pp. 95, 101; *Solms-Braunfels Archives*, Vol. XLVIIIa, p. 157). Willke: a former lieutenant in the Prussian army, Ludwig Willke (1818–1893) and his family already lived in Texas when Solms arrived. Solms appointed him depot overseer and commander at Carlshafen. In later years Willke was postmaster (1858–1860) of Spring Branch, west of New Braunfels, and a surveyor (1866–1870) for Kendall County. Willke's brother-in-law was apparently Mathias Sander (Geue and Geue, *A New Land Beckoned*, p. 134; Everett Anthony Fey, *New Braunfels: The First Founders*, New Braunfels, Texas: Comal County Genealogical Society, 1994, Vol. I, pp. 512 and 611).

[11] Saulter: identity unknown.

[12] Castle of Indolence: Solms used an analogy from the Scottish poet James Thomson (1700–1748). In the poem "The Castle of Indolence" Thomson describes the ills of indolence and the blessings of industry. But the name given to Fordtran's place, however, was not of Solms's making, he simply expanded on it. Moritz Tiling remarked that "after settling in Texas [Friedrich] Ernst called his place 'Industry,' while Fordtran's farm received the less inviting name of 'Indolence' or 'Lazytown,' as it was generally called" (Moritz Tiling, *History of the German Element in Texas from 1820–1850*, Houston, Texas: privately published, 1913, p. 18). Fordtran had been appointed as caretaker by Count Boos-Waldeck and continued to serve in this position under Prince Solms until the arrival of a colonial physician at Nassau Farm (Rudolph L. Biesele, "Prince Solms's Trip to Texas, 1844–1845" in *Southwestern Historical Quarterly*, Vol. XL, p. 11). Ferdinand Jacob Lindheimer (1801–1879): born in Frankfurt on the Main, emigrated to Illinois, USA, in 1834 but soon left for Mexico. In 1836 he returned to New Orleans to participate in the Texas Revolution. In the early 1840s he started to collect Texas flora for other botanists. Joining the Society in 1844, he settled in New Braunfels and married in 1846. When the *New Braunfels Zeitung* was established, he became editor. Much of his life he devoted to collecting plants. Called "the father of Texas botany" he is credited with having found several hundred plant species (*The New Handbook of Texas*, Vol. IV, pp. 203–204). Louis Cachand Ervendberg (1809–1863): his early years in Europe before his arrival in the U.S. around 1836 are slowly coming to light. He established Protestant congregations in Illinois where he also met and married Maria Sophia

Dorothea Luise Muench in 1838. Late the following year the family came to Houston, Texas. After a brief stay in Houston he moved with his family to Colorado County where he ministered to the local German settlers. When Solms arrived in Texas Ervendberg sought employment with the Society. He relocated his family to New Braunfels and organized a Protestant congregation there (1845). When the settlement was struck by an epidemic that left children parentless he established the Western Texas Orphan Asylum in New Wied, Comal County. He also tried to establish the West Texas University. In the mid-1850s Ervendberg left his wife and departed for Mexico accompanied by a teenage orphan girl. There he worked as a naturalist collecting plants for clients in the U.S. He reportedly was shot for his money in 1863. (*Ibid.*, Vol. II, p. 885; Al Dreyer, "Louis Cachand Ervendberg a.k.a. Christian Friedrich Ludwig Cachand," in *The Journal*, German-Texan Heritage Society, Vol. XXII, No. 2, pp. 27–29; Bill Stein, et al., "Introduction to the Kirchenbuch of Louis Cachand Ervendberg," in *Nesbitt Memorial Library Journal*, Columbus, Texas, January 1992, Vol. II, No. 1, pp. 41–44).

[13] Jordt: Solms spelled the name also Yordt (see also note 19 this chapter). The Jordt in question was very likely a son of Detlev Thomas Friedrich Jordt. D. T. F. Jordt arrived in Texas about 1833 and under the pseudonym of Detlev Dunt wrote one of the earliest German books on Texas, (*Reise nach Texas* [*Journey to Texas*], Bremen, Germany: Carl W. Wiehe, 1834) while he lived with Friedrich Ernst in Industry. Jordt returned to Germany to have his manuscript published as well as to bring his family back with him to Texas. This included his wife Dorothea, née Heeder (ca. 1802–1870), sons Karl Friedrich Sophus (1820–1879) and Hermann Emil Mathias (ca. 1824–1863) and daughter Henriette Elise Rebecca (1829–1906). D. T. F. Jordt died ca. 1833. It is assumed that one of the sons accompanied Solms (Biesele, *German Settlements in Texas*, pp. 2–3; Walter Struve, *Germans & Texans*, Austin, Texas: The University of Texas Press, 1996, pp. 44 and 68; letter to W. M. Von-Maszewski from Bill Stein, Nesbitt Memorial Library, Columbus, Texas).

[14] Honnen: first name unknown. Church records for the German community on Cummings Creek list a Mr. and Mrs. Honnen at the Maundy Thursday service in 1843 and only a Mr. Honnen at the Good Friday service in 1844. The death register reveals that a Sara Gesina Honnen, neé Booker, age thirty-nine, died in childbed on 27 October 1843 (Bill Stein, et al., "Kirchenbuch of Louis Cachand Ervendberg" in *Nesbitt Memorial Library Journal*, Vol. II, No. 1, pp. 56 and 58). von Röder: identity unknown, several von Röders were in Texas at this time.

[15] Rutersville, Fayette County: organized in 1839 with the purpose of

establishing a Methodist college there. When the Congress of the Republic of Texas granted the charter in 1840, it became the first Protestant college established in Texas. Dr. A. P. Manley: physician and Methodist minister. La Bahia Road was readily reached from Nassau Farm. On its southern leg, it followed Highway 237 to Oldenburg and from there Highway 159 through Rutersville to LaGrange.

[16] LaGrange, Fayette County, had a population of approximately 300 (Hunt and Randel, *A New Guide to Texas*, p. 57). Solms met Mad. Schneider previously on the boat trip from Galveston to Houston (see entry for 3 July 1844). Rohde: The 1850 Census identifies a H. (or Henry) Rhode, born in Germany, forty-five years old and a merchant by occupation (*1850 U.S. Census, Fayette County, Texas*, p. 208A, National Archives Microfilm M432, Roll 910). William Brookfield, Fayette County, Charles Fordtran's father-in-law. At LaGrange the Colorado River was crossed and on an almost southerly direction, the party passed approximately where present-day Ammansville and Dubina are located. Brookfield's place was along the trail in the vicinity of the present-day community of Hostyn. In his diary entry for 25 July, Solms summarizes the distances covered on this journey. Besides mentioning the stop at Brockhaus, he gives an additional reference, Mrs. Lyons, a location in the southeast corner of Fayette County. The party followed approximately the route of present-day Highway 77 (see Charles Pressler's Texas map of 1859).

[17] Solms crossed the Navidad River in present-day Fayette County. Schadouens: probably Thomas Chaudoin, a prominent early settler in the northeast part of Lavaca County (Paul C. Boethel, *Colonel Amasa Turner, The Gentleman from Lavaca*, Austin, Texas: Von Beckmann-Jones Co., 1963, p. 110). Mixon Creek: in Lavaca County. Mitchell: Isaac Newton Mitchell (1810–1853) settled three miles north of the Hallet settlement which later became Hallettsville (Paul C. Boethel, *The Free State of Lavaca*, Austin, Texas: Weddle Publications, 1977, p. 120). The sketch of the camp is apparently a site along Mixon Creek (*Solms-Braunfels Archives*, Vol. XLVIIIa, p. 161). The trail continued on its southerly course crossing the Navidad River and Mixon Creek. The location of the camp may be on Mixon Creek.

[18] LaBacca: Lavaca River; this portion of the river is located in Lavaca County. In his diary, Solms was not consistent in the spelling of the river and the community of Port Lavaca, e.g., LaBacca, LaVacca, DaBacca. Father Edward A. Clarke: In his book about Texas Solms refers to the stopover at Clarke's as the "Catholic School of Father Clarke" which explains Bishop Odin's presence there (*Texas 1844–1845*, Houston, Texas: The Anson Jones Press, 1936, pp. 79 and 84). Another source observes that

"while in the heart of the Lavaca settlements he [Bishop Odin in 1841] visited with [Fathers] Haydon and Clarke and was impressed by the school being built by them. It consisted of a two story log house with a passage or hall down the center (Carlos Eduardo Castañeda, *Our Catholic Heritage,* Vol. VII, Austin, Texas: Von Beckmann-Jones Co., 1958, p. 73). The trail intersected the Gonzales Road in the vicinity of Halletsville. Solms took the Gonzales Road (Highway 90A). It crossed the Lavaca River and touched on the Clarke's settlement. This location may correspond to the present site of St. Mary's Church and Brown School off SH 90A on FM 390, about 3 miles west from Hallettsville.

[19] Yordt: the proper spelling of the name is "Jordt," Solms occasionally spelled it "Yordt" (see note 13 this chapter).

[20] Brockhaus: Charles Braches (1813–1889), born in Germany, moved from the United States to the Republic of Texas in 1840 and lived on a plantation on Peach Creek eight miles east of Gonzales. During the Seventh Congress of the Republic of Texas, 1842–43, he represented Gonzales in the House. The 1850 Census enumerates besides him his wife Sarah Ann Ashby McClure, thirty-nine, their two small children, Sarah's child from her first marriage, Joel D. McClure, eleven, born in Texas, as well as her brother William Ashby, twenty-four, and his wife Francis, twenty-two years, both born in Kentucky (*1850 U.S. Census, Gonzales County, Texas,* p. 326, National Archives Microfilm M432, Roll 910). From Clarke's settlement the trail followed Highway 90A to Brockhaus' plantation on Peach Creek in present Gonzales County.

[21] Smith had been hired as a guide to succeed Fordtran (*Solms-Braunfels Archives,* Vol. XLVIIIa, p. 162). Gonzales in Gonzales County: in 1846 Alwin Sörgel described Gonzales as a community consisting of about thirty buildings (Alwin H. Sörgel, *A Sojourn in Texas, 1846–47,* translated and edited by W. M. Von-Maszewski, Southwest Texas State University, San Marcos, Texas: German-Texan Heritage Society, 1992, p. 46). San Marco [River]: should be San Marcos [River]. Mathieu: probably William A. Mathews. John G. King's boarding house west of Gonzales. (Hermann Seele, *The Diary of Hermann Seele & Seele's Sketches from Texas,* translation, introduction and notes by Theodore Gish, Austin, Texas: German-Texan Heritage Society, 1995, p. 253). After passing through Gonzales, the San Marcos River was crossed. Ten miles west of Gonzales on a course that would coincide with present-day Highway 90A the Solms's party arrived at King's place which was frequented by travelers as an overnight stop.

[22] Mill Creek in Guadalupe County. Gerwin: identity unknown. Seguin (town) in Guadalupe County. Johnstone: identity unknown. Señor Flores: Manuel Flores (1801–1868), south side of Guadalupe River. Many early

travelers through this part of Texas remarked that the Guadalupe and San Marcos Rivers were emerald-green and clear. Viktor Bracht quoted Sörgel's passage when he rhapsodized about the Guadalupe River (see: Sörgel, *A Sojourn in Texas,* p. 48; Viktor Bracht, *Texas in 1848,* translated by Charles F. Schmidt, San Antonio, Texas: The Naylor Printing Co., 1931, p. 99; Ferdinand Roemer, *Texas,* pp. 87, 92). The trail approached Seguin from the east. At the time this settlement had a population of about 50 (Hunt and Randel, *A New Guide to Texas,* p. 61).

[23] The brothers Jose Antonio Navarro (1795–1871) and Jose Luciano Navarro (1800–1869) owned large ranches to the north of Seguin. With Jose Antonio Navarro still imprisoned in San Juan de Ullva prison, Mexico, for participating in the Santa Fe expedition, it must have been Jose Luciano who visited with Solms. After General Woll's invasion of San Antonio in 1842, anxiety continued about a repeated Mexican invasion of the Republic of Texas.

[24] Santa Clara Creek in Guadalupe County. Cibolo Creek forms the boundary between Bexar and Guadalupe Counties. Salado Creek in Bexar County. San Fernando Cathedral: not to be mistaken for the present-day structure which was built in 1868 upon the foundation of the old Spanish parish church. The structure referred to today as the Alamo (Spanish for "cottonwood") was originally the chapel of Mission San Antonio de Valero. Abandoned in 1793, it became a military post for the Mexican army in later years. In 1836 the former chapel became a fortress for the Texians in their fight for independence from Mexico. After the fall of the Alamo, the building was practically in ruins (*The New Handbook of Texas,* Vol. I, p. 82). Dhaun: the reference is to Castle Dhaun near the town of Kirn, State of Rheinland-Pfalz, Germany. Schmidt: may be the same person whom Solms calls Smith in his entry for 22 July 1844. Hays: John Coffee (Jack) Hays (1817–1883), surveyor and legendary captain of the Texas Rangers. Johann Jacob Rahm (ca. 1806–1845), from Canton Schaffhausen, Switzerland, fought in the Texas War for Independence and joined John Hays' Texas Rangers in 1843. He also assisted Solms in spring 1845 when the site of New Braunfels was located. In gratitude Solms presented Rahm with a four and one-half acre lot in town for a butcher shop. Rahm was the official butcher for the German Emigration Society. The following year Rahm was killed in a duel (Biesele, "Prince Solms's Trip," in *Southwestern Historical Quarterly,* Vol. XL, p. 10n; Fey, *New Braunfels,* Vol. I, p. 481; "Swiss" in *The New Handbook of Texas,* Vol. VI, p. 182). Jose Cassiano (1791–1862), a native of Italy, a wealthy individual, resided in San Antonio since the 1820s (Evelyn M. Carrington, editor, *Women in Early Texas,* Austin, Texas: Texas State Historical Association, 1994, pp. 49–55). One

memoir states that Cassiano's house "fronted on the Main Plaza, was bounded south by Dolorosa Street and extended half way back to the Military Plaza" (Rena Maverick Green, editor. *Samuel Maverick, Texan, 1803–1870,* San Antonio, Texas: privately published, 1952, p. 74). Francois Guilbeau (1813–1879), born in France, arrived in San Antonio in 1839, where he operated a successful bakery and wine shop. Among his other business interests he developed an extensive transportation network in the Gulf coast region. He served as acting mayor for San Antonio in 1841 and was appointed French vice-consul for that region. Also a horticulturist, he helped save the French viniculture from total destruction by the phylloxera when he shipped cuttings from the Texas mustang grapevine to be grafted on the French stock. He was appointed the Society's agent in San Antonio (*The New Handbook of Texas,* Vol. III, p. 371). On the last leg of the journey the trail continued to follow Highway 90A. It crossed Santa Clara Creek, Cibolo Creek, Salado Creek, and along Commerce Street ended at the Alamo.

[25] Mrs. Lyons: The home of the Lyons family was near the present town of Schulenberg (Lonnie R. Weyland and Houston Wade, *An Early History of Fayette County,* LaGrange, Texas: LaGrange Journal, 1936, pp. 71 and 72).

[26] Sister Auguste: presumably Auguste Louise Therese Mathilde (1804–1865), Solms's sister (Information to W. M. Von-Mazewski from Schloß Braunfels, Braunfels, Germany, 9 June 2000). As an empresario Castro recruited in Alsace, Switzerland and Germany for a land grant west of San Antonio where he established the colony of Castroville. Major George T. Howard, sheriff of San Antonio. Johann J. Rahm, "savior of the unfortunate": referred to his personal care and help of Castro's stranded colonists which he financed from his own meager funds (Biesele, "Prince Solms's Trip" in *Southwestern Historical Quarterly,* Vol. XL, p. 10n).

[27] The missions of San José y San Miguel de Aguayo, San Juan Capistrano, Nuestra Senora de la Purisima Concepcion de Acuna, and San Francisco de la Espada, located south of town along the San Antonio River, were established in the early 1700s to Christianize and educate the local Indians. After secularization in 1794 the structures gradually deteriorated. The mill referred to here is very likely the "Old Mill" located to the north of town on the east bank of the San Antonio River (Map of "San Antonio in 1835" in Henderson Yoakum, *History of Texas,* Two Volumes in One, New York: Redfield, 1855, Vol. II, map opposite page 26). Torzinsky: identity unknown.

[28] James Goodman: gunsmith and blacksmith, reported to be of a volatile personality (Jesus F. de la Teja, editor, *A Revolution Remembered:*

Juan N. Seguin, Austin, Texas: State House Press, 1991, p. 43; Solms-Braunfels, *Texas, 1844–1845,* p. 57).

[29] July heroes: In the entry for the previous day Solms states that the Alsatians, French subjects, flocked around him. The mass could be the French celebration of *Trois Jours Glorieux* (The Three Glorious Days, 27, 28 and 29 July), the July Revolution in 1830 when Charles X, King of France, was overthrown and driven into exile. Demoiselle Mendjak: identity unknown. Mlle. Seguin: identity unknown. William A. Elliott: San Antonio merchant. The 1850 Census gives his age as forty years and his place of birth as South Carolina *(1850 U.S. Census, Bexar County, Texas,* p. 246, National Archives Microfilm M432, Roll 908). Oketown: an Indian chief; the tribe is unknown.

[30] Chiefs Roon & Ltzeti: apparently of the Lipan tribe who occupied the lands between the San Marcos and San Antonio Rivers. John McMullen: merchant in San Antonio, offered the Society his land located along the Medina River. Castro arrived in San Antonio from Washington about 18 July and left again on 25 July to inspect for the first time his land grant in the west, including the potential settlement sites on the banks of Lake Quihi and the banks of Hondo Creek (Bobby D. Weaver, *Castro's Colony, Empresario Development in Texas 1842–1865,* College Station, Texas: Texas A&M University Press, 1985, p. 44).

[31] Castro, on his trip to the west, saw McMullen's land and wanting it for his own colony, made McMullen an offer. With two potential buyers vying for the land, McMullen raised the price at which time the Society dropped out (*Solms-Braunfels Archives,* Vol. XLVIIIa, p. 169). Jose Cassiano also possessed extensive land holdings. Glewin: possibly Gerwin (see entry for 23 July).

[32] Armory: location unknown.

[33] This inspection trip was to the Bourgeois-Ducos grant west of San Antonio and north of the Henry Castro grant (Biesele, *German Settlements in Texas,* pp. 72, 104; see also note 5 this chapter and the map on page 59).

[34] John James (1819–1877), district surveyor for Bexar County (*The New Handbook of Texas,* Vol. III, p. 905). Rilcipi: Indian scout, either a Lipan or Tonkawa since both tribes were at peace with each other and lived in the same general area. Tom Lyons: Texas Ranger (Frances Terry Ingmire, compiler, *Texas Ranger Service Records 1830–1846,* St. Louis, Missouri: Ingmire Publisher, 1982; p. 90). Samuel Hamilton Walker (1817–1847): born in Maryland, he arrived in Texas in 1842, joined John C. Hays's company of Texas Rangers in 1844 and later volunteered for service in the Mexican War where he was killed in action. He also successfully modified a revolver known thereafter as the Walker Colt (*Ibid.*, p.

154; *The New Handbook of Texas,* Vol. VI, p. 797). Leon Creek: joins the Medina River in south Bexar County.

[35] Arroyo Medio: in Bexar County. Medina River: rises in Bandera County, flows through Medina and Bexar Counties before it joins the San Antonio River. Presidio: reference likely to the road going to the presidio. Lucky Spring: should be Leon Creek. Very likely Solms traveled on an established trail, the Upper Presidio Road. It crossed Medio Creeks and the Medina River about three miles west of the confluence of Sauz Creek and the Medina River. After crossing, Solms left the trail and continued upriver on the right side of the Medina (A. Joachim McGraw and Kay Hindes, "The Development of the Regional Road Network: Southern Frontier Trails to San Antonio," in *The Old San Antonio Road and the Caminos Reales,* Austin, Texas: Texas State Department of Highways and Public Transportation, 1991, p. 154).

[36] Quihe: Should be Quihi River, Medina County. Solms would have continued upriver to a point, about eight miles above present Castroville, where the hills give way to an open plain that offers easy excess to Quihi Creek. Retracing his steps he arrived at the Canyon Road crossing on the Medina River about three miles below the confluence of San Geronimo Creek and the Medina (Hollon and Butler, *Bollaert's Texas,* p. 352).

[37] Potruaka Creek: should be Potranco Creek, Bexar County. San Lucas Springs: or San Lucas Creek, in western Bexar County. Leon Creek: in Bexar County. Bexar: another designation for San Antonio. In his *Second Report,* dated 20 August 1844, Solms stated regarding his inspection of the Bourgeois-Ducos grant, as well as the McMullen grant, that he considered it a good fortune that Bourgeois-Ducos contract had been annulled because portions of the land had already been settled resulting in not enough land remaining for German immigrants to be settled in one area (Geue and Geue, *A New Land Beckoned,* p. 26). Traveling east, the party crossed Big Sauz and its branches, Potranco, San Lucas, and Leon Creek before it arrived in San Antonio.

[38] Capt. Mendjak: Antonio Menchaca (1800–1870) fought on the Texian side during the Texas War for Independence, served several terms as alderman in San Antonio, highly respected by Sam Houston (Amelia W. Williams and Eugene C. Barker, editors, *The Writings of Sam Houston,* Austin, Texas: Pemberton Press, 1970, Vol. IV, p. 251; Vol. VII, p. 452). Hill: identity unknown.

[39] In honor of Princess Sophie's birthday Solms made a donation of "$30 to the poor." This gesture was misunderstood by Castro who did not look after the welfare of his own colonists in Texas. Many of Castro's colonists, consequently, found themselves in destitute conditions and in San

Antonio they were willing to join the Society's colonization project. Consequently, when Solms distributed this money Castro construed this as an attempt to lure his colonists away from him (*Solms-Braunfels Archives,* Vol. XLVIIIa, p. 176).

[40] Anticipating a Mexican invasion into Texas the Anglo population was leaving San Antonio. Because of this, the merchant Wilson Riddle offered his house to Solms (*Ibid.*, Vol. XLVIIIa, p. 177).

[41] Tuwig: Joseph A. Tivy, private, Texas Ranger, served under Captain John C. Hays in the San Antonio area between June and October 1844. Later he worked as a surveyor and sold land in the Pedernales Valley (Ingmire, *Texas Ranger Service Records,* p. 148; *The New Handbook of Texas,* Vol. VI, p. 509). Sam Houston, in his letter to Solms dated Washington [-on-the-Brazos], 2 August 1844, apologized for his absence due to sickness when Solms called on Washington. The president went on to say that he approved of the Society's goals in Texas but regretted that recent legislation by congress would hamper the enterprise. Congress, over the president's veto, on 30 January 1844, repealed all laws that authorized the president to issue colonization contracts as well as forfeit such already in force, where the conditions had not been strictly complied with. Houston, apparently as a show of faith, stated that he was enclosing a copy of his veto message of 10 January 1844, to congress (Williams and Barker, *The Writings of Sam Houston,* Vol. IV, pp. 351–352; Gammel, *The Laws of Texas,* Vol. II, p. 958).

[42] Erasmo Seguin (1782–1857): his ranch near present Floresville, Wilson County, was a stopping-over place for travelers (*The New Handbook of Texas,* Vol. V, p. 965). Chief Chiquito: Captain Chicito, Lipan Indian chief (Dorman H. Winfrey and James M. Day, editors, *The Indian Papers of Texas and the Southwest 1825–1916,* Austin, Texas: Texas State Historical Association, 1995, Vol. II, p. 97). The road to Cassiano's ranch and next to Seguin's ranch followed State Highway 181 from San Antonio to Floresville. According to *J. de Cordova's Map of the State of Texas* (1849), the trail continued in a southeasterly direction to Goliad and Victoria, crossing Marcilenas Creek and Cibolo Creek in Wilson County. In his book *Texas 1844–45,* page 82, Solms gives the distances from San Antonio to Cassiano's Ranch and on to Seguin's Ranch as twenty-four miles and ten miles, respectively.

[43] Marcellino: Marcelinas Creek, Wilson County. Passo del Capote: in Karnes County. (Not to be mistaken for Capote Hills in Guadalupe County.) San Antonio River: rises in the city of San Antonio, flows to the southeast, and empties into the Guadalupe River. From Seguin's Rancho the party traveled the Bahia Road to Cassiano's Rancho on Cibolo Creek.

From here the party turned south looking for Passo del Capote. When the goal eluded it, Solms's group turned west and camped overnight by the San Antonio River.

[44] St. Rochus Day, 16 August: named for Roch of Montpellier, France, who devoted his life to the services of the plague-stricken. Rochus Chapel is situated on the Rhein near Bingen. Pelikan: Solms meant "pemmican" but what he ate apparently was "jerky." Placing an object in the mouth stimulates the flow of saliva and thus helps still the thirst; today, the use of lead for that purpose is considered a health hazard. The following day, on a southeasterly course, the party reached the confluence of the Cibolo and San Antonio River in present Karnes County. They retraced their steps, reached their camp of the previous night, and on a WNW course came across La Bahia Road at the Marcelinas crossing.

[45] Salado Creek: crosses eastern Bexar County and enters the San Antonio River. Mr. Jack: William B. Jacques. Mrs. Jacques ran a boarding house at the southwest corner of Commerce and Yturri (Green, *Samuel Maverick, Texan*, p. 140). The journey to San Antonio followed, in reverse, Highway 181 to the Salado Creek crossing and into San Antonio proper.

[46] In his reports to Europe, Solms mentions his physical conditions and his plans to visit a health resort when he returns to Europe. Although the incident of the ranger's survival is correct, his name was Cicero Rufus Perry. During a scouting trip in August 1844, to ascertain if a Mexican invasion into Texas could be expected, four Texas Rangers camped at the Nueces River. While two of the Rangers, John Carlton and James Dunn bathed in the river, the other two, Christopher H. "Kit" Acklin and Cicero Rufus "Rufe" Perry, were suddenly attacked by Indians. Acklin and Perry fought back as best as they could while they retreated to the river to link up with their comrades. In the melee both were severely wounded. They lost sight of each other and found refuge in a nearby thicket. Carlton and Dunn believing these two dead, rode 110 miles to San Antonio. Acklin and Perry badly wounded, and not knowing of each other's fate, walked separately to San Antonio. Here Solms's account picks up (John Henry Brown, *Indian Wars and Pioneers of Texas*, reprint, Austin, Texas: State House Press, 1988, p. 269).

[47] "Wrote the entire day," could refer to his writing of the *Second Report* dated 20 August 1844 (Geue and Geue, *A New Land Beckoned*, p. 25).

[48] Christopher H. Acklin: see note 46 this chapter.

[49] Solms presumably selected Dr. Meyer for the task of special messenger, to ride to Galveston and bring back any mail addressed to the Society officials in Texas (*Solms-Braunfels Archives*, Vol. XLVIIIa, p. 185).

[50] Friedrich Wilhelm von Wrede Jr. (1820– ?) came first to the U.S.

with his father in 1836. They traveled extensively before their return to Germany 1843. His father compiled and published their experiences in a book (see Chapter IV, note 36). The young Wrede left Europe in June or July and arrived in San Antonio on 23 August 1844. From that time, he was Solms's constant companion, serving him as his secretary. Wrede brought from Germany communiqués from the Society's directors, one such communiqué instructed Solms to dismiss Bourgeois d'Orvanne as Colonial Director because it was unlikely that the Republic of Texas would renew his land grant contract. In 1847 he accompanied John O. Meusebach (see Chapter V, note 40), Solms's successor as general commissioner, to make a peace treaty with the Indians. Wrede settled in Fredericksburg where he entered into private business but also served as county clerk of Gillespie County (1850–1851) and represented that area in the Eighth Texas Legislature (1859–1861). He married Sophie Bonzano, sister of Mary Bonzano Kessler Fisher (see Chapter III, note 24). Sometime in 1865 the family left permanently for Wiesbaden, Germany (*The New Handbook of Texas*, Vol. VI, p. 1088; Biesele, "Prince Solms's Trip" in *Southwestern Historical Quarterly*, Vol. XL, pp. 21–22; Dorothy E. Justman, editor, *Henry Francis Fisher, Saint or Sinner?*, Houston: privately published, 1989, p. 282).

[51] Correspondence with Bourgeois: This may be d'Orvanne's dismissal as Colonial Director when it became certain that his colonization grant had not been renewed (Geue and Geue, *A New Land Beckoned*, p. 35). Powder House: located east of the Alamo on the road to Gonzales.

[52] Solms's writing coincides with the *Third Report* dated 26 August 1844 (*Ibid*, p. 34). The Indian attack may refer to the convoy from Galveston to San Antonio. One cart fell behind, was ambushed by Indians and its occupant, nineteen-year-old Ziliax Rheen, killed (Weaver, *Castro's Colony*, p. 48).

[53] Mr. Ridel: Wilson Riddle, San Antonio merchant. Michael Erskine (1794–1862), owner of Capote Ranch east of Seguin. On the home-bound journey to Nassau Farm, at Brache's farm on Peach Creek, the party took the Gonzales-Columbus Road. Southeast of present-day Moulton in Lavaca County, the La Bahia Road was taken north to LaGrange and Nassau Farm. Because of the intense summer heat travel was limited to the early morning and the late afternoon hours.

[54] Cristwell: Leroy Vanoy Criswell lived where later the community of Black Jack Spring, Fayette County, developed along present Farm Road 609 (Marion Day Mullins, *Republic of Texas: Poll Lists for 1846*, Baltimore, Maryland: Genealogical Publishing Co., Inc., 1974, p. 38; Bracht, *Texas in 1848*, p. 203).

[55] Charles Fordtran was inspector at Nassau Farm (see also note 9 this chapter), William Etzel the general manager, and Denman the overseer (Biesele, *German Settlements in Texas*, p. 103; Geue and Geue, *A New Land Beckoned*, p. 24).

[56] James: a Negro whose primary duties were that of a blacksmith for Nassau Farm (*Verein Papers*, Yale University, Box 15, Folder 92). Wrede, probably Wrede Jr. (see note 50 this chapter).

[57] Richard: a Negro on Nassau Farm (*Ibid*, Box 15, Folder 92)

[58] Enumeration data for 1850 states that William Sutton was born in Virginia in 1783, married, farmer by occupation with real estate valued at $2,000 (*1850 U.S. Census, Fayette County, Texas*, p. 192B, National Archives Microfilm 432, Roll 910). The community of Shelby is located in northwestern Austin County, Texas.

[59] Deutschland hoch!:

Durch des Weltmeers Wogen,
Getrennt vom Vaterland
Sind wir hergezogen,
Von manchem Liebesband.
Auf muthigen Rossen durchzieh'n
Wir Texas' heisse Prairien,
Und kürzen den Weg mit Gesang,
Der schallet in diesem Klang.
Hoch Deutschland, Deutschland hoch!

Lagern wir im Kreise
Ums helle Feuer hier,
Gedenken in der Ferne
Der trauten Lieben wir,
Und spiegelt den seltnen Wein
Des Feuers Widerschein;
Wir würzen den Trunk mit Gesang,
Der schallet in diesem Klang:
Hoch Deutschland, Deutschland hoch!

Geht es nun zum Kampfe,
Mit Indiern wild und graus,
Zum blutigen Schlachtentanze
Dann Du deutsches Schwert heraus!
Und wer den Tod hier fand
Starb auch für's Vaterland.

Er kämpft und starb mit Gesang,
Der schallet in diesem Klang:
Hoch Deutschland, Deutschland hoch!

Separated by ocean waves from our Fatherland,
we've come here, [drawn] by many a bond of love.
We cross Texas's hot prairies on spirited steeds
and shorten our way with song that resounds with
a toast to Germany!

When we're drawn around bright campfires,
from afar do we remember our dear ones,
and the choice wine reflects the fire.
We spice our drink with song that resounds with
a toast to Germany.

If it now comes to a fight with wild and terrible Indians,
then you'll be drawn, O German sword!
And whoever found death here died for the Fatherland as well;
he fought and died with song that resounds with
a toast to Germany.

Hermann Seele states that Solms wrote the poem and that Captain Alexis Baur set it to music. In some quarters this is considered the first example in German-Texan literature (Herman Seele, *The Cypress and Other Writings of a German Pioneer in Texas,* translated by E. C. Breitenkamp, Austin, Texas: The University of Texas Press, 1979, p. 74; Hubert P. Heinen, "The Consciousness of Being German: Regional Literature in German Texas," in *Eagle in the New World: German Immigration to Texas and America,* Theodore Gish and Richard Spuler, editors, College Station, Texas: Texas A&M University Press, 1986, p. 132–134). Washington: refers to Washington-on-the Brazos. Fuller: see note 9 this chapter. Solms followed basically the same route to Washington-on-the-Brazos and back that he did in July.

Chapter Three

Sunday, Sepember 8th. In the saddle and on the way to Independence at 6 A.M. Breakfast at Jacobs's store. Mrs. Jacobs, a flirtatious woman, came to visit in the inn. Thunderstorm. Continued at 3 o'clock, arrived at Washington at 5:30. Stayed at Roberts'. A good evening meal. Slept in the meeting hall of the Congress, a good bed. Talked to Dr. Anson Jones and Mr. Miller.[1]

Monday, September 9th. Slept wonderfully until sunup. Good breakfast, then off to the saddler, prepared for Dr. Jones; extended discussion with him. Mr. Miller joined me for the noon meal. Talked also with Major Western. In the evening sat in front of the house for a long spell. Supper. Had a headache.[2]

Tuesday, [September] the 10th. Didn't close an eye the entire night because of my headache. Slept at noon, ate, and then off to Independence where I arrived at 6 o'clock. Stayed at Mr. Lee's, his wife received me with courtesy. "Soiree musicale" at Mrs. Jacobs's. May God have mercy. She flirts terribly. Late to bed.[3]

Wednesday, [September] the 11th. At 6 A.M. on the way; at 10 o'clock at Capt. Fuller's where we had lunch. Fordtran left from here, we continued at 3 o'clock and arrived at Nassau at 5 o'clock. Wilke reported about growing tobacco; brought books with him.

Thursday, [September] the 12th. Wilke rode to LaGrange and returned with Schiller's works. Read in the evening. Earlier Mässchen arrived, who is from Sachsen-Coburg on the Schwarzburg border. I gave him the program.[4]

Friday, [September] the 13th. Wilke rode home. He was hardly gone when a man arrived wearing a Hanoverian military coat. It was Lt. von Bauer from the 7th Regiment, ate with us, and we accompanied him on his ride. When it became dark, we turned around.[5]

Saturday, [September] the 14th. Early, at 6 o'clock, we rode by way of Fordtran to Ernst who was flattered. Mad. Ernst, Mad. Bartels. Ernst's land has only tobacco (4 feet by 2 feet to 2 feet by 2 and one-half feet) so the plough can pass through. Dinner at Fordtran's, Mr. and Mrs. Lewis, he was elected to Congress, he is a fool. Reached Nassau in darkness. Two silly letters were waiting at Shelby, Spilander had opened one, in spite of my distinct orders to the contrary. Returning home I found Thome from the Cumings Creek Settlement there. He wanted to join the company of soldiers. He is an intelligent man. He spent the night here.[6]

Sunday, [September] the 15th. Very hot. In the evening went horseback riding for a short while; then read *Wallenstein*.[7]

Monday, [September] the 16th. Ehrenberg, pastor of the Cumings Creek Settlement, came in the morning, stayed all day, wants to be employed. At noon Fordtran arrived, had the rifle welded. In the evening looked for hens; afterward read.[8]

Tuesday, [September] the 17th. Rain from morning until the afternoon, the thermometer ranged from +30° to +16° R. Philippi went to LaGrange to get flour, the horses escaped. Anton, Wrede, Denman, all looked for them. They were finally found at Capt. Sutton's. The cook is malicious. In the evening a fire in the fireplace and punch. Read *Wallenstein*. Long conversation.[9]

Wednesday, [September] the 18th. Rain and storm! A lucky day! The Dr. arrived and brought letters from my Sophie! My angel. I could not stop looking at her handwriting. There was also a letter from Brunet. He [the Dr.] brought with him Algeyer and Michel; as for himself, he has fever. In the evening a fire in the fireplace and punch. Yesterday the thermometer dropped to +16° R, today to +17° R.[10]

Thursday, [September] the 19th. During the night we had a hard frost. Rifle target was broken in. Dickens with Algeyer. After the meal went riding on the prairie.[11]

Friday, [September] the 20th. Mail day. A letter to Sophie and one to Brunet. The men shot at targets.[12]

Saturday, [September] the 21st. Algeyer and Michel rode away. The latter took the packet of letters to Houston. In the morning I had them ride on the square, afterward target practice; after dinner went horseback riding, found a deserted house and two graves.

Sunday, [September] the 22nd. Had them practice riding (the saddler Heidtmeyer rode along; Wilke fell off). Received a letter from Ernst, an invitation and about Fordtran's target practice. The mattresses and the wine arrived. Rhein wine. Champagne by moonlight until 1:30. Singing.[13]

Monday, [September] the 23rd. Allowed the gentlemen to ride. Fordtran, pointed out things to him. Target practice. Sang in the evening until 11:30.

Tuesday, [September] the 24th. Wrede, Wilke and the saddler on business to Cumings Creek. Went riding in the evening. Temperature during the day +21° R, in the evening +18° R.[14]

Wednesday, [September] the 25th. Rain in the morning. Temperature +20° R. The gentlemen didn't return last night; showed up this morning. Thome's song book! Sang in the evening.[15]

Thursday, [September] the 26th. At 8 A.M. the saddler Heidtmeyer arrived with Thome, the three Bruhn brothers, one a tailor, the other two shoemakers, one a former cavalryman of the guard with the 7th Cavalry Guard Squadron. Joseph accused the Dr. yesterday. I believed that I took care of the matter; today he insisted that everything that was said was true. Couldn't do anything because of the visitors. They left in the afternoon.[16]

Friday, [September] the 27th. Slept until 9:30! Unbelievable. The Dr. will not accept the blame. Likely story! Since yesterday a fabulous storm and rain. Temperatures: noon +16° R, at 9 P.M. +10° R.[17]

Saturday, [September] the 28th. Temperature +8° R in the morning. Wrote Herrscht because the Dr. is still here. In the evening a fire in the fireplace and punch.[18]

Sunday, the 29th. The weather improved. Rode to Fordtran. Returned at 3 o'clock. In the evening read *Geisterseher.*[19]

Monday, [September] the 30th. Otto von Roeder came to take the Dr. to a duel. It did not take place because of the Dr.'s illness. Went riding. Singing in the evening.[20]

Tuesday, October 1st. Fordtran arrived at noon, in the afternoon Schmidt. Business about the acceptance of stolen goods. F[ordtran] talked himself out of it and produced the collected signatures regarding Ernst. Rode to Shelby, to look at Dr. Bell's horses, a beautiful chestnut bay stallion, a small stallion and a 3 year-old gelding.[21]

Wednesday, October 2nd. Ernst's letter to Esq. von Baur. Rode to Shelby, no mail. Decided to make the trip to Houston. Singing in the evening. Had a bad night.

Thursday, October 3rd. A major clean up in the morning, afterward spoke to the workers and the gentlemen. At 3 P.M. on the way. Past Fordtran, to Ernst. Mrs. Ernst's plum cake. The sound of a lute and a twangy piano. Ernst as minstrel, Mrs. von Roeder as waitress. Gossiped until midnight.[22]

Friday, October 4th. On the road 5 minutes to six; at McCampbell's at noon, 24 miles, then another 9 miles to the Brazos, crossed over at Jones Ferry, then 4.5 to 5 miles (3 miles through the Brazos bottom) to Miskill. Rested and cleaned up. Supper. Wilke's wife has beautiful eyes, seems she was formerly a seamstress in Berlin; accompanied her part of the way.[23]

Saturday, October 5th. Left 5 minutes to five. On to Old Habermacher, an Alsatian, his wife was born in Turin. A pleasant area, flat prairie aspect. 28 miles. Rested until 1:30. Then another 16 miles to Houston. The pony became lame, had no more willpower. Wrede stayed behind with it. By 4 o'clock at Mad. Kessler's. Müllerchen was also there. Cleaned up in the Houston House. Wrede arrived. Called on Mad. Kessler. Supper, and to bed at 9 o'clock.[24]

Sunday, [October] the 6th. Breakfast at 8 o'clock. Slept well. Visited by Müllerchen and Capt. Payne. The former ate with me. In the evening rode leisurely to Rothaase. It's a very bad location. Wine cultivation, the grass arbor protects the grapes from the sun's heat. Garden with roses. His plans and sketches. Visit with Mad. Kessler. On the way back a backwoodsman had a delusion of the worst kind, wanted to barter. When we drew our weapons, he went crazy and shouted again and again: "I have found the man with a feather in his hat." That is as far as it went.[25]

Monday, [October] the 7th. Purchases. Visits. Dinner at Major Neighbours' place. Superviel, Houston's mayor, and God knows who else, a rather good dinner prepared by Sencihal. Afterward rode to the arsenal and from there to Schrimpf; pictures of King Otto's farewell in Munich, and of old Pappenheim as well as Crewall of Frankfurt. In the evening Capt. Payne.[26]

Tuesday, [October] the 8th. The steamer arrived. A good night. Visit. Superviel ate here, then Georg Fisher from Belgrade; discussion about the Baarzer Comitat. Leisurely ride on the race track. In the evening a visit to Mad. Kessler with sharpened sabers.[27]

Wednesday, [October] the 9th. Bad night. Superviel gave me a mirror as a gift. Visits. Ate at 2 o'clock, wanted to board at 3 o'clock, it became 5 o'clock, departed at 5:30 o'clock. Superviel, Mr. Anney, Capt. Stirret, in Harrisburg at 9 o'clock. Supposed to arrive in Galveston at seven next morning. The Americans played throughout the night except for Garcia and Huesmann. To bed at 10 o'clock.[28]

Thursday, [October] the 10th. In the morning at 4 o'clock, with a rather high tide, ran onto Clopper's Bar. Woke at 6 o'clock. We were stuck, nothing happened. There was no boat available to us. Finally at 9 in the evening a float was built, a boat fetched and Capt. Stirret got a flatboat. To bed at 10.[29]

Friday, [October] the 11th. A schooner anchored close to us; the flatboat carried bales of cotton, some to shore, some to the schooner. At 4 o'clock another attempt was made to get the boat unstuck. The ropes tore since they were old and bad. The larger part of the company boarded the schooner. At 5 o'clock I transferred my three horses, they stood on eight cotton bales. It was two miles to shore and from there one mile to Col. Morgan's neatly furnished home. I was well received there. Col. M. was in Houston. His son was at home. His wife is expecting soon. Supper. In bed at 9 o'clock.[30]

Saturday, [October] the 12th. I was wakened at 4 A.M., the boat was at shore ready to sail. The horses were put on board again; on the way by 5 o'clock; in Galveston by 10 o'clock. Being off-loaded, a horse fell in the water. Cobb and Baumgarten showed up. To the Tremont House. Stephenson, then to Klaener. Holstein & Rainer. Ate at 3 o'clock. Spent the evening with Arcieri. Early to bed. Before that with Stephenson on horse to Kennedy who was not at home.[31]

Sunday, [October] the 13th. Called on Klaener, Hockley, and Stephenson. The latter was not in. At noon Arcieri. In the evening to Maas. Mad. Maas sings very beautifully. A little Jewish person from Cologne (Offenbach); to bed at 11:30 o'clock.

Monday, [October] the 14th. Called on Kennedy, took care of things. Dinner at 3 o'clock. In the evening on horse with K. to the beach, afterward tea at his place. Mrs. Kennedy is an extremely well-mannered lady. Turned in at 11 o'clock.

Tuesday, [October] the 15th. Took care of things in the morning. Stephenson lunched with me at noon, afterward on horseback on the beach, it was a fun day. In the evening a party at Maas's (Rainer, Stephenson, Miss Tyza).To bed at midnight.[32]

Wednesday, [October] the 16th. Called on Mrs. Kennedy. Arcieri had dinner with me. In the evening rode along the beach, then Mr. Rainer, talked about the cultivation of tea.

Thursday, [October] the 17th. Rain in the morning. Visits by Ruthven, Jacob and Steph. Then to Mrs. Jacob; ate alone since Wrede was hunting. In the evening at Maas's; in bed at midnight.[33]

Friday, [October] the 18th. Awoke at 5:30 o'clock, a raging thunderstorm, went back to sleep until 9:30 o'clock. North wind and cold. Flowers from everywhere. Dinner celebrating the 18th. Kennedy, Stephenson, Holstein & Rainer. Stayed until 10:30 o'clock.[34]

Saturday, [October] the 19th. Rode horseback in the morning. Lunch at Kennedy's. Hockley, Stephenson, Colquhoun. Wrede slipped away. Stayed until 11 o'clock. The *Star Republic* was sighted.[35]

Sunday, [October] the 20th. Arrival of the *Republic*. Holstein brought the news, Anton woke me to tell the news, also that Fischer was here. Met him at 9:30 o'clock. Talked with him, afterward went riding, then letters! Two from my angelic Sophie. Dinner with Fischer, talked until 12 o'clock.[36]

Monday, [October] the 21st. Went riding in the morning, hot and foggy. In the evening at Stephenson's, later to Kennedy, with him to Capt. Hoydt. St[ephenson] gives me the reliquaries and Hoydt a sword.[37]

Tuesday, the 22nd. Long discourse with Kennedy. I went horseback riding in the afternoon. At noon Fischer had lunch with me. In the evening Mad. Maas & Mr. Rainer who had supper with me.

Wednesday, [October] the 23rd. Started to write. Interruptions. Alone in the evening. Went horseback riding.

Thursday, [October] the 24th. Wrote, constant interruptions, business with Fischer. Went riding in the evening. Then to Kennedy. Returned home at 9 o'clock. Rainer and Holstein joined me at supper. The new clock stopped at 9:15 P.M. May God see to it that no harm befell my Sophie. Fischer traveled to Houston.

Friday, [October] the 25th. Wrote in the morning. Dinner at Holstein's & Rainer's. In the evening walked by moonlight and made a courtesy call at Ostermann's.[38]

Saturday, [October] the 26th. Wrote, ate and finally went riding. In the evening at Mad. Maas's.

Sunday, [October] the 27th. Wrote in the morning. Learned from Cobb that Spilander is a petty crook. A letter to Cobb on that subject; his answer. In the evening at Kennedy's, later at Maas's.[39]

Monday, [October] the 28th. Wrote in the morning. Went riding on the beach, in the evening tea and song at Maas's.

Tuesday, [October] the 29th. Bourgeois arrived last evening. Saw him today, his imaginary colony! In the evening said farewell at the Mass's, then I went to Kennedy. Arrived home at 1:30 o'clock, his sherry is bad.[40]

Wednesday, [October] the 30th. At 10 A.M. departed for Virginia Point. Brock accompanied us. Crossed over in a wonderful boat, but had a difficult landing. Then onward, to a farm, far off to the right, where a strange fellow stood with his gold lorgnette. At 4 o'clock at Henri Bequin's, through a cane swamp on the road finally. A clean and good bed and supper. He is from Neufchatel, his medallion (10 miles from Virginia Point).[41]

Thursday, [October] the 31st. We were on the way at 7:30, with much difficulty made it to Benson's house on Dickinson Bayou. Shouted but when no one answered, looked for a trail and chose a direction. At a mustang run came across a trail, followed it (a prairie ghost), reached the Brazos bottom at 3 o'clock. Another three miles to Mr. [?]'s house. Horrible group of people there. At 6:30 o'clock back in the saddle with Schreier as a guide who took us to Houston (20 miles). Arrived at 10 o'clock. Supper and to bed. Rode 55 miles this day.[42]

Friday, November 1st. Long discussion with Fischer in the presence of his mother. Dinner at Mad. Kessler's in the evening. In bed at 9:30. A rat kept me awake, so a terrier had to be put in my room. Miller introduced Gen. Tyrrel.[43]

Saturday, November 2nd. Conversation with Tyrrel. Letters to Kennedy and Klaener as well as to Dr. Anson Jones by Miller and to Castell & Sophie via Tyrrel to Heath Furse. Schubert returned from his trip. He dined with me in the evening.[44]

Sunday, November 3rd. In the morning long consultation with Fischer. *Dejeuner a la fourchette* [a breakfast with meat] at 2:30. [From Houston] to the entertainment house. It was dirty, bad, miserable. I fell into a swamp. In the night children's screams, barking dogs, and fleas.[45]

Monday, November 4th. On the way at 6:30 o'clock, at Miskill's at 2 o'clock. Called on Wilke. What a pitiful domicile! He and his wife spent the evening at Miskill's. To bed at 9 o'clock.[46]

Tuesday, November 5th. As a group on the way to San Felipe at 7:30 where I went ahead to Wildcat Spring. The Dr.'s hut (brush shelter), he is sick. Took his horse with us. At Ernst's at 2 o'clock. There I wrote a circular and a letter to Ervendberg. Pancakes and salad. Then on home, arrived there at 6:30. Great joy. Brunert & Müller were there as well as Heidmeyer. The song "We are faithful to our prince."[47]

---

[1] Jacob: identity unknown. Roberts: identity unknown. Mr. Miller: presumably Washington D. Miller, Sam Houston's private secretary.

[2] Major Thomas G. Western: see Chapter II, note 7.

[3] Mr. Lee: identity unknown.

[4] Johann Friedrich Schiller (1759–1805): German dramatist and poet. Mässchen: could be Sebastian H. C. Möschen, farmer, age thirty-eight, from Saxe-Gotha, who arrived with his wife and daughter Friedericke, age eight, on the brig *Weser*, from Bremen on 8 July 1844. (*Secretary of State, Record Group 307, Colonization Papers,* Archives and Information Ser-

vices, Texas State Library [ARIS-TSL], Austin, Texas; Herman Seele, *The Cypress and Other Writings of a German Pioneer in Texas*, Austin: The University of Texas Press, 1979, pp. 122 and 127). Sachsen-Coburg on the Schwarzburg border: today this area is within the state of Thuringia. "Gave him the program," could indicate that Solms offered information about the Society's plans in Texas.

[5] Lt. von Bauer: Alexis von Bauer's presence on this date invalidates the information in Geue & Geue (p. 78) that he came to Texas in 1845. He apparently arrived in Galveston on the brig *Weser* on 8 July 1844 (*Ibid.*). Solms eventually put Bauer in command of the Society's militia. Very little else is known about this individual (see also Chapter II, note 59).

[6] Mad. Bartels: wife of Wm. Gerhard Bartels (Miriam K. York, *Friedrich Ernst of Industry*, Giddings, Texas: privately published, 1989, p. 62). Mr. & Mrs. Lewis: Samuel K. Lewis elected to Congress 1844–45 (*Biographical Directory of the Texan Conventions and Congresses, 1832–1845*, p. 125). Spilander: identity unknown (see also note 39 this chapter). Mr. Thome: very likely Carl Wilhelm Thomae (1819–1880) whom Solms employed for the Society in a clerical capacity. Thomae's presence in Texas can be established as early as December 1843. He became New Braunfels' first postmaster in 1846. The following year he married Johanna Lessmann (1824–1908). Three children were born to this union: Eduard, Theodor, and Carl. Sometime in 1862/63 the family moved to Mexico to escape the effects of the Civil War ("From Coblenz to Colorado County, 1843–1844: Early Leyendecker Letters to the Old Country," in *Nesbitt Memorial Library Journal (Columbus, Texas)*, Vol. I, No. 6 (Aug. 1990), p. 183; additional information provided by Linda Sito of Missouri City, Texas, a descendant of Carl W. Thomae). Cummins Creek Settlement: an area loosely settled by German immigrants along Cummins Creek in Colorado County. Frelsburg's origin goes back to this settlement. The remark "company of soldiers" most likely referred to Solms's entourage. In Texas, Europeans as well as Anglos ridiculed Solms for following traditions of the European nobility. In addition, the type of uniform that he chose for his retainers was quite unsuitable to the frontier. One contemporary observer described the uniform thusly: "This outfit is always worn by the soldiers in the pay of the Society who belong to the company of light cavalry formed by the Prince of Solms. Their uniform consists of tall boots, gray pants, gray blouse and a white hat with a wide brim adorned with a wild turkey feather. The weapons are a long cavalry saber, a pair of saddle pistols, and a German-made carbine with the inscription: *For the Immigrants in Texas* (M. Maris, *Souvenirs d'Amerique. Relations d'un Voyage au Texas et en Haiti*, Brussels, Belgium, 1863, p. 90; translation by Betty Von-Maszewski; Sörgel, *A*

Sojourn in Texas, p. 165; Rena Maverick Green, editor, *Memoirs of Mary A. Maverick*, Lincoln, Nebraska: University of Nebraska Press, 1989, p. 81).

[7] *Wallenstein*: A trilogy by the German writer and poet Friedrich Schiller (1759–1805) with the action set in the Thirty Years War (1618–1648).

[8] When Solms speaks of hens, he could be referring to wild turkeys. Ervendberg, like other German settlers from the Mill Creek and the Cummings Creek area, came in hopes of finding employment with the Society.

[9] Temperature conversion to 100° to 68° Fahrenheit, respectively. Philippi: identity unknown.

[10] Algeyer: It is not clear if this was the same person who in 1842, with the name of U. Algauer from the area of Industry, was one of the petitioners asking that the Texas Congress grant a charter for Herrman University (Biesele, *German Settlements in Texas*, p. 216). Michel: identity unknown. Temperature conversions to 68° and 70° Fahrenheit, respectively.

[11] Dickens: identity unknown.

[12] Mail day coincides with *Fourth Report* dated 20 Sept. 1844 (Geue and Geue, *A New Land Beckoned*, p. 39). Brunet: see Chapter I, note 2.

[13] Heidtmeyer: Johann Friedrich Heidemeyer (1814–1886) appeared to have already been in Texas when the Society's settlers arrived at which time he joined the Society. Solms recognizing his military ability appointed him a non-commissioned officer in the militia. Heidemeyer is considered one of the founders of New Braunfels and was elected an Alderman in the city's first election. Later he had a saddlery business in town (*Secretary of State, Colonization Papers*, ARIS-TSL; Frey, *New Braunfels*, pp. 364–366).

[14] Temperature conversions to 79° and 73° Fahrenheit, respectively.

[15] Temperature conversion to 77° Fahrenheit.

[16] Brothers Bruhn: should be Brune: Georg, Ludwig, August, and Edward. Georg Christoph Brune (1807–1869), wife Ernestine Henriette (von Zabiensky) Brune (married in Herford, Westphalia, Germany, in 1839); Ludwig (Louis) August Brune (1816–1883); August Brune; and Edward Brune (1820–1869) arrived on the ship *Albert* in New Orleans on 20 December 1843 (Ronald Vern Jackson, editor, *Texas 1870 Mortality*, North Salt Lake, Utah: Accelerated Indexing Systems International, Inc., 1983, p. 12; *Church Registers, Sankt Marien-Stift Evangelisch*, Herford, Westphalia, Germany; *The Cemeteries of Austin County, Texas*, Bellville, Texas: The Austin County Historical Society, 1991; *New Orleans Passenger Lists, 1820–1902*, National Archives Microfilm M259, Roll 23, Document 434). Joseph: identity unknown. Dr.: likely refers to Dr. Emil Meyer.

[17] Temperature conversion to 68° and 55° Fahrenheit, respectively.

[18] Temperature conversion to 50° Fahrenheit. Herrscht: identity unknown.

[19] *Der Geisterseher* (1789), an unfinished rather popular novel by Friedrich Schiller treating the then topical theme of experiments in the supernatural.

[20] Otto von Roeder (1807–1878): son of Ludwig Siegismund Anton and Caroline Louise (Sack) von Roeder. The parents and their children arrived in Texas 1834. They settled in the area that became the community of Cat Spring, Austin County. Otto von Roeder purchased Nassau Farm from the bankrupt *Adelsverein* in 1848; however, the creditors held him liable for the *Adelsverein's* debt. When he refused to pay, the property was attached and sold at a sheriff's sale. The legal fight over Nassau Farm continued until 1865, when in the end the Supreme Court ruled against Otto (Flora L. Von Roeder, *These Are The Generations: A Bibliography of The von Roeder Family and Its Role in Texas History*, Houston: Baylor College of Medicine, 1978, p. 117).

[21] Esq. Schmidt: identity unknown. Dr. Bell: identity unknown.

[22] Mrs. Ernst: Mrs. Louise Ernst, wife of Friedrich Ernst. Mrs. von Roeder: identity unknown.

[23] McCampbell: identity unknown. Jones Ferry: likely at San Felipe on the Brazos River. Elizabeth Miskell (Miskill), widow of William A. Miskell. At the time Solms visited here the area was part of Austin County with Waller County not yet organized (*1850 U.S. Census, Austin County, Texas*, p. 95B, National Archives Microfilm M432, Roll 908; *Austin County [Texas] Deed Records*, Vol. B, pp. 192, 278). Wilke's wife: Elizabeth Sander, wife of Ludwig Willke and sister of Mathias Sander (Fey, *New Braunfels*, Vol. I, p. 512; see also note 46 this chapter). From Industry Solms's party traveled the Gothier Trail, passing in the vicinity of Cat Spring. It crossed SH 36 north of present-day Sealy and passed the McCampbell's place. The Brazos River was crossed at San Felipe and the trail led to Miskell's place on the Samuel C. Haddy League, six miles east of San Felipe. This placed the party in the vicinity of present-day Clemons Community along FM 1458 in Waller County (*Map of Austin County*, 1860; courtesy of the Texas General Land Office).

[24] Thomas and Marie Habermacher. The family was in Texas since the early 1830s. Thomas Habermacher and his son Stephen, both of Harrisburg, worked on William Stafford's cotton gin on Oyster Creek in May 1834. (Dilue Rose Harris, "The Reminiscences of Mrs. Dilue Harris," in *Southwestern Historical Quarterly*, Vol. IV, p. 107). When Solms visited them, Thomas Habermacher had been residing for several years on the 107 acres in the W. Hardin League (*Harris County [Texas] Tax Rolls 1837–1910,*

Microfilm Roll 1, taxes for 1841 on p. 10, taxes for 1843 on p. 8A, taxes for 1844 on p. 10, and taxes for 1845 on p. 7A). Mad. Kessler: Mary Bonzano Kessler, widow of Henry Kessler. Henry F. Fisher had his office in the Kessler's building. After her husband's demise Fisher became her notary public in 1841 when her husband's estate, for its time considerable, was probated. On April 10, 1845, she became Henry F. Fisher's wife. Four children were born to this union, three daughters and a son (Marie Russell, compiler, *Marriage Records, Harris County, Texas, 1837–1865*, Houston, Texas: privately published, 1980, Vol. I, pp. 8 and 31; *Harris County [Texas] Probate Records*, Vol. E, p. 386; Dorothy E. Justman, *German Colonists and Their Descendants in Houston*, Houston, Texas: privately published, 1974, p. 323). Müllerchen: apparent belittling of Burchard Miller (formerly Müller) who was a business partner of Henry F. Fisher not only in land speculation but other matters as well. At the probate settlement of Henry Kessler's estate Müller was appointed guardian of Julia, daughter of Henry and Mary B. Kessler (*Harris County Probate Records*, Vol. E, p. 386). Houston House: boarding house that was located on the corner of Main and Franklin Streets (*Telegraph & Texas Register*, 8 May 1844, p. 3, col. 3). From Miskell's place the trail took a southeasterly course, skirting present-day Katy in the north, crossing the Buffalo Bayou at Highway 6 where Elisabeth Wheaton, widow of Joel Wheaton, farmed on the banks of the bayou. The trail continued south of Buffalo Bayou to Thomas Habermacher's place and from there took an easterly course to Houston. (*Connected Map of Austin Colony*, commenced by S. F. Austin, 1833, and completed by J. F. Perry, 1837; map courtesy of Texas General Land Office, Austin, Texas).

[25] Capt. Payne: B. Owen Payn, Captain of Ordnance (Williams and Barker, *The Writings of Sam Houston*, Vol. III, p. 232; Vol. IV, p. 292). Rothaase: Friedrich Jacob Rothaas was surveyor of the Harrisburg and Brazos Railroad (1840), city surveyor of Houston (1841–45), and an artist. *George Allen's Residence* (1845), a watercolor by him, shows Allen's two-story, frame plantation house near Houston. He was also an avid viticulturist. Wine cultivation was a recurrent interest in German settlements throughout the 1800s. The warm climate of Texas was thought to be suitable for viniculture. In the *[Houston] Telegraph & Texas Register*, 21 February 1844, Rothaas advertised "grape vine, a large and choice assortment of American grapes, roots, or cuttings" (*The New Handbook of Texas*, Vol. I, plate 15; S. W. Geiser, "Men of Science in Texas, 1820–1880" in *Field & Laboratory*, Vol. XXVII, No. 4, p. 189).

[26] Neighbours: Robert Simpson Neighbors (1815–1859), appointed on 12 February 1845, agent to the Lipan and Tonkawa Indians for the

Republic of Texas (Kenneth F. Neighbours, *Robert Simpson Neighbors and The Texas Frontier 1836–1859,* Waco, Texas: Texian Press, 1975, p. 24). Superviel: Antoine Superville arrived on the ship *Medford* in New Orleans from Havre on 15 October 1843. In the 1850 he is identified as born in France, forty-two years old, merchant by occupation, and a resident of Houston (*New Orleans Passenger Lists,* National Archives Microfilm M259, Roll 23; *1850 U.S. Census, Harris County, Texas,* p. 22, National Archives Microfilm M432, Roll 911). Mayor of Houston in 1844: Horace Baldwin (1801–1850), from New York state, became the sixth mayor of Houston; brother-in law to Augustus C. Allen who with his brother John K. Allen were early settlers and founders of Houston (*Dr. Jonas C. and Mrs. Betty Baldwin, Founders of Baldwinsville, New York,* Baldwinsville, N. Y.: Hawley, 1977, p. 42; *The New Handbook of Texas,* Vol. I, p. 108). Sencihal: A. Senechal of Harris County (Mullins, *Poll Lists For 1846,* p. 151). Johann Wilhelm Schrimpf: offered the following information about himself in 1850: forty years old, butcher, born in Germany, resident of Houston (*1850 U.S. Census, Harris County, Texas,* p. 19, National Archives Microfilm M432, Roll 911). King Otto: identity unknown. Pappenheim: identity unknown. Crewal: identity unknown.

[27] The "steamer" is the *Dayton,* John H. Sterrett (1805–1879), master, which plied between Galveston and Houston. Later in the year (September) the 111-ton sidewheeler steamship suffered an inglorious end when it sank in Corpus Christi Bay following a boiler explosion. It was contracted by the U.S. Army to transport troops and supplies to General Zachary Taylor's troops in Corpus Christi before the Mexican-American War (*The New Handbook of Texas,* Vol. II, p. 544). Georg Fisher (1795–1873), born in Hungary. He came to America in 1814, arriving in Texas in circa 1829. During the next decades he served as diplomat, immigration agent, attorney, land promoter, and commission agent (*Ibid.,* Vol. II, p. 1010). "Baarzer Comitat": identity unknown. The statement "mit geschliffenen Säbeln" [with sharpened sabers] could imply that he and Mad. Kessler had points of difference. Possibly Kessler's impending marriage (in April 1845) to Fisher did not sit well with Solms. First of all, he was smitten with her and secondly he developed a dislike for Henry F. Fisher because Fisher's interest was in himself and not in the Society.

[28] Mr. Anney: possibly Robert M. Hanney who is also mentioned as a founding member of the Galveston Chamber of Commerce in 1845 (Hayes, *Galveston,* Vol. II, p. 718; Ephraim D. Adams, "British Diplomatic Correspondence Concerning the Republic of Texas," in *Southwestern Historical Quarterly,* Vol. XIX, p. 93). Capt. John H. Sterrett (Stirret): see note 27 this chapter. Steamboats left Houston in the evening and arrived in

Galveston in the morning which allowed businessmen to conduct their affairs during the day (David G. McComb, *Galveston: A History,* Austin: University of Texas Press, 1986, p. 47). Garcia: identity unknown. An individual by the name of F. W. Huesmann was one of the citizens of Austin and Colorado Counties in 1842 who signed a petition asking the legislature for a charter to establish Hermann University (York, *Friedrich Ernst,* p. 74).

[29] Clopper's Bar: a sandbar across from Morgan's Point obstructing the passage between Galveston Bay and San Jacinto Bay and consequently the traffic between Houston and Galveston.

[30] James Morgan (1786–1866): resided on his plantation Orange Grove next to the town site of New Washington. Morgan remarked in a letter that while he was absent from his home that the prince visited his home (Feris A. Bass, Jr. and B. R. Brunson, editors. *Fragile Empires.* Austin, Texas: Shoal Creek Publishers, Inc., 1978, p. 260).

[31] Baumgarten: F. W. Baumgarten (Hayes, *Galveston,* pp. 364 and 365). Henry Stephenson: see Chapter II, note 3. Diedrich Hermann Klaener: left Germany as a young man, worked in mercantile establishments in Central and North America; arrived in Galveston about 1840 where he went into business for himself. The Society appointed him agent in Galveston with the task of assisting the newly arrived German immigrants to continue their journey to Indianola/Carlshafen in Lavaca Bay (Franz Joseph Pitsch, *Die wirtschaftlichen Beziehungen Bremens zu den Vereinigten Staaten von Amerika,* p. 86). Mr. Holstein: probably H. W. Holstein whose name appears with D. H. Klaener on the summary report of emigrants arriving on the *Johann Dethard, Herschell,* and *Ferdinand* in 1844 (*Secretary of State, Record Group 307,* ARIS-TSL). Mr. Rainer: from the firm D. H. Klaener, Galveston, Texas. The *Eighth Report* by Solms leaves the impression that Rainer was an accountant (Geue and Geue, *A New Land Beckoned,* p. 63).

[32] Miss Tyza: identity unknown.

[33] Archibald St. Clair Ruthven (1813–1865), born in Edinburgh, Scotland, came to Texas in 1839, was a businessman in Galveston and Houston in the 1840s (Michael Kelsey, et al., *Texas Masonic Deaths with Selected Biographical Sketches,* Bowie, Maryland: Heritage Books, Inc., 1998, p. 124). Jacob: identity unknown.

[34] "Dinner celebrating the 18th": meaning unknown.

[35] Ludovic Colquhoun (1804–1882): during the Mexican invasion of San Antonio in 1842 he was taken prisoner by General Adrian Woll and sent with other San Antonians to Perote Prison. Released in 1844, he returned to San Antonio (*The New Handbook of Texas,* Vol. II, p. 231). *Star*

Republic, Hendsley, master, arrived in Galveston on 19 October 1844, after a passage of twenty-two days from New York. This fast-sailing packet ship on the New York-Galveston run carried news and dispatches not only from the East Coast but also from Europe (*The Civilian and Galveston Gazette,* 26 October 1844, p. 1, col. 1; Hayes, *Galveston,* Vol. I, p. 468).

[36] A local newspaper offered this quote "The steam packet *Republic,* Crane, master, arrived in Galveston on October 20, 1844, from New Orleans having left the city on October 16" (*The Civilian and Galveston Gazette,* 26 October 1844, p. 1, col. 1). When the Republic of Texas declined to extend d'Orvanne's grant, the Society discharged him as Colonial Director in August. In Germany, in the meantime, Henry Francis Fisher (1805–1867) secured the Society's interest in the Fisher-Miller grant and returned to Texas on 15 September 1844. Fisher and Burchard Miller received this grant of about three million acres for settlement from the Republic of Texas on June 7, 1842. The grant was located between the Llano and Colorado Rivers, and extended into the western portion of Texas (Biesele, *German Settlement in Texas,* p. 76; *The New Handbook of Texas,* Vol. II, p. 1014; see also map on page 112).

[37] Capt. Hoydt: probably Capt. N. Hoyt, Texian Navy (Hollon and Butler, *Bollaert's Texas,* p. 57n). Reliquaries: meaning unknown.

[38] Solms's writing coincides with the *Fifth Report* dated Galveston 25 October 1844 (Geue and Geue, *A New Land Beckoned,* p. 41). Joseph Ostermann (1779–1861) arrived in Galveston in 1837 to continue his mercantile career which he began in Philadelphia (Hayes, *Galveston,* Vol. II, p. 891).

[39] Spilander: identity unknown; see also note 6 this chapter.

[40] Bourgeois's colony: After his dismissal from the Society (see Chapter II, note 51), Bourgeois d'Orvanne struck out on his own, advertising the potential of the land he saw between Cibolo Creek and San Antonio River. He praised its fertility as well as its suitability for the settlement of European immigrants. Other advantages were the location of the land midway between San Antonio de Bexar and the Gulf of Mexico where the town of "San Bartolo" would be established and the potential of making the San Antonio River navigable from the junction of Cibolo Creek to the Gulf which all combined would help divert commerce from Mexico, which presently went to San Antonio, to this promising area (*Telegraph & Texas Register,* 30 October 1844, p. 2, col. 4; *Solms-Braunfels Archives,* Vol. XLVIIIa, p. 197+).

[41] Brock: identity unknown. Henri Bequin: The 1850 census identifies a Henry Bigham, born in Switzerland, thirty-six years old, a farmer, as residing in the Clear Creek and Dickinson Bayou Precinct, Galveston

County (*1850 U.S. Census, Galveston County, Texas*, p. 285A, National Archives Microfilm M432, Roll 910). Virginia Point: located on the mainland shore opposite Galveston Island where today the causeway connects with the mainland, seven miles west of the city of Galveston (*The New Handbook of Texas*, Vol. VI, p. 760).

[42] The 1850 Census identifies a Herman Benson, born in Germany, thirty-eight years old, and farmer by occupation, as living in the Clear Creek and Dickinson Bayou Precinct (*Ibid.*, p. 283B). Schreier: identity unknown. When Solms writes "reached the Brazos bottom" this would have taken him in a round-about way to Houston, certainly more than the fifty-five miles he claims to have traveled that day. On his way from Virginia Point to Houston it is more likely that he crossed Clear Creek.

[43] General Tyrrel: George Whitfield Terrell (1803–1846), attorney general in Sam Houston's administration (1841–1842); Indian Commissioner for Texas (1842–1844); chargé d'affaires to France, Great Britain and Spain (December 1844–1845).

[44] Miller: presumably W. D. Miller, Sam Houston's private secretary. Heath Furse & Co.: business in London that expedited correspondence to and from Solms in Texas (*Solms-Braunfels Archives*, Vol. XLIX, p. 146; Vol. LI, p. 37). Schubert: very likely Friedrich Armand Strubberg (1806–1889) born in Kassel, Germany. After involvement in a duel in which he wounded his adversary, the family shipped him to America in 1826. There he represented European businesses. In 1829 he went back to Germany but finding the family business in other hands he returned to America. After a few courses at a medical school in Kentucky he adopted the name "Dr. Schubert." In late 1844 he arrived in Texas where he joined F. H. Fisher in the attempt to establish a settlement on the San Gabriel River in present-day Milam County. In 1846, on recommendation by Fisher, Schubert was employed by the Society as physician and administrator for the new settlement of Fredericksburg. Proving to be an inept administrator, he was removed from office the following year. He moved and took possession of Nassau Farm. A dispute arose between Schubert and the Society because the agreement to lease the plantation to him had been withdrawn. Matters escalated to an armed confrontation that cost two lives, one of which was the Swiss artist Carl Casper Rohrdorf. Charges followed countercharges. Schubert lost Nassau Farm and in 1848 left Texas for Arkansas. He returned to Germany in 1854 where he began publishing under the pen name Friedrich Armand fictionalized accounts of his experiences in North America and Texas (Armin O. Huber, "Frederic Armand Strubberg, Alias Dr. Shubbert, Town-Builder, Physician, And Adventurer, 1806–1889" in *West Texas Historical Association Year Book*, Vol.

XXXVIII (October 1962), p. 37–71; *Solms-Braunfels Archives*, Vol. XLI, p. 236; Vol. LVI, pp. 225–226; *Bell County Reprinted Biographies* reprinted from *A Memorial and Biographical History of McLennan, Falls, Bell and Coryell Counties,* Texas [Chicago, Illinois: Lewis Publishing Company, 1893], Honey Grove, Texas: Newhouse Publications, 1991, p. 92).

[45] Entertainment House: apparently a generic term for a roadside inn. A travel guide for this period makes this statement: "There is a House of Entertainment. Every attention given to make man and beast comfortable" (Jacob Raphael DeCordova, *Texas: Her Resources and Her Public Men,* Philadelphia: J. B. Lippincott & Co., 1858, p. 199).

[46] Wilke: most likely Louis (Ludwig Willke, also Wilke Sr. or Wilke I (see also note 23 this chapter and note 10 in Chapter II). It appears that Solms followed the same trail from Houston to Nassau Farm that he used once before (see notes 23 and 24 this chapter).

[47] Wildcat Spring: Cat Spring, Austin County. Dr.'s hut: presumably Dr. Emil Meyer's hut. Brunert & Müller: identities unknown. Heid[e]meyer: see note 13 this chapter. Solms retraced his steps from Houston to Nassau, see notes 23 and 24 this chapter.

Chapter Four

Wednesday, November 6th. Fordtran showed up. He and I rode to Marshall. Wilke and Wrede as well as Bohnert and Koch arrived.[1]

Thursday, November 7th. Otto von Röder, Lindheimer, and Schmidt. They stayed for the meal, afterward went horseback riding with Baur. Torey off to LaGrange.[2]

Friday, November 8th. Scheerer promises to bring horses, Schmidt brought cigars. Lewis arrived with three different mules, one laughs constantly. Disgusting creatures. Rode off to York, has no horses. Torey off to Industry. Mad. Mäßgen would not go along for fear of Indians. I gave a scolding speech. In the morning with Gim looked for gold rocks, found metal in the rocks.[3]

Saturday, November 9th. Went with Gim prospecting for rocks. Scheerer came with horses. Fordtran chased off. Ernst accompanied us. In the afternoon to the farm to watch Gim wash the rocks. Kray arrived.[4]

Sunday. November 10th. Thome and Brunert came in the morning and the 2 Brunerts. Ernst and Dr. Frank (from Hannover) arrived at noon. Concern over staples. Accompanied Ernst. People sang in the evening. Dr. Frank spends the night here.[5]

Monday, November 11th. Wilke went to Industry. Wrede to LaGrange to look at horses. Found nothing. In the evening I read *Faust*.[6]

Tuesday, November 12th. Looked at horses in the morning. Wrede wanted to leave for Washington at 3 o'clock. Met Fischer and returned with him in the evening. Wrote letters to Hays, Guilbeau, and Rahm as well as Ewing.[7]

Wednesday, [November] the 13th. Thome to Port La Bacca. In the afternoon Fischer went to Ernst, I accompanied him. Read *Faust.*

Thursday, [November] the 14th. In the morning, Fordtran, in the afternoon Fischer with Ernst Jr. To the farm. In the evening the settler from higher up. Talked with Fischer until midnight.[8]

Friday, [November] the 15th. Business, letter to Guilbeau. In the afternoon Fischer to the farm. Fordtran was there. Talked at length in the evening. Fordtran discharged.

Saturday, [November] the 16th. At 8 o'clock departed with the entire company. Everyone sang. At Kray's on Cumings Creek at noon, 16 miles. Mr. and Mrs. Brun and Rohde. The little child was baptized by Ervendberg ($15) and named Carl. On the way again at 2 o'clock, visited on the trail with the Englishman Mr. [?]. At 6 o'clock at the Colorado [River] ferry. The young boy did not want to carry us across, but had no choice. At 7 o'clock at Robertson's, 14 miles. A big Scotsman with a long, black beard. A bitter cold norther passed through, some people slept in the open. It rained in at my place. A good supper and grog. Mr. Hegler, surveyor of Colorado City. The tailor Mahleskum, a tall fellow. ("Don't talk so much."). Preciosa's song.[9]

Sunday, [November]the 17th. Day of rest. Turned the command over to Baur. Terrible rain. Song and drink. Mr. Ridel from San Antonio stopped on his way.[10]

Monday, [November] the 18th. Continued the march at 9 o'clock. I rode ahead with Wrede, Anton, and Joseph. To Tyrrel's on the Navidad, 20 miles. Looked for a crossing, Anton swam across, the current caught him on the way back. When the horse went under I shouted to him to let go of the horse. His spurs became entangled in the rope. I threw him another one and pulled him out. The chestnut bay climbs out by itself. The remainder of the party arrived. Camp; we built a float. The night was cold but clear. I brought up the idea of field training. Rheinwein, then pleasant sleep.[11]

Tuesday, [November] the 19th. Crossed the Navidad at 9 o'clock; the horses swam across; I rode ahead, 14 miles to Foley's, an old, deaf man. Large cotton farm and a cotton gin (80 Negroes). Someone else put me on the trail to Clarke. 5 miles to Mrs. Hallies's. 4 miles to Clarke. The bishop was there, sick. From there 2 miles and I was at Glais's. The Abbé took me there, he looked sick. Camp. I slept in the house.[12]

Wednesday, [November] the 20th. Early on the road, 21 miles to a creek. Had our noon meal there, from there 14 miles to McHenry. Friendly woman. Everyone put up under a roof. A billy goat strangled. A norther during the night.[13]

Thursday, [November] the 21st. Marched on at noon, only 12 miles to the Jonosso. Beautiful but cold camp close to the river. Wrede bathed and ate crayfish like an Indian.[14]

Friday, [November] the 22nd. Early in the saddle, Wrede and I out front. 30 miles to Port La Vacca. 9 miles of poor trail. A wagon driver believing us for Indians took defensive measures. Arrived at noon. Ewing and his sister who wears glasses. Her husband was killed during the attack on Linnville and she was taken away by the Indians. In the afternoon I killed an ox with my rifle. When I followed up with the second shot the rifle exploded in my hand, the wing nut and both locks were gone and the barrel split half way down. And no injury to me—God is great! The men arrived in the evening and were put up. In the evening Judge Hays arrived with letters from Sympton. I sent him immediately to Passo Cavallo.[15]

Distances:

Nassau to	Cumings Creek:	16 miles
	Columbus:	14 mi.
	Tyrrel (Navidad):	20 mi.

Foley:	14 mi.
Clarke:	9 mi.
McHenry:	35 mi.
Jonosso (Arenosa Creek):	12 mi.
Port La Vacca:	30 mi.
	150 miles

Saturday, [November] the 23rd. Bad water gave Thome and Anton the stomach ache. Everyone had one to a lesser or greater degree. Sympton arrived at noon; with him came Stephenson. Letters from Sophie and from Flersheim and Klaener. My Sophie is an angel! In the evening, because of the wound fever, I was too tired to write.

Sunday, [November] the 24th. After breakfast handed my letters to Sympton. Got him on board of his ship, 3 miles below Indian Point. Back by evening on the [sloop] *Tom Jack*, Capt. Parker.

Monday, [November] the 25th. In the morning off for Tapon, arrived there at 2 o'clock. On horseback. The land is high and good, wooded, 2 creeks, several smaller ones. Back on board by 5 o'clock. The boat got stuck. Had a good night sleep until the mosquitoes overwhelmed us.[16]

Tuesday, [November] the 26th. Early underway to put ashore the sick Wilke. Baur on board. Gone again from Port La Vaca by noon. At 10 o'clock across from Duncan's house. Ewing wanted to continue, we got stuck on a sand bar. Had a pleasant night.[17]

Wednesday, the 27th. Fischer arrived in the morning. We went to Capt. Bridges at Port Austin. His wife and daughter. Good dinner. A good night.[18]

Thursday, [November] the 28th. With Baur and Fischer on board the *Tom Jack* under sail for Galveston. Letters to Wrede, Wilke, Hays, and Rahm; with the help of Ewing to P[ort] La V[aca]. (Tapon is the prettiest place but the water is only 4' deep. Port Austin is quite bare, but has a good harbor.) Departed at 12 o'clock. On board wrote to Sophie. At 12:30 P.M. at Decrow's Point.[19]

Friday, [November] the 29th. The Capt. busied himself so long that it was 12 o'clock before we got away. Unfavorable wind. In the evening he expected a norther, we did not. Bad journey. Everyone got sick except for me. Flat coastline.

Saturday, [November] the 30th. We finally saw Cedar Lake, then the mouth of the Brazos with Velasco and Quintana (evening). The Capt. did not want to land, I feared a norther. It arrived at 2 A.M. [20]

Sunday, December 1st. We were 28 miles from Galveston. (Brewster's [?]) at anchor, on which our lives depended. Terrible cold. Stayed in bed for most of the day.

Monday, [December] the 2nd. At 3 A.M. the storm let up. We forced the Capt. to sail. Arrived in Galveston at 10 o'clock. *Joh. Dethart* has been there since Nov. 23rd. Holstein had the people transshipped. How stupid! This in spite of my instruction! Business. Found Capt. Kingston, then Kennedy. Had Holstein, Rainer, and Lüdering over for dinner. On board the *Joh. Dethart*, a beautiful ship. Afterward to Maas. In the evening discussion with Fischer, then to bed.[21]

Tuesday, [December] the 3rd. Wrote in the morning. At noon on board the *Alert.* Contracted another good ship. [blank in diary] tons. Sails very well. Storm at night, the water was luminous. The wind let up by 12 o'clock. The sea ran very high, [the ship] rolled and pitched, a terrible situation. The wind shifted around 1 o'clock. The ship sailed as quick as an arrow to San Louis. It carried only the jib [sail] nothing else. Then drifted from 2 until 6 o'clock.[22]

Wednesday, [December] the 4th. Only an occasional wind blew, but the seas were very high. At 12 o'clock crossed the sandbar, in Galveston at 2 o'clock. Fischer arrived and I had to go immediately to look at houses. Cleaned up, dinner at 4:30. Afterward business; to bed at 10:30 (Rainer to supper).

Thursday, December 5th. Slept heavenly. Business, wrote afterwards. Dinner. In the evening wrote on Kennedy's behalf.

Princess Sophie of Salm-Salm
Courtesy Sophienburg Musuem & Archives

Mary Bonzano Kessler
Courtesy of Roland Getze

Henry Francis Fisher
Courtesy of Roland Getze

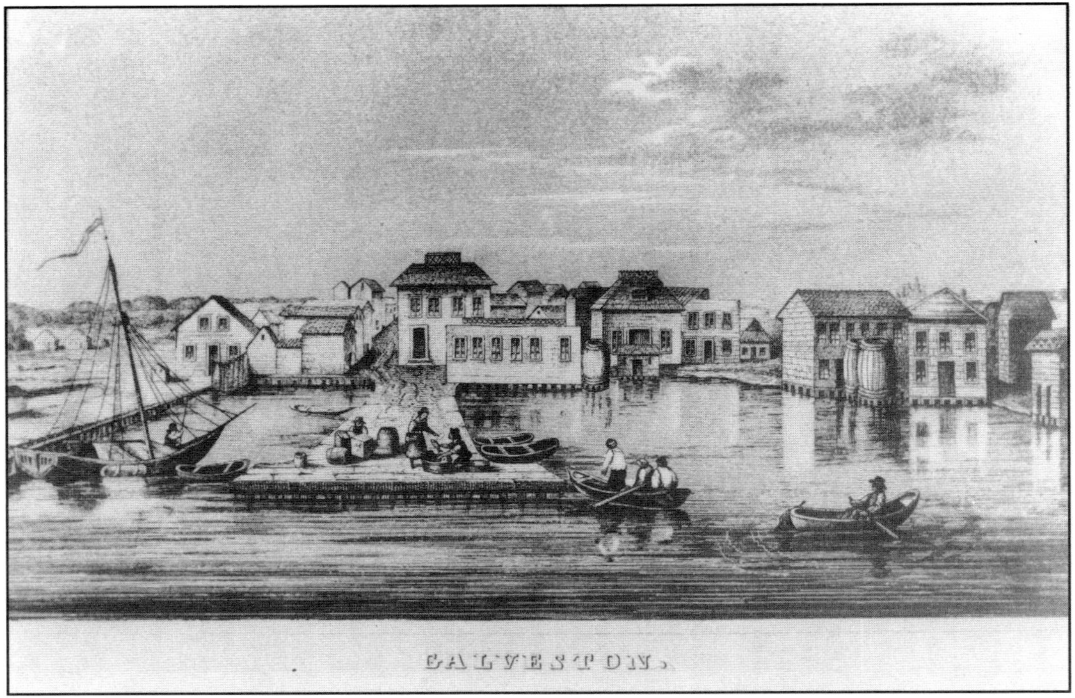

Galveston
C. V. Sommer, *Reise nach Texas im Jahre 1846*,
Bremen, Germany: Heyse, 1847

Early Scene on Buffalo Bayou
A. E. Sweet and J. A. Knox, *On a Mexican Mustang Through Texas*

Houston, Capital of Texas
(One of several perceptions by European artists who clearly never visited the town)
Courtesy Texas Room, Houston Public Library

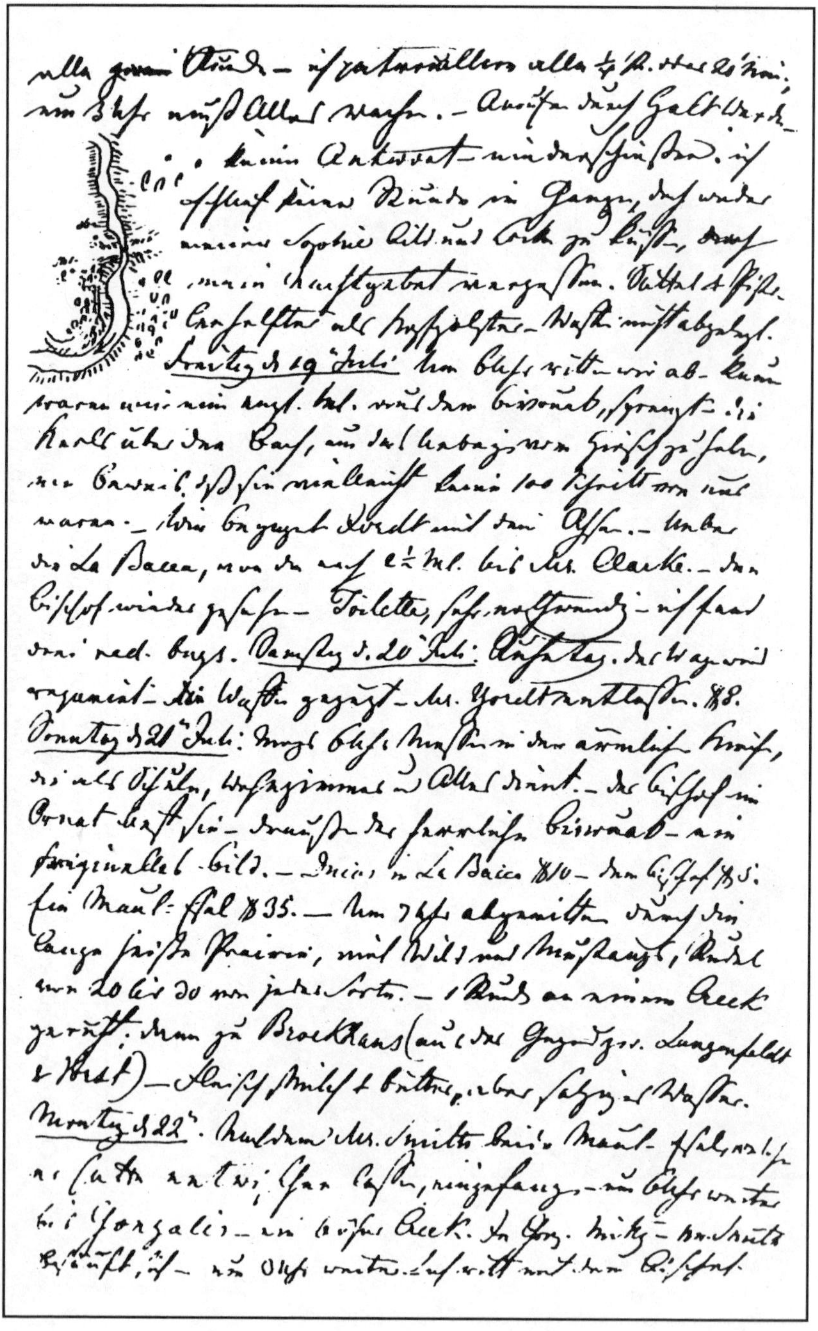

Diary entries for July 19–22, 1844

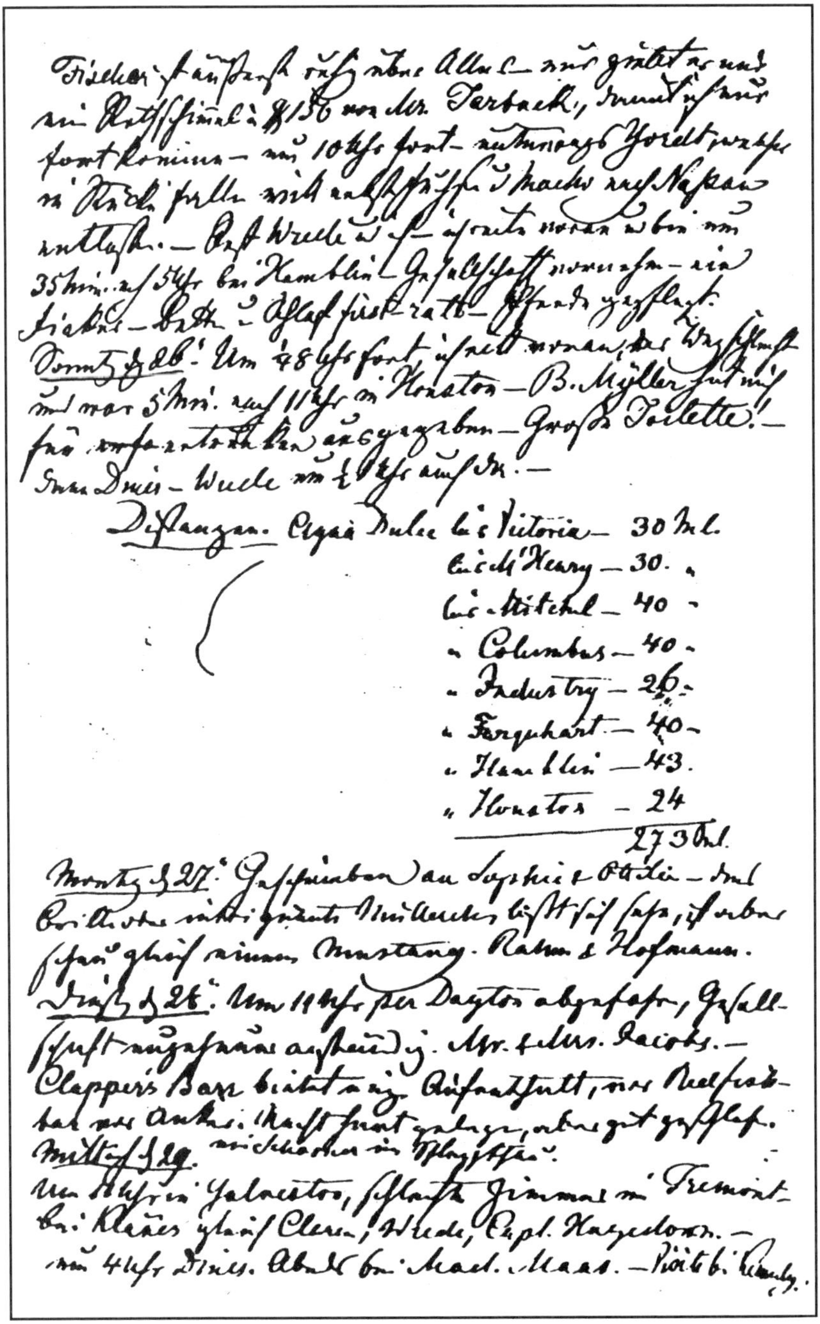

Diary entries for January 26–29, 1845

San Antonio de Bexar, by Hermann Lungkwitz (ca. 1856)
Courtesy of the Witte Museum, San Antonio, Texas

Friday, December 6th. In the morning called on Kennedy; dinner. Afterwards made copies of my letters and in the evening had tea with him at his place.

Saturday, December 7th. In the morning Capt. Elliot came ashore from the *Spartan* (38 guns), brought me letters, one also from Sophie. Dinner, in the evening correspondence.[23]

Sunday, December 8th. Correspondence. Elliot ate with me. Wrote again in the evening. Prepared for my trip.

Monday, December 9th. At noon on board the *Alert*. Eggers is along. Good but cold weather. The storm increased by evening. Ten knots per hour.[24]

Tuesday, [December] the 10th. At 1 A.M. at anchor before the sand bar, in the morning terribly cold, at noon with 7.5 feet water crossed the bar, tacked that long (4 hours). At Decros Point at 4 o'clock. Judge Sommerville is a drunken bore. Went ashore after supper. Maverick and sister. The judge again on board in the evening. History of republicanism.[25]

Wednesday, [December] the 11th. Under sail at 7 A.M. Calmness, got stuck three times on different sand bars. At six in the evening in P[ort] de Vacca. Off Indian Point two cannon shots, off P[ort] de V[acca] four shots. The crew answers with rifles and cheers! (Dr. Köster). Package of letters from Castell.[26]

Thursday, [December] the 12th. To the camp at 11 o'clock. Some of the people complained about the treatment on the *Joh. D.* They quarrel among themselves. I established my headquarters there. Late dinner. Letter to Mr. Jones.[27]

Friday, [December] the 13th. Rahm went off to Victoria. I was at the warehouse. Afterward dinner, in the evening a few gentlemen to supper. Count Henkel gave me Alexander's letter.[28]

Saturday, [December] the 14th. At 9 A.M. to Texana, crossed three creeks and the de Vacca, accompanied by Rahm & Perry & Oliver Jenkins. Halfway we met Lindheimer & Dr. Wales. The latter showed me the area. In Texana I found Müller, Brun & Ervendberg. The land is beautiful but flat and unhealthy, the place itself awful. Ate in camp. Very eerie night in a decrepit house.[29]

Sunday, [December] the 15th. Oppressive heat, looked at the land with Jones. At 2 o'clock in camp. Rain. Dinner. Grand supper in the evening. During the night a norther arrived with heavy rains and cold temperatures.[30]

Monday, [December] the 16th. To Indian Point in spite of the terrible storm. Accompanied by Dr. Köster, Thielepape, Count Henkel, Ewing as chief forester "Molepas." Arrived at 2 o'clock. White not at home. Prepared for the night as well as we could. Very cold.[31]

Tuesday, [December] the 17th. White returned and led us through the swamp. The land belongs to George & Hatchet. The first station, 12 miles from Indian Point. At 3 o'clock back in camp; dinner; tea in the evening, had a good night's sleep. The norther subsided.[32]

Wednesday, [December] the 18th. Hoffman from Houston wants to leave, letter to Fischer. Changed at Mad. Wilke's. In camp in the evening. A terrible runny nose and headache. White called in the evening.[33]

Thursday, [December] the 19th. Wrede, accompanied by Perry, rides off to Corpus Christi. I with Thielepape, Eggers, Schubert, Müller, Wilke, Imhof, Schulz go to Indian Point; White's boat. Departed at 11 o'clock. Underway in Capt. Talbot's boat (schooner *Mary*), ate on board the schooner, a beautiful ship. Made soundings in the afternoon. On board in the evening.[34]

Friday, [December] the 20th. With Wilke, Thielepape & Imhof on the beach, the others in the boat. Laid out Carlshafen. Stayed with White for the evening.[35]

Saturday [December], the 21st. Departed in White's boat by 11 o'clock. In Port La Vacca at noon. Capt. Hatch, meeting at Chocolate Creek regarding Leiningen. Found the group from Texana in the camp, announcement regarding church service.

Sunday, [December] the 22nd. Church service in camp, festive & touching. Dinner, wrote prior it.

Monday, [December] the 23rd. Wrote all day. In the evening von Wrede Sr. arrived with news and letters.[36]

Tuesday, [December] the 24th. In three and three quarters hours to Carlshafen, accompanied by Zink, Köster, Lünzel, Reuter, Henkel, Baur. Joyful welcome of the immigrants in camp as well as on the schooner. Zink's family. Lt. Müller and wife. Returned on the *Alert* at 4 o'clock; we met Sympton who took command of the boat. Walked by moonlight to the camp. Sophie was in my thoughts!!! Christmas tree. C.z.S. Supper. (Employed Fritsche.)[37]

Wednesday, [December] the 25th. Church service. Correspondence. Answered Bourg. Ate at five P.M., afterward distributed gifts to the children. Great joy and cheers.

Thursday, [December] the 26th. Previous evening reprimanded the soldiers, during the night a scandal by them. I chased them all to hell. Departed for Carlshafen at 11 o'clock, arrived there at 2 o'clock. Dinner. Church service (Lindheimer slept behind the altar). Christmas presents given to the children. A cold norther, [spent] the night under open sky.

Friday, [December] the 27th. Returned to camp. Pistol practice. Early to bed. (Rahm arrived.) Chased soldiers from the camp.

Saturday, [December] the 28th. To La Vacca, business matters. Wrede arrived. Chased soldiers out of the warehouse. In the evening the old Wrede & Klaren. Lindheimer's group started for Leiningen.

Sunday, [December] the 29th. Church services in camp, afterward off to Leiningen where Zink arrived with the people. Late lunch, at 5 o'clock.

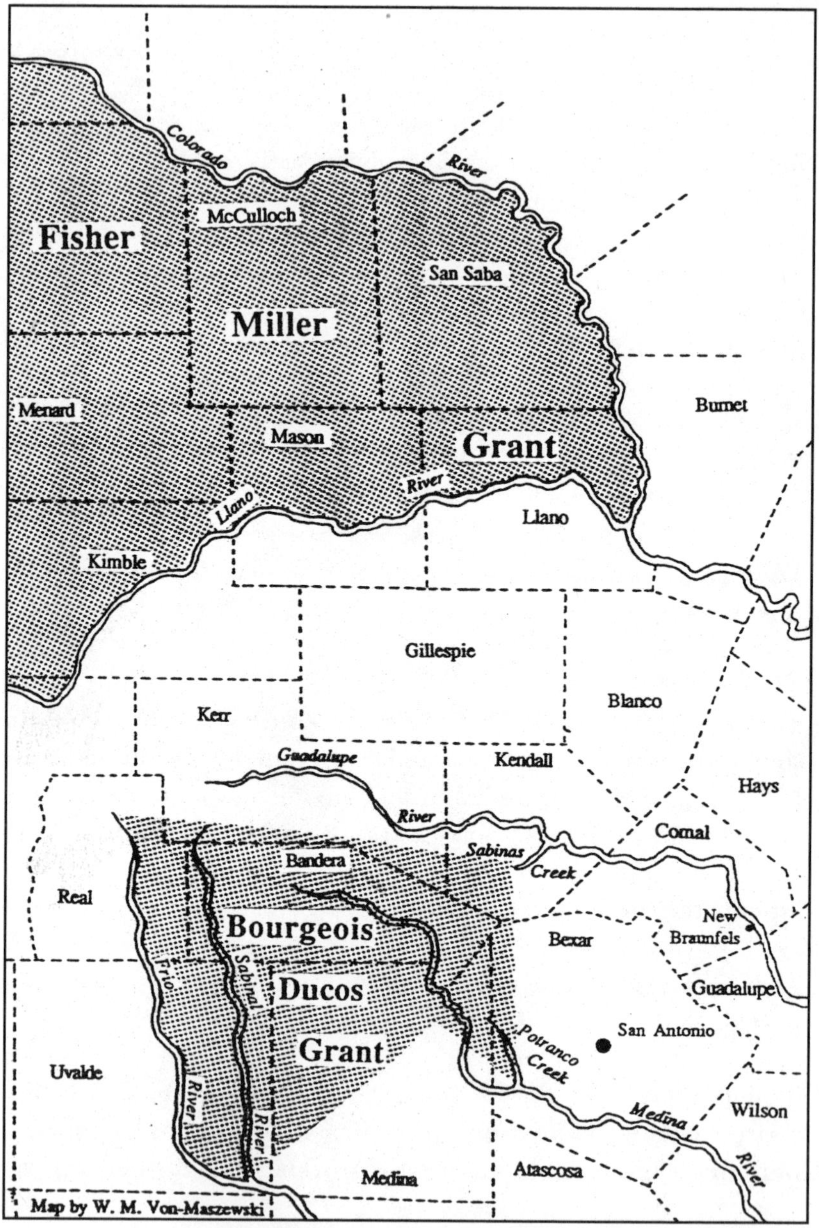

Location of the grants

Monday, the 30th. To La Vacca; von Kloudt [*sic*] with a letter from Coll. Baur's quarrel with Anton. Dinner, afterward pistol practice.[38]

Tuesday, [December] the 31st. Rest; wrote in the tent. Wilke, Imhof went to Carlshafen. Supper at night (Hofmann in the swamp). At midnight rifle volleys by the soldiers and cheers. I addressed the group.[39]

Wednesday, January 1, 1845. Letter to Sophie, afterward rode to Carlshafen by way of Leiningen. Everywhere there were new year's congratulations. Note to the Dr. I have a beautifully decorated tent in Carlshafen. Zink does not have the equipment.

Thursday, [January] the 2nd. Rode back to the camp which had been struck. Coll accompanied me. (Klondt did not show up). Rain during the night.

Friday [January] the 3rd. Headquarter transferred to the Agua Dulce. The second tent was left behind. Baur is useless. I slept wonderfully this night.[40]

Saturday, [January] the 4th. In the morning business matters, then I took care of correspondence. Dinner, Zink arrived. In the evening a group went to Carlshafen, all the ox drivers were drunk. Terrible racket. Correspondence. Coll departed.

Sunday, [January] the 5th. Church service at 11 o'clock, followed by Miss Bremer's baptism. Correspondence. Coll arrived with Holstein's letter. I talked with him. He presented me with his expenses. There was a strong wind.[41]

Monday, [January] the 6th. Coll rode away. Capt. Kraatz arrived with Fischer's letter. Kraatz dispatched again. Wedemeyer was at dinner, afterward I looked at horses. One of Schlichting's children died. Coll and Zink returned from Carlshafen.[42]

Tuesday, [January] the 7th. First meeting of the Colonial Council, afterward, business matters for the remainder for the day. Preparations for the Second Council.[43]

Wednesday, [January] the 8th. Duel between von Coll and Dr. Köster, plenty aggravation, plenty spectacle. Ate late. Seconds: Cloudt, Zink, Lüntzel, Wedemeyer.

Thursday, [January] the 9th. Second meeting of Colonial Council. Posting of the Camp's legal regulations. Lüntzel at lunch.[44]

Friday, [January] the 10th. A gradual distribution of food. Completed swearing in of the company and the inspection of the horses.[45]

Saturday, [January] the 11th. Third meeting of Colonial Council. Inspection of all men able to bear arms. Call for volunteers, everyone responded. Election of officers. I addressed them.[46]

Sunday, [January] the 12th. Church service. Business matters. Dinner a la [?]. Selected horses.

Monday, [January] the 13th. Business matters and packing up of papers. At noon I went from camp to Carlshafen. After lunch, at three o'clock, boarded the [sloop] *Sarah Foyle*. This ship is peculiar in that it has three captains, no sailors, no cook and for this reason a very smelly cabin. (Mrs. White, Thielepape and Bäschen, also the peculiar Müller). At 10 P.M. ran aground at Decros Point, quickly afloat again, dropped anchor. I spent the night sleeping on deck.[47]

Tuesday, [January] the 14th. In the morning to Decros Point. Rolling sea, contrary wind. Didn't cross the bar. At 3 o'clock back at Decros Point. Col. Maverick & mistress are refined but he didn't give any horses and he is tough. Spent the night with Judge Sommerville who is a scoundrel.[48]

Wednesday, [January] the 15th. At 7 A.M. back to Carlshafen, at 2 o'clock back in camp. Wrede followed. Reports from Zink & Coll. I had a lot to do.

Thursday, [January] the 16th. Wedding of Röser and Therese von Kroitsch. Heine, the Jew, is useless and dull and will be let go. Less useful still is Schellenträger on whose head a tent collapsed with barrels being damaged. George Brune was enraged.[49]

Friday, [January] the 17th. A pleasant norther passed through during the night which soaked everyone's bedding. In spite of the cold, jollity prevailed. In the evening there was a good supper and grog.

Saturday, [January] the 18th. Beautiful weather. A lot of business affairs. Schellenträger inquired. (Martin, the best one, had asked in Decros already and had been accepted). Finished my letters to Germany at Decros in the evening of the 24th. Young Saalmühle wants to go to Mexico, seduced by the Jew. After talking to him he changed his mind but not the Jew, [?] unfortunately for nothing with the [?] looked up.[50]

Sunday, [January] the 19th. *"Dejeuner a la four chatte"* (meat breakfast). At 11:30 I went to Victoria, with Wrede, Anton, Yordt, and Joseph; it is a very good trail. Trailor at the lead was excellent. In Victoria at 5 o'clock. Company there rather rude.[51]

Monday, [January] the 20th. In the morning looked in on Thome. Departed at 8 o'clock. Good trail. At McHenry's at 2 o'clock. In the evening started the list of [?]. Anton remarked that [?] and he wants to jump out of his skin.[52]

Tuesday, [January] the 21st. (Ellichen's birthday) Departed at 7:15 for Mitchell's by way of Mrs. Hallis. Poor lodging. Good trail.[53]

Wednesday, [January] the 22nd. The big Fordtran lost [?] and became unhappy. Wrede assured me that he cannot [?] for this reason he was left with Mitchell and in his stead we purchased a blind plow horse for $10. Departed at 8 o'clock. Slow pace, passable trail, at Robson & Low in Columbus at 4 o'clock. Drank to Ellichen's health.[54]

Thursday, [January] the 23rd. Purchased a stallion and a *Macho* for $120. On the trail at 9 o'clock. At Cumings Creek at 12 o'clock. Pastor Ervendberg's wife (where did she work before?). Mad. Brune was busy with calving so we continued [?] and arrived at Ernst's at 4 o'clock. Since I did not feel well these past five days I asked Dr. Rikleff to prescribe me a [medicinal] powder which took its effect during the night. Rather cold. Ernst as ballad-singer. Mr. Sand. [?] wants to ride with us tomorrow. Endivin Salad.[55]

Friday, [January] the 24th. Left at 8:15 A.M. Joseph with the plow horse (with whom he [?] yesterday) and Fuchs Fordtran to Nassau. Five miles past Ernst, Anton unhitched and returned to Nassau by way of Ernst's. Gave him $20. At Farquhart's by 6 P.M. (Passed through two towns: Brenham & Jacksonville). Miserable company and a senator who disturbed our slumber. Judge Bilbury [arrived]. Message to our "dear Fischer".[56]

Saturday, [January] the 25th. The lecture had its desired effect. He [Fischer] arrived at 8 A.M. and was rather restrained. If we depend on Congress we will not succeed. Fischer is very calm about everything. To get rid of me he gave me a roan (Rothschimmel) that he bought from Tarbuck for $150. I left at 10 o'clock. On the road, Yordt who was close to going to pieces was sent to Nassau with Fuchs and Macho. This left Wrede and me. I rode ahead, and reached Hamblin at 5:35. Distinguished company, a coach. Beds and sleep *first class.* Horses were taken care of.[57]

Sunday, [January] the 26th. Departed at 7:45; I rode ahead, the trail was bad. Arrived in Houston at 11:05. B. Müller had spread the word that I had drowned. Thorough cleaning! Afterward dinner. Wrede arrived at 12:30.

Distances:

Aqua Dulce	to Victoria:	30 miles
	to McHenry:	30 mi.
	to Mitchell:	40 mi.
	to Columbus:	40 mi.
	to Industry:	26 mi.
	to Farquhart:	40 mi.
	to Hamblin:	43 mi.
	to Houston:	24 mi.
		273 miles

Monday, [January] the 27th. Wrote to Sophie & Ottilie. [?] glasses of the intriguing Müllerchen allows himself to be seen but is as shy as a mustang. Rahm & Hofmann.

Tuesday, [January] the 28th. At 11 o'clock departed on the *Dayton*. The company was exceptionally respectable. Mr. & Mrs. Jacobs. Clopper's Bar forced a delay; anchored off Redfish Bar. Spent the night on a hard surface but slept well. A schooner in tow.[58]

Wednesday, [January] the 29th. In Galveston at 11 o'clock. Inferior room in the Tremont. Claren, Wrede, Capt. Hagedorn were at Klaener's. Dinner at 4 o'clock. In the evening at Mad. Maas's. Called on Kennedy.[59]

Thursday, [January] the 30th. Wrote in the morning, later made some purchases. Drank Bavarian beer on board the *Ferdinand.* (The great unknown on the *Apollo.*) At noon Capt. Hagedorn came to dinner. In the evening at Mad. Maas's.[60]

Friday, [January] the 31st. Did correspondence. Dinner at 4 o'clock. Saw Elliot & Saligny. In the evening a foursome of whist. Called on the bishop.[61]

Saturday, February 1st. The steamer *McKinney* arrived. Big to-do about General Navarro. Galveston's militia paraded on this occasion. Impressive sight. Cannon salute during which I wrote to Castell, *about what?* Visit from Elliot. Foursome of whist.[62]

Sunday, February 2nd. Rebecca & Arcieri sang at morning mass. Visit from the latter. Dinner at Saligny's. Visited Maas in the evening.[63]

Monday, [February] the 3rd. Didn't feel well. Stayed in bed for a long time. Visits from Maas, Holstein, Dr. Aschhof, etc. Fischer & Müller arrived. Played whist in the evening.[64]

Tuesday, [February] the 4th. Still didn't feel well. Letter from Fischer. I answered it. Beautiful weather, went horseback riding to the Fort with the Spanish cannons; in the evening a foursome of whist.[65]

Wednesday, [February] the 5th. Did correspondence. The *Neptun* arrived (Klaener and his wife were on board as well as ten emigrant families). Dinner. In the evening played whist.[66]

Thursday, [February] the 6th. Visited Klaener. Wrote until late. Called on his wife, a charming woman. A foursome of whist. Spoke to the Napoleon emigrant who joined [the Society].[67]

Friday, [February] the 7th. After all these days of correspondence with Fischer; my first impression of him has proven correct (he is a scoundrel). Conference with Rose. Many interruptions, also from Illies. Called on Mad. Illies, nee Pappenheim. Letter and picture of her father Albrecht. Did correspondence until late in the evening. Prior to that a visit from the Dutch naturalist.[68]

Saturday, [February] the 8th. Did paper work all day until late in the evening.[69]

Sunday, [February] the 9th. Continued same early in A.M. Visited Mad. Klaener, Kennedy, Mrs. Jacobi. On board the *McKim*. A beautiful quadroon on board. Dined with the Stewards. In the evening, but not until 8 o'clock, at Maas's.

Monday, [February] the 10th. My letters left with the *McKim*, the *New York* in view. Fischer sent emigrants of the *Neptun* to an uncertain future by advising them to go with Schubert. Asked Klaener about this who confirmed this to be true. A letter dated December arrived with Sophie's picture. Oh, what joy! I answered it immediately.[70]

Tuesday, [February] the 11th. I did correspondence all day. Played whist in the evening.

Wednesday, [February] the 12th. The *New York* left at noon, Wrede and Klaener are on her. Simpton arrived. Dined at Saligny's. In the evening visited at Maas's.

Thursday, [February] the 13th. Plans for the departure. Dinner at Kennedy's. A soiree at my place in the evening. Stephenson and his tales.

Friday, [February]the 14 th. Went horseback riding. I was in a bad mood. Called on Mad. Maas. Dinner at Saligny's. I had an audience with Dr. Meyer.

Saturday, [February] the 15 th. Wrede left with the horses. I ate at Saligny's; at the Maas's in the evening.

Sunday, [February] the 16th. Stepped out in the morning. Dinner at Saligny's. Whist at my place in the evening.

Monday, [February] the 17th. Slept badly last night. In the morning I went to Major Cook & Klaener. Holstein dined with me. Expected Simpton. Plan for the contract with the English government. I was at Rainer's in the evening.[71]

Tuesday, [February] the 18 th. Wrote to Castell & Sophie. Simpton didn't come. How awfully boring. At Saligny's at noon. In the evening at Maas's.

Wednesday, [February] the 19th. Did correspondence in the morning and read the Weser newspaper. Ate at home. Played whist in the evening.[72]

Thursday, [February] the 20 th. Simpton still has not arrived! Went out walking. The *New York* arrived in the evening and with her arrived Klaener and the news of Benton's annexation bill.[73]

Friday, [February] the 21st. Visited Kennedy in the morning. Ate at Saligny's at noon. Whist at my place in the evening.

Saturday, [February] the 22nd. At night a norther with heavy thunderstorms and lightning struck at Elliot's & St. Martin's. The *McKim* arrived; Lewi Jones "public narration about prolonging the libations, when the pronunciation came. He has been out of the pale of Christ. society for his political, social and financial state." Dinner at Saligny's. Evening at Kennedy's. Fordtran and the scene which I had with him.[74]

[1] Marshall, Bohnert, and Koch: identities unknown.

[2] Schmidt: possibly H. Schmidt whose name appears on the petition for Herman University in 1842 (Biesele, *German Settlements in Texas*, p. 216).

[3] Scheerer: could be Bernard Schirrer (York, *Friedrich Ernst*, p. 83). Lewis: identity unknown. York: possibly John York (1800–1848) who lived on Mill Creek in Austin County before he moved to newly established DeWitt County (*The New Handbook of Texas*, Vol. VI, p. 1124). Mad. Mäßgen: maybe Möschen, see Chapter III, note 4. Gim: possibly Solms's phonetic spelling for Jim, a Negro at Nassau Farm (see also Chapter II, note 56).

[4] Kray: Henry Krey and Susan Saltin were married by Ervendberg on 2 April 1841 (*Marriage Records, Colorado County, Texas*, Book B, p. 22).

[5] Brunert: identity unknown. Dr. Frank: A Dr. E. Frank who apparently lived near Industry, Texas, served as trustee for the proposed Hermann University 1845–50 (*Trustees' Minutes, Hermann University*, manuscript, information by courtesy of Ann Lindemann, Industry, Texas).

[6] *Faust*, the well-known drama by Johann Wolfgang von Goethe (1749–1832).

[7] William G. Ewing, formerly a merchant in Linnville, Texas, was engaged by the Society in Port Lavaca (Donaly E. Brice, *The Great Comanche Raid*, Austin, Texas: Eakin Press, 1987, p. 31).

[8] Ernst Jr.: very likely Johann Friedrich ["Fritz"] Ernst Jr. (York, *Friedrich Ernst*, pp. 40–44).

[9] Brun (Mr. & Mrs.): probably Georg and Henrietta Brune (*New Orleans Passenger List, 1820–1902*, Microfilm M259, Roll 23, for 20 December, 1843; *1850 U.S. Census, Colorado County, Texas*, p. 34B, National Archives Microfilm M432, Roll 910). Rohde: see Chapter II, note 16. Robertson's: probably Robert Robson who moved to Texas from Dumfries, Scotland in 1839. He built a castlelike structure on the south bank of the Colorado River outside Columbus. Damaged by a river flood in 1869, the building was finally torn down in 1883 (*Colorado County Chronicles*, compiled by the Colorado County Historical Commission, Austin, Texas: Nortex Press, 1986, Vol. I. p. 54). Grog: an alcoholic drink diluted with water. Hegler: possibly William R. Hensley (1800–1849) who was active as a surveyor in Fayette and Colorado Counties during the 1830s (*The New Handbook of Texas*, Vol. III, p. 566). Colorado City: a guide for the period offers the description that "Colorado City is a name which has been given to a very beautiful and romantic prairie, on the west side of the Colorado [River], just above the town of LaGrange. It is more celebrated for the beauty . . . than for its improvements" (Geo. W. Bonnel, *Topographical Description of Texas*, reprint, Waco, Texas: Texian Press, 1964, p. 59). Mahleskum: identity unknown. Preciosa's Song: meaning unknown. From Nassau the trail

led in a southerly direction along the course of Cummins Creek to Columbus. After crossing the Colorado River the party rested at Robson's place. Since the last stop at Kray's the party traveled a distance of fourteen miles.

[10] Mr. Ridel from San Antonio: see Chapter II, note 53.

[11] Wrede: Solms is very clear in his entries about which of the two Wredes, father or son, that he is writing. The elder Wrede he addresses as "von Wrede Senior" or "von Wrede I" (see entries for 23 December, 17 April, 3 May, and 1 June), while the younger Wrede he simply refers to as "Wrede." Joseph: identity unknown. Tyrrel: The 1850 Census gives this information on a Henry Terrell: born in Georgia, forty-three years old, farmer, with a real estate value of $8,500. His wife Maria, born in Alabama, was thirty-two years old. The couple's six children ranging in age from three to thirteen years were all born in Texas. On 29 July 1843, Terrel purchased 526 acres in the James Bowie Survey, located in Colorado County, extending east from the Navidad River. The present community of Oakland was established on this survey (*1850 U.S. Census, Colorado County, Texas*, p. 29A, National Archives Microfilm M432, Roll 910; *[Colorado County] Deed Record*, Book E, p. 380; *Colorado County Chronicles*, Vol. II, p. 778).

[12] Washington Green Lee Foley (1780–1874) arrived in Texas in 1838 and established a plantation on the west side of Mixon Creek in Lavaca County. It included a mill, gin, blacksmith shop, and slave quarters. County tax rolls for 1851 list him as owning ninety-five slaves and over 12,000 acres of land. His plantation was separated from that of Isaac N. Mitchel's (see Chapter II, note 17) by only a lane (*The New Handbook of Texas*, Vol. II, p. 1049). Clarke: Clarke's settlement on the Lavaca River, see Chapter II, note 18. Mrs. Hallies: Margaret L Hallett (1787–1863) operated a trading post and donated adjacent land for a town site which grew into Hallettsville (*Ibid.*, Vol. III, p. 419). Glais: identity unknown.

[13] McHenry: probably John McHenry (1798–1878) whose place was six miles west of the Lavaca River in present Jackson County (*Ibid*, Vol. IV, p. 409).

[14] Jonosso: should be Arenosa Creek, which forms a boundary line between Victoria and Jackson Counties.

[15] La Bacca, the port and the river, is today spelled Lavaca. Juliet Constance Watts was William G. Ewing's sister. She was married to Hugh O. Watts for less than a month when Indians killed him during the raid on Linnville on 8 August 1840. Juliet was carried off by the Indians. A few days later at the Battle of Plum Creek in Caldwell County, she was rescued (Brice, *The Great Comanche*, pp. 45, 95 and 99). Passo Cavallo or Cavallo

Pass connects Matagorda Bay with the Gulf of Mexico. In the nineteenth century this was a major point of entry through Lavaca and Indianola to the Texas interior (*The New Handbook of Texas*, Vol. I, p. 1045). Judge Hays: referring to John Coffee (Jack) Hays, Texas Ranger (see also Chapter II, note 24). Sympton: Capt. Simpton of the Texas revenue cutter *Alert* (Biesele, "Solms's Trip to Texas," in *Southwest Historical Quarterly*, Vol. XL, p. 17; Mary A. Maverick, *Memoirs of Mary A. Maverick*, Rena Maverick Green, editor, Lincoln, Nebraska: University of Nebraska Press, 1989, p. 85). From Robson's place Solms's party traveled in a southwesterly direction, possibly on the Atascosito Trail, to Clarke's settlement, five miles west of present-day Hallettsville, and from there on a southern course to Port Lavaca.

[16] Tapon: identity unknown.

[17] Duncan: identity unknown.

[18] Captain Thomas Bridges, wife Hannah H. (Williams) Bridges and daughter Alice Williams Bridges came from Massachusetts in 1836, or shortly thereafter. Bridges with two partners established the town of Port Austin in Matagorda County from his league on the east side of Tres Palacios Bay, 31 May 1838 (*Historic Matagorda County*, compiled by the Matagorda County Historical Society, Houston, Texas: D. Armstrong Co., Inc., 1986, Vol. I, pp. 51 and 301).

[19] Ship *Tom Jack*: Herrman Seele wrote in 1844 that this boat was named after his friend Thomas Jack of Brazoria County, Texas, on whose farm it was built (Seele, *The Diary of Hermann Seele*, pp. 190 and 229). Decrose Point: Decrow's Point, on the western tip of Matagorda Island.

[20] Cedar Lake: Creek in Brazoria County. Brazos [River] empties into Gulf of Mexico. Velasco: located slightly upriver from the Gulf of Mexico on the east bank of the Brazos River in Brazoria County. Quintana: located on the west side of the mouth of the Brazos River in Brazoria County.

[21] *Johann Dethardt*: a brig, 86 ft long, 21 ft wide, 11 ft draft; Theodor Lüdering, master and co-owner (Fey, *New Braunfels*, Vol. I, p. 41). Capt. Kingston: identity unknown. Fischer: presumably Henry Fisher.

[22] Ship *Alert*: see note 15 this chapter. San Louis: San Luis, located at the western end of Galveston Island

[23] G. B. Elliot, captain of H.M.S. *Spartan*: cousin of Charles Elliot, British chargé d'affaires in Galveston (Tom H. Wells, *Commodore Moore and the Texas Navy*, Austin, Texas: The University of Texas Press, 1960, p. 144).

[24] Eggers: (no first name given) appointed agent for Kauffmann & Co. at Port Lavaca.

[25] Judge Sommerville: most likely Alexander Somervell (1796–1854), collector of customs at Port Cavallo on Matagorda Island. Samuel Augustus Maverick (1803–1870): In nineteenth-century fashion, he addressed his

wife's sister Elizabeth Adams as "sister" or "sister Lizzie." Maverick was born in South Carolina and came to Texas in 1835 in time to participate in the siege of Bexar (December 1835). A participant in the Texas Revolution, he established his home in San Antonio after Texas gained its independence from Mexico. In 1839 he was elected the town's mayor. When General Woll and his soldiers invaded San Antonio in 1842, Maverick was one of the prisoners carried to Perote Prison in Mexico. He was released in 1843. Elected to the Seventh and Eighth Congress of the Republic of Texas he advocated that Texas be annexed by the U.S. In late 1844 he moved his family to Decrows Point on Matagorda Island. They returned permanently to San Antonio in 1847. Maverick continued to be active in politics, serving in the Fourth through Ninth State Legislature, 1851–1863 (Green, *Samuel Maverick, Texan,* pp. 199, 238, 260, and 264; *The New Handbook of Texas,* Vol. IV, pp. 574–575).

[26] Port da Vacca: today spelled Port Lavaca (on Lavaca Bay). Indian Point: on Lavaca Bay in Calhoun County. Dr. Theodore Köster (1817–1877): arrived in Texas on the brig *Johann Dethardt* in November 1844. He had been hired in Germany as the colony's physician. In that capacity he also served as member of the Colonial Council, or the Society's governing body in Texas. The immigrants were divided in their opinion as to Köster's demeanor and his medical practice. Sörgel related that Köster may have been no licensed physician but a pharmacist's assistant in Germany who failed his examination. Köster settled in New Braunfels, married, raised a family and practiced medicine there (*Secretary of State, Record Group 307, ARIS-TSL;* Fey, *New Braunfels,* Vol. I, pp. 410–415; Sörgel, *A Sojourn in Texas,* p. 87).

[27] Camp: temporary camp near the town of Lavaca for the first group of the Society. Mr. Jones: President Anson Jones (see Chapter II, note 7).

[28] Rahm: see Chapter II, notes 24 and 26. Warehouse: storehouse in Lavaca for Society's provisions. Count Henkel: Arnold Count Henkel von Donnersmark (1820–1850) arrived on the *Johann Dethardt* in 1844. Later became proprietor of a tavern in New Braunfels (Seele, *The Diary of Hermann Seele,* p. 267). Alexander Friedrich Ludwig (1807–1867), Solms's brother (Information to W. M. Von-Maszewski from Schloß Braunfels, Braunfels, Germany, 9 June 2000).

[29] Texana, Jackson County, on the Navidad River, originally Santa Anna, renamed Texana after the Texas Revolution in 1836. County seat of Jackson County until 1883. "Rahm & Perry & Oliver Jenkins": only Texas Ranger Johann Rahm can be identified; see Chapter II, notes 24 and 26, and note 28 this chapter. Dr. Wales: probably Dr. Francis Flournoy Wells. He and his sister-in-law Pamelia McNutt Porter founded the town of Texana

in 1832 (*The New Handbook of Texas*, Vol. VI, p. 269). Theodore Müller of Kaufmann & Co., Galveston, was appointed the Society's agent at Indian Point. Georg Brun: identity unknown. Erfenberg: Ervendberg (see Chapter II, note 12). Several Germans from the Cummins Settlement went to Nassau Farm as well as to the coast in hopes of finding employment with the Society. See also Chapter III, note 6. Camp: near Texana established by the immigrants from the ship *Weser* who arrived in Galveston on July 8, 1844, as part of a contingent from another colonization company but were left to their own devices. Solms took this group into the Society's project (Fey, *First Founders*, p. 29).

[30] Jones: identity unknown.

[31] Wilhelm Carl August Thielepape (1814–1904) arrived in Texas in 1844. He settled in Carlshafen before moving to San Antonio where he was an engineer and architect, Reconstruction mayor, founder of the *Beethoven Gesangverein*, and organizer of the city's German-English School. In his professional activities, he surveyed the town site of Uvalde and designed the San Antonio Casino as well as the Comal County Courthouse. In 1874 he moved to Chicago (*Ibid.*, Vol. VI, p. 459). Ewing as chief forester "Molepas": meaning unknown. Samuel Addison White (ca. 1805–1869) held title to the land at Indian Point. White arrived in Texas in 1830, fought in the battle of Velasco (1832), was captain in the Texas army in 1835 and 1836, and took part in the battle of Plum Creek in 1840 (see note 15 this chapter). Later he served in the senate of the Sixth and Tenth (Texas) Legislature, served as mayor of Victoria and was district judge in 1865 (*Ibid.*, Vol. IV, p. 931).

[32] George: identity unknown. Hatchet: Sylvanus Hatch (1788–1885) held title to the land on Chocolate Creek. Hatch was born in Massachusetts and by 1811 lived in Louisiana. Became a veteran of the War of 1812. During a trip to Texas in 1828 he met Stephen F. Austin who invited him to become a member of his colony. Hatch returned to Texas in 1829, bringing with him his family and settled on his land grant on the Lavaca River near the community of Texana. When the Texas Revolution came, he enlisted and when Calhoun County was created (1846) he was one of the two first commissioners to serve the county (Ira T. Taylor, *The Cavalcade of Jackson County*, San Antonio, Texas: Naylor Co., 1938, pp. 401–403). First Station: At Agua Dulce (Spanish "sweet water") on Chocolate Creek in Calhoun County. Solms named it Camp Leiningen in honor of Prince Carl of Leiningen, a member of the Society.

[33] Hoffman; identity unknown. Fischer: most likely Henry Fisher. Madame Wil(l)ke: Elizabeth Willke, wife of Lt. Ludwig Willke (see also Chapter III, note 23).

[34] Heinrich Imhof and Johann Heinrich Schulze: arrived in Texas in 1844 (Fey, *New Braunfels*, pp. 392 and 540, respectively). Capt. Talbot: identity unknown.

[35] Carlshafen: Solms wanted a harbor facility that would exclusively serve the Society's German immigrants. He named it in honor of Prince Leiningen-Armorbach, Count Castell, both directors of the Society, and himself, all three having the given name Carl. Previously the place was called Indian Point or Powderhorn, after the Society's demise it became Indianola (Biesele, *German Settlements in Texas*, p. 110). Count Carl of Castell: see Chapter I, note 5.

[36] Solms's writing coincides with the *Sixth Report* dated Camp at Port Lavaca, 23 December 1844. Friedrich Wilhelm von Wrede Sr. (1786–1845), attained the rank of captain in the Hessian military service. In the early 1840s he traveled in the central and eastern parts of the United States as well as Texas and returned to Germany in 1843 where he joined the Society as an official. He arrived in Texas in the early part of December, possibly on the brig *Herschel*. From Galveston he wrote a letter to Henry Fisher on December 17, 1844, in which he talks about his journey and the plans to move groups of immigrants from Galveston to Matagorda Bay. Solms entrusted him with various important duties on behalf of the Society and as manager of Nassau Farm (Geue and Geue, *A New Land Beckoned*, p. vii; Friedrich W. von Wrede, *Sketches of Life in the United States of North America and Texas*, translated by Chester W. Geue, Waco, Texas: Texian Press, 1970; Justman, *Henry Francis Fisher*, p. 314; see also Chapter II, note 50 and note 59 this chapter).

[37] Zink: Nicholas Zink (1812–1887) a civil engineer and former Bavarian army officer moved with his wife to Texas in 1844. Solms put him in charge of logistics, moving the immigrants from Carlshafen to the future town of New Braunfels. There he also supervised the erection of a palisade to enclose the tent settlement, named in his honor Zinkenberg, where the newcomers lived until permanent homes were built. Zink surveyed the future site of New Braunfels and the adjoining farmland. In 1847, divorcing his wife, he left New Braunfels and settled on land on Sister Creek. This was the beginning of Sisterdale, a Latin settlement. In 1850 he and his second wife Elisabeth Mangold moved and operated a gristmill south of Fredericksburg; in 1853 he lived in Comfort. By 1870 he was a shingle maker and had taken a third wife. He finally settled in Spanish Pass (today Welfare), between Comfort and Boerne (*The New Handbook of Texas*, Vol. VI, p. 1154; Fey, *New Braunfels*, Vol. I, pp. 619–621). Christoph Lünzel (1820–1858): arrived in Texas in November 1844. On the emigrant list generated by the Society his occupation is given as

being a lawyer (*Secretary of State, Record Group 307*). Wilhelm Reuter (1820–1863): arrived in Texas in November 1844. Lt. Müller and wife: identities unknown. C.z.S.: possibly initials for Carl zu Solms-Braunfels. Fritsche: identity unknown.

38 Von Kloudt: Richard von Cloudt (1817–1904) emigrated to Texas in 1844 and arrived in New Braunfels in April 1845. A former 2nd lieutenant in Germany he volunteered for service in the Mexican War. When he returned from the war, he settled in Gillespie County. About 1855 he moved to Kimble County to be near his children (*Ibid.*: Fey, *New Braunfels*, Vol. I, pp. 324–325). Jean Jacques von Coll (1814–1852) was a retired 1st lieutenant of the Duchy of Nassau. He arrived in Texas in 1844. Solms appointed him the colony's financial officer. In 1846 he helped in the founding of Fredericksburg. Elected mayor of New Braunfels in 1852, he was killed shortly thereafter in a dispute (*Ibid.*, Vol. I, pp. 326–329).

39 The statement "wrote in tent" coincides with *Seventh Report* dated 1 January 1845. Hof(f)mann: not clear if this is Gustav or Joseph Hoffmann.

40 Agua Dulce: see note 32 this chapter.

41 Heinrich Christian Bremer (1811–1880) and family: arrived in Texas in 1844. The child baptized was Caroline Ann Bremer (*Secretary of State, Record group 307*). Solms's writing coincides with Postscript to the *Seventh Report* dated 5 January 1845 camp on Agua Dulce (Geue and Geue, *A New Land Beckoned*, p. 54).

42 Capt. Kraatz: probably Louis/Lewis Kraatz born in Germany. For his participation in the battle of San Jacinto the Republic of Texas patented to him 640 acres of land in Victoria County in 1842. He died in 1857 and is buried in the Independence Cemetery, Washington County, Texas (Thomas L. Miller, *Bounty and Donation Land Grants of Texas, 1835–1888,* Austin, Texas: The University of Texas Press, 1967, p. 799; Charles F. Schmidt, *History of Washington County [Texas]*, San Antonio, Texas: Naylor Co., 1949, p. 43). Adolph Wedemeyer (1822– ?): emigrated to Texas in 1844. He was one of the early settlers of New Braunfels and ran a ferry at the confluence of the Comal and Guadalupe Rivers. In 1847 he sold his business and acreage and left for parts unknown (Fey, *New Braunfels*, Vol. I, p. 584–586). Friedrich Schlichting: arrived in Texas in December 1844. It was his three-year-old daughter Dorothea who died (*Ibid.*, p. 531).

43 Colonial Council: established to assist Solms in the care, protection, and transportation of the immigrants into the interior. This council was composed of the General Commissioner, a minister, an engineer, a bookkeeper, and a doctor (Fey, *New Braunfels*, Vol. I, p. 66; Biesele, *German Settlements in Texas*, 87).

[44] Legal regulations: military code of conduct defining order and discipline to be adhered to by the Society's militia (Fey, *New Braunfels*, Vol. I, pp. 71–74).

[45] Distribution of food: the Society had agreed to supply immigrants during their early months in Texas. "Swearing in of company": the organization by Solms of a militia from the ranks of the immigrants. This company would protect the immigrants from Indian attacks as they were moved into the interior.

[46] This confirms that the first three Colonial Council meetings were held at the camp on Agua Dulce.

[47] Mrs. White: presumably the wife of Samuel Addison White (see note 31 this chapter). Bäschen: German for "little (female) cousin;" identity unknown. "peculiar Müller": apparently another instance of Solms's derogatory reference to Burchard Miller (Müller), Henry Francis Fisher's partner in the Fisher-Miller land grant (see also Chapter III, note 24).

[48] Col. Maverick and mistress: Samuel Augustus Maverick and Mary Adams Maverick (1818–1898), his wife. Mary kept a diary during much of her married life and it offers an interesting as well as important insight to life in Texas in the 1830s and 1840s. In it she mentioned that Solms called on them in 1844 while they resided at Decrows Point on Matagorda Island. (Mary's granddaughter edited the diary for publication in 1921: Mary Adams Maverick, *Memoirs of Mary A. Maverick*, edited by Rena Maverick Green, San Antonio, Texas: Alamo Printing Co., 1921; reprint, Lincoln, Nebraska: University of Nebraska Press, 1989). Judge Alexander Somervell (1796–1854): see note 25 this chapter.

[49] Röser: Heinrich Roser (1811–1854) arrived in Texas in December 1844. He married Theresa von Kreusser. Jud Heine: identity unknown. Philip Schellenträger: on 30 January 1846, *post facto*, Klaener, agent of the Society in Galveston, submitted to the Secretary of State in Austin a composite listing of passengers arriving in 1844 on the brigs *Johann Dethard*, *Herschell*, and *Ferdinand*. F. [sic] Scheelentrager, cooper, single, age 24, is listed among them (*Secretary of State, Record Group 307*; see also Chapter III, note 4). Geue and Geue in *A New Land Beckoned*, p. 136, state that he arrived with his wife Pauline from Eisenach. An individual named Schellenträger appears on the Victoria County poll list in 1846 as well as on the 1850 and 1860 censuses for that county with the only difference that this person is ten years older than the one listed by the Society. He has a wife Paulina and six children, the three oldest born in Germany. The 1850 census lists also a six-month-old male being their first Texas-born child (Mullins, *Texas: Poll Lists*, p. 152; *1850 U. S. Census, Victoria County, Texas*, p. 238, National Archives Microfilm M432, Roll 916; *1860*

U. S. Census, Victoria County, Texas, p. 60, National Archives Microfilm M653, Roll 1307). Georg Brune: appointed wagon master for the Society, possibly on account of his past military experience (see Chapter III, note 16). He assisted in moving immigrants from Carlshafen to the future town of New Braunfels.

[50] Martin: Ludwig Martin and Saalmühle: Friedrich Saalmüller arrived in Texas on the *Johann Dethardt* in 1844 (Geue and Geue, pp. 119 and 134).

[51] Trailor: probably Winn Trailor who had extensive land holdings around Victoria and whose farm along the Guadalupe River served as the third stopping place, Camp Castell, on the trail to New Braunfels. Camp Leiningen at Agua Dulce was located in the proximity where present-day's Highway 35 and Farm-to-Market Road 2541 intersect. From this camp the trail to Victoria followed approximately present-day Highway 87.

[52] McHenry: see note 13 this chapter. "Lists of Cadenat": Recognizing in the arriving male settlers the younger sons of families who under the laws of primogeniture were not entitled to any of the family land in Germany, the prince may have made a list to be used at the time of land distribution. He addressed this subject in reference to Nassau Farm in a letter of 15 July 1844. "*. . . Das einzige was wir mit Nassau thun können, ist, es in 8 Theile zu theilen und jede einzelne Parzelle an irgend einen Cadet de famille zu verkaufen, der sich hier Wohlstand erarbeiten kann.*" (. . . The only thing to do with Nassau is to divide the property into eight portions and to sell each to a young son who can achieve prosperity here.) (*Verein Papers,* Yale University, Box 12, Folder 77; see also Chapter II, note 9 in reference to Solms's dislike of Nassau Farm for a German settlement). From Victoria the party traveled on a northeasterly course, possibly on the Atascosita Road, to reach McHenry's place.

[53] Mitchell: located apparently around Brushy Creek east of Hallettsville. Mrs. Hallis: see note 12 this chapter. From McHenry's Solms took the trail north to Hallettsville and here picked up the road to Columbus (Pressler's Map).

[54] Robert Robson & John Low were business partners in Columbus (Information by courtesy of Bill Stein, Columbus, Texas; see also note 9 this chapter). The trail followed from Victoria to Columbus would be the Atascosita Trail. It started at Goliad, passed through Victoria, the Atascosita Crossing on the Colorado River below Columbus, crossed the Brazos River in the vicinity of San Felipe, and continued to the Trinity River (*The New Handbook of Texas,* Vol. I, p. 274).

[55] Ervendberg: see Chapter II, note 12. Riklef: A Dr. A. Ricklefs served as trustee for the proposed Hermann University in 1845 (*Trustees' Min-*

utes, Hermann University, manuscript, information by courtesy of Ann Lindemann, Industry, Texas). Ferdinand Lindheimer mentions a Dr. Bickleff [sic] from this area (Goyne, *A Life Among The Texas Flowers*, p. 103). Madame Brune: see note 9 this chapter. Mr. Sand: identity unknown. Solms on his way to Washington apparently by-passed Nassau Farm and stayed overnight in Industry.

[56] Farquhart: The 1850 Census identifies a James L. Farquhar, born in North Carolina in 1807, a farmer with 6,000 acres of land (*1850 U.S. Census, Washington County, Texas*, p. 319A, National Archives Microfilm M432, Roll 916; see also endnote 44). Brenham: became the county seat of Washington County in 1844. Jacksonville: former community, 3 miles north of Chappel Hill in Washington County. Judge Bilbury: probably Timothy Pilsbury (1780–1858), served Brazoria County in the Senate, at the Ninth and final Congress of the Republic. He had also held offices of Chief Justice and Judge of Probate for Brazoria (*Biographies of the Texan Conventions and Congresses, 1832–1845*, p. 154). "dear Fischer": reference is to Henry F. Fisher.

[57] Congress was in session in Washington-on-the-Brazos through February 3, 1845. It appears that Solms requested that Fischer come from Washington to Farquhar's place for a discussion on the Society's affairs with Congress. Tarbuck: Lyman Tarbox. The 1850 Federal Census for Austin County, Texas (p. 152B, line 33) shows him 37 years old, stage contractor, estimated evaluation of $10,000, born in New York state, and married with one child. He became partner with J. F. Brown in the fall of 1845 when both their names appear in the ads for regular stage service from Houston to Washington-on-the-Brazos and beyond (e.g., *Telegraph and Texas Register* of 5 November 1845). W. K. Hamblin: see Chapter II, note 6. Solms must have left Farquhar's place without going to Washington. On his way to Houston he stayed overnight at Hamblin's on Big Cypress Creek.

[58] Redfish Bar: a shoal that crosses Galveston Bay midway which before the dredging of the Houston Ship Channel made navigation difficult and dangerous. Steamer *Dayton*: see Chapter III, note 27. Mr. & Mrs. Jacobs: identity unknown. Solms made the overnight boat trip to Galveston.

[59] Oscar von Claren (1812–1845), emigrated to Texas in 1844. Because of his military background, a lieutenant in the Hanoverian artillery, Solms appointed him at the Second Colonial Council Meeting to be in charge of the militia's artillery. Claren was with the first group of settlers to arrived in New Braunfels. In 1847 he and Friedrich von Wrede Sr. (1786–1845) were killed and scalped by Indians on their return trip from Austin to New Braunfels (Friedrich W. von Wrede. *Sketches of Life in The*

United States of North America and Texas, translated by Chester W. Geue, Waco, Texas: Texian Press, 1970, p. viii); see also Chapter II, note 50 and note 36 this chapter. Capt. Alexander Hagedorn: captain of the *Ferdinand.*

[60] *Apollo,* a schooner (dimensions: length, 82ft; breadth 25ft; draft, 12 ft), it was launched on 31 March 1835 and for the next 20 years was owned by Friedrich Leo Quentell of Bremen. On this trip it was captained by Tönjes Stürje (Peter-Michael Pawlik, *Von der Weser in die Welt: Die Geschichte der Segelschiffe von der Weser und Lesum und ihre Bauwerften 1770 bis 1893* [*From the Weser into the World: The History of Sailing Ships from the Weser and Lesum and Their Shipyards 1770 to 1893*], Bremerhaven, Germany: Deutsches Schiffahrtsmuseum, 1993, p. 374). "the great unknown": identity unknown.

[61] Captain Charles Elliot (1801–1875), Royal Navy, British chargé d'affaires to the Republic of Texas. Elliot sought to secure an armistice between Mexico and Texas and worked against the annexation of Texas by the United States. Alphonse Dubois de Saligny (1809–1888), French chargé d'affaires to the Republic of Texas, who also opposed the annexation of Texas by the United States. (*The New Handbook of Texas,* Vol. II, pp. 711–712 and 828). The unnamed bishop most likely was Bishop Jean Marie Odin.

[62] Steamer *McKinney*: should be *McKim.* After the initial misspelling of the name, in subsequent entries Solms gives the ship's correct name. A contemporary account gives the following description of the ship: "Steam Ship *John McKim,* valued at $32,000. The length of this vessel is 175 feet, breadth of beam 23 feet and depth of hold 9 feet and is rated at 244 tons burthen. She is worked by two of Erickson's propellers, eighteen and a half feet in diameter, moved by two engines of 125-horse power. Her ordinary speed is 8 miles an hour with steam alone; under canvass alone, she is capable of running nearly at the same rate with a fair wind" (*Telegraph & Texas Register,* 15 January 1845, p. 2, col. 5). General Navarro: José Antonio Navarro (1795–1871). From 1813 to 1860 he served in the legislatures of Mexico and Texas. Captured by Mexico as a traitor while serving as Santa Fe Expedition Commissioner, he escaped from Mexico and returned to Texas in 1845. The *Telegraph and Texas Register* (5 February 1845, p. 2, col. 3) reported: "Mr. Navarro arrived at Galveston on the steamship *McKim* and was cordially welcomed by the citizens. The military companies turned out, and he was escorted to his hotel, accompanied by a large concourse of people" (see also Chapter II, note 23).

[63] Rebecca: identity unknown.

[64] Dr. Aschhof: presumably H. Aschoff, a 36 year-old physician born in Germany (*1850 U.S. Census, Galveston County, Texas,* p. 240B, National Archives Microfilm M432, Roll 910).

[65] "Fort with Spanish cannons": identity unknown.

[66] *Neptun*: built for the Bremen firm of C. L. Brauer & Son in 1844. Made its maiden voyage, Ficke Haeslop, master, with 24 passengers from Bremerhaven (23 December 1844) to Galveston (5 February 1845) (Peter-Michael Pawlik, *Von der Weser in die Welt*, p. 205).

[67] Napoleon emigrant: identity unknown.

[68] In 1842 a Robert Rose officiated as a notary public in Galveston (*Compiled Index to Elected & Appointed Officials of the Republic of Texas*, Austin, Texas: State Archives Division, Texas State Library, 1981; p. 105); and in 1850, as a 35 year old, he was a general land agent enumerated in the household of Andrew J. Yates, attorney at law (*1850 U.S. Census, Galveston County, Texas*, pp. 256B and 268A, National Archives Microfilm M432, Roll 910). See also remark in Solms's *Eighth Report* (Geue and Geue, *A New Land Beckoned*, p. 53). John H. Illies of J. H. Illies & Comp., representative of the Dhanis Company in Galveston (Cornelia English Crook, *Henry Castro: A Study of Early Colonization in Texas*, San Antonio, Texas: St. Mary's University Press, 1988, p. 111). Albrecht Pappenheim: see Chapter III, note 26. Dutch naturalist: In all probability M. Maris who related his experiences in *Souvenirs d'Amerique. Relations d' un Voyage au Texas et en Haiti* (Brussels, 1863). In a letter of 18 April 1845, Lindheimer made the comment that "a Belgian has arrived [in San Antonio] who says he is collecting specimens of natural history but is neither a collector of natural history nor a Belgian" (Goyne, *A Life Among the Texas Flora*, p. 113).

[69] Solms's writing corresponds with the *Eighth Report* dated Galveston, Texas, 8 February 1845 (Geue and Geue, *A New Land Beckoned*, p. 55).

[70] Schubert: the name taken by Friedrich Armand Strubberg (1806–1889). See also Chapter III, note 44. In collusion with H. F. Fisher, he recruited also among Society immigrants in Galveston to join their proposed colony in present western Milam County. On 11 February 1845, five immigrants who had just arrived on the bark *Neptun* from Bremen, Germany, F. J. Mädgen, H. Lohmann, H. Heinemann, J. Schmidtzinsky and J. Pfeiffer, signed an affidavit in Galveston stating that on advice from Henry F. Fisher they were disassociating themselves from the Society and joining Schubert's colony (*Solms-Braunfels Archives*, Vol. XL, p. 97). This episode is also mentioned in a contemporary account because the observer was acquainted in Germany with two of these immigrants (Seele, *The Diary of Hermann Seele*, pp. 226 and 227). Schubert's colony was located on the San Gabriel River, six miles up river from the present community of San Gabriel. Persistent Indian depredations forced the settlers to safer areas. Johann Schmidtzinsky joined the German settlers in Fredericksburg, Texas (*Pioneers in God's Hills*, compiled by the Gillespie

County Historical Commission, Austin, Texas: Eakin Press, 1960, Vol. I, pp. 133 and 240). Franz Josef Mädgen persevered; he and his family settled and farmed in Milam County (*Bell County Reprinted Biographies,* p. 92). H. Heinemann, J. Pfeiffer and H. Lohmann: identities unknown, although a John Pfeiffer is listed in Galveston County and a J. G. Pfeiffer in Comal County (Mullins, *Republic of Texas Poll Lists,* p. 133) and a Henry Lomann and family lived in Travis County (*1850 U. S. Census, Travis County, Texas,* p. 147B, National Archives Microfilm M432, Roll 915). Schubert gave up his colonization endeavor and in 1846 was in the employ of the German Emigration Society in Fredericksburg. (Biesele, *German Settlements in Texas,* p. 142n).

[71] Major Cook: possibly William Gordon Cooke (1808–1847), Republic of Texas secretary of war (*The New Handbook of Texas,* Vol. II, p. 307). "contract with English government": meaning unclear. Solms considered the annexation of Texas detrimental to Great Britain. Rainer: see Chapter III, note 31.

[72] Weser newspaper: This particular issue arrived on a recent immigrant ship which started its voyage from the Weser River. The newspapers were shipped over for Solms. See entry for 29 August 1844.

[73] Benton's annexation bill: Pro- and anti-factions in the Republic of Texas, the United States as well as the governments of Great Britain, France, and Mexico debated and hoped to influence the question about the annexation of Texas in one way or the other. From 1842 on bills were introduced in the U. S. Congress but all came to naught. On 5 February 1845, Thomas H. Benton, Senator of Missouri, introduced a new bill that specified no precise terms of annexation (Justin H. Smith, *The Annexation of Texas,* New York: Barnes & Nobles, Inc., 1941, p. 337).

[74] St. Martin: identity unknown. Ship *McKim*: see note 62 this chapter. Lewi Jones: should be Levi Jones (see Chapter I, note 35); unable to clarify his statement.

Chapter Five

Sunday, [February] the 23rd. At 11 o'clock the *Olive Branch* from the Sabine, Simpton's arrival very uncertain. At noon rode off with Claren & Eberhardt. After 30 miles to San Louis, there was a bad crossing of the West Pass, not much better at the main channel. ($4.50) The island, a mile wide, is a waste land, deserted and with decaying wooden buildings. Four travel companions, among them the innkeeper from Velasco; from San Louis to there 18 miles. Crossed Oister Creek. Romantic scene, this cavalcade with roaring sea and whistling and howling winds. In Velasco by 8 o'clock. I was dead tired riding the white horse, a pacer. The money bag also pressed a lot. Good bed, slept heavenly. ($5.75)[1]

Monday, [February] the 24th. On the road at 9 o'clock. Ferry across the Brazos ($1.50). At 10 o'clock continued on the other side. From there, 10 miles up to the San Bernard. Neither a ferry, a ferryman nor dwellings except for two decaying buildings was to be seen. I made a quick decision: undressed, swam across and returned with a very small boat. We stayed two and one-half hours. Two people on horses, two people in the boat, moved away. The horses crossed over. Traveling like this is terrible business. Crossed Cedar Lake and Caney [Creek]. The water and waves touched the pistol holsters. Arrived at Jeman's around 5:45; poor quarters; his wife is German, from Dittlingen near Bingen!!! (She left 11 years ago.) In the evening wrote to Holstein and in my diary.[2]

Distances:

Galveston	to San Louis:	30 miles
	to Velasco:	18 mi.
	to San Bernard:	10 mi.
	to Cedar Lake:	5 mi.
	to Caney:	11 mi.
	to Jeman's house:	10 mi.
		84 miles

To bed at 9:30.

Tuesday, [February] the 25th. At 9 A.M. in Yeomans' boat; an open boat; hardly any wind; 16 miles to Matagorda; 10 miles [down the course] were two ships at anchor; another 28 miles to Carlshafen. At anchor from 7 to 11 o'clock, the moon rose at 9 o'clock. Although it was hard surface, we slept soundly.[3]

Wednesday, [February] the 26th. In Carlshafen at 1 A.M. which we found after being lost for a long time. I threw myself upon Wrede's bed who had returned from Decros Point the previous day. Got up late, inspected Carlshafen. Dinner and fish and oyster party. In the evening Thielepape played the part of a *Minnesänger*.[4]

Thursday, [February] the 27th. Departed at 9 o'clock. Bad road with many muddy spots all the way to Mr. Poland. At 6:30 in Victoria where Fischer & Müller had just arrived. Supper at Zink's and a wonderful bed. Wedemeyer played the piano.[5]

Friday, [February] the 28th. Rode to the camp. Joyful welcome with cannon fire. Discussion with Zink. Letter to Hays; played the piano in the evening. Rain & storm.[6]

Saturday, March 1st. Discussion with Fischer! Led to nothing, made demands on Müller's behalf. Wants him on the Colonial Council and receive a salary commensurate to the position. A lot of business.

Sunday, March 2nd. Birthday of my dear, departed Mother! On the way at 10 o'clock; nice, beautiful, hilly trail. Met Renner & Fordtran.

In camp at 6:30. Coll & Lüntzel, Hoffmann & Assel met me on the trail. Supper and grog! (Wrede)[7]

Monday, March 3rd. Storm and rain, wind from the north. In spite of all this Zink arrived, lengthy discussion with him and Coll. Fischer arrived in the evening.

Tuesday, [March] the 4th. Colonial Council meeting. Meeting from 10 A.M. until 2 P.M., then from 4 until 6:30 P.M. Outcome is known. Champagne in the evening.[8]

Wednesday, [March] the 5th. Correspondence and also discoursed with Fischer. Zink rode away.[9]

Thursday, [March] the 6th. At 11:30 A.M. Louis off to Galveston. A discussion with Dr. Köster, he was suspended; Cloudt became uncouth; Baur is less than nothing; very malicious. It was too late to ride.[10]

Friday, [March] the 7th. Inspection of the company. I praised Heidtmeyer because he trained them. On foot and in the field they still need additional training. Turned everything over to Heidtmeyer. Rahm returned in the evening.[11]

Saturday, [March] the 8th. Departed for Gonzales at 10 o'clock. Arrived at King's at 6:45 P.M. Supper, slept on the porch. Saddle for a pillow, a lot of dog barking and children shouting. American tobacco, chewing and spitting.[12]

Sunday, [March] the 9th. Off at 7 o'clock, on the trail there came a cold norther. Breakfast in spite of the rain. At the San Jeronimo at noon, from there struck out to the north, 4.5 miles. I arrived at Don Antonio Navarro's at 2 o'clock. He is an interesting man. His description of the march to Santa Fe (160 miles, from there [Santa Fe] high mountains with snow and ice). The broad prairie only accessible through the Passo del Norte. Water holes for the buffaloes. His imprisonment in Vera Cruz. Mr. Veramendi was introduced to me. Dinner and supper left something to be desired. The same for the night lodging. Many fleas and a hard bed. Feathers on wood.[13]

Monday, [March] the 10th. Departed at 8 o'clock, going to Manuel Flores where we ate and waited for Veramendi. He did not come so we left at 12 o'clock. Wrede, Hoffmann and Pluto stayed behind two miles on this side of the Cibolo Creek. There was a wolf in the Canyon Viejo. At 6 o'clock we were on high ground with a view of San Antonio ahead of us. My travel companions were joyous. Lodged at Rahm's [favorite] old hotel [operated] by McCamel. Howard arrived in the evening.[14]

Tuesday, [March] the 11th. Called on Signor Calvo. Saw the church and the tower. Then at Mrs. Jaques. Looked at the Alamo. Visited Veramendi and Signor Garza. Lunch was bad. Talked with Devine, then to Riddle & Robinson. Took a walk, afterward saw Cassiano. Supper. In the evening very tired, therefore early to bed.[15]

Wednesday, [March] the 12th. In the morning I had discussions with Veramendi and de Vine. I called on Signor Meadjaka. (Alexander's birthday, letter to him). (My companions on the trip were Wrede, Anton, two orderlies from Lindheimer's company, from the militia Lüntzel & Hoffmann.) In the evening more discussions with the Mexicans, they no longer made brash demands. Supper, Mauris, a Belgian naturalist, present. Met him in Galveston.[16]

Thursday, [March] the 13th. In the morning I completed my business with the Mexicans. Breakfast, called on Guilbeau, then on Mrs. Jaques. Talked about [?]. Dinner, afterward rode to the San Pedro Springs and the Powder House.[17]

Friday, [March] the 14th. Letters to Fink and Coll. Rahm rides to the camp. Completion of the document by Signor Rodriguez (Maria Antonea Veramendi-Garza, a beautiful woman). Rode with Lüntzel & Lindheimer to Mission La Concepcion. At noon ate there with Guilbeau. I walked in the evening.[18]

Saturday, [March] the 15th. At 9 A.M. to Rodriguez. Signing of the documents. Morgan is drunk. I wrote correspondence the entire day.[19]

Sunday, [March] the 16th. At 10 A.M. de Vine accompanied me. We rode to Seguin. Breakfast along the Cibolo. At Flores at 5 o'clock. Wonderful day, beautiful light on the waterfall. Wrede & Hoffmann arrived in the evening.

Monday, [March] the 17th. At 11 o'clock Zink and Coll arrived with 13 men. Dr. Meyer came also. At 3 o'clock we continued our journey. We camped at a spring not far from the Guadalupe. During the night a norther blew in. It was bitterly cold.

Tuesday, [March] the 18th. In the saddle at 10 o'clock. We arrived on the Comal tract at 3 o'clock. Put up tents, ate late, then went to bed.[20]

Wednesday, [March] the 19th. We awoke to a snowstorm. I rode out to outline the horse exercise area. Afterward I went with Rahm, Wrede, Lüntzel, Zink into the woods; with hunting knives and axes we cut a trail to the spring, 4 miles. Course NE—N—NW—W. We stopped where we came to a meadow. It was bitterly cold. In the morning there was snow on the tents.

Thursday, [March] the 20th. With Coll, Lindheimer and five men I went on a long ride through the country. On horseback we climbed up to an outcropping, through cedars to the top of a plateau (Lindheimer killed a deer so we named the hill Lindheimer's Peak). Two deer and two turkeys were shot. Eggers brought mail from Europe (January's mail).[21]

Friday, [March] the 21st. (Beginning of spring and Good Friday). Crossing of the first 15 wagons, but what toil and what difficulty it was. Finally they are *here*! Change of the camp to higher ground.

Saturday, [March] the 22nd. Zink wanted to leave on account of a misunderstanding. I calmed him down. The camp was marked off. I rode to the nearby spring. Rain again. I have the colic and am miserable.

Sunday, [March] the 23rd. (Easter Sunday) I am very miserable, but regardless I rode out with Coll over the land which is hilly and covered with [?]. Rain again. The sky cleared up in the afternoon. In the evening there were signs of a norther. (Full moon)

Monday, [March] the 24th. I am still miserable. There is a bitter-cold norther. I had to remain in bed for half the day. The Dr. prescribed oak bark with red wine. Things improved. In the evening immigrants crossed the Guadalupe.

Tuesday, [March] the 25th. Rahm arrived from San Antonio bringing news that 1,000 Indians were in Corpus Christi. I discussed matters with Zink and Coll. A few more wagons crossed the Guadalupe. I brought them in myself.

Wednesday, [March] the 26th. Heinrich the butcher went with two wagon to San Antonio. I held discussions regarding fortifications. During the pitch-black night the dogs were restless. Dr. Frank was on guard duty, Wrede stole a horse. I patrolled the camp for half the night.[22]

Thursday, [March] the 27th. The first patrol went out at 4 A.M. I did correspondence during the day. In the evening I led the militia on the second patrol.[23]

Friday, [March] the 28th. From now on, there will be patrols in the morning and in the evening. Serious talk by Zink. Getting ready for a defense, palisades are cut and erected. What chore it is to get the people to work! In the evening there was unrest again. Although there were no wolves there was still unrest.

Saturday, [March] the 29th. In the morning Wrede left for Galveston. At 9:30 Henkel, Dr. Meyer, Anton, Louis, Brun and I were off for San Antonio. Nice area along the Cibolo and near the San Pedro. Arrived in San Antonio at 3:45. I stayed at Mrs. Campbell's.[24]

Sunday, [March] the 30th. I had business with Veramendi, the Chief Justice Morgan, and afterward with Guilbeau. In the evening I rode to La Concepcion. I shot a black moccasin snake.

Monday, [March] the 31st. I had lunch at Guilbeau's and took care of business matters. Then I rode to the Powder House and upriver.

Tuesday, April 1st. I conducted business with Addicks and Veramendi Jr. Things are finally coming together. Dr. Meyer & Verron went to the Lipan Indians.[25]

Wednesday, [April] the 2nd. Coll arrived at 10 A.M. with Lindheimer and 13 men. The church, the Alamo. In the afternoon I visited the mission.

Thursday, [April] the 3rd. I arrived back in camp at 4 P.M. On the way I killed three rattlesnakes, two of whom were copulating. The palisades have not yet been finished.

Friday, [April] the 4th. Arrival of a few wagons, rather hot temperature.

Saturday, [April] the 5th. Ten more wagons arrived, including Dr. Köster. Drawing of lots for farm land (Zink's confusion).

Sunday, [April] the 6th. Lipan Indians with Dr. Meyer & Verron. Terrible thunderstorm during the night, the day was cold.

Monday, [April] the 7th. Meeting of the Colonial Council. Imhof departed. Fear of the Lipan Indians! Rahm returned.

Tuesday, [April] the 8th. The Lipan Indians rode off in the morning. Walked with Zink & Thomae to the spring. Enormous detour.

Wednesday, [April] the 9th. Guilbeau arrived in the afternoon. Moved into Sophienburg today. Anton & Louis constructed the building.[26]

Thursday, [April] the 10th. With Guilbeau & Phillippi to the Loma de la Mission. Great amount of physical effort to go up and back down again. We had pistol practice in the evening.[27]

Friday, [April] the 11th. A norther at night, rain during the day. Guilbeau departed, Verron left for Victoria. Meeting of the Colonial Council. Quarrel between Coll and Zink and Zink and Dr. Köster.

Saturday, [April] the 12th. The day was almost bright. In the evening a leisurely ride with the Zink ladies.

Sunday, [April] the 13th. It rained so hard in the morning that the sermon was interrupted. In the evening such a terrible storm with thunder that my tent and two others were flattened. Everything was wet in the cabin. Slept well on the buffalo hides.

Monday, [April] the 14th. Sunshine only for a brief moment. Had just turned in for the night when it rained hard again. I was swimming in my bed. Slept in a wet shirt bundled in buffalo hides on the floor. Slept comfortably. [?] with the cook who was given a beating.

Tuesday, [April] the 15th. Tolerable weather with the exception of a shower. All the creeks are very high. There are wagons and livestock on the other side of the Guadalupe. Didn't sleep well during the night.

Wednesday, [April] the 16th. Discovery of the plot hatched by Hartz, Holekamp & followers. Unbelievably ungrateful people. Wrote to Sophie. Moret, Bellmer, Lüntzel arrived with the news that Verron's body was found. Dr. Köster and I and 12 men attend to the post-mortem examination. The indications are that he took his life with a shot in the mouth. Dr. Meyer played the comedy of being horrified. (Zink's behavior!). Hays arrived in the evening.[28]

Thursday, [April] the 17th. It was brought to my attention that 31 bottles of wine and some bottles of whiskey were stolen. Wrote a letter to Guilbeau. Wrede crossed the Guadalupe River.

Friday, [April] the 18th. Wrede Sr. was brought across the river. In the afternoon Zink and Thome sounded the alarm concerning Indians. Guards set up, mounted scouts went out. Even the Brunes (Louis & August) claimed to have seen Indians. Checked the guards several times during the night. Kept my horse saddled. Slept with boots and spurs on. Dr. Frank confessed to have stolen the wine.

Saturday, [April] the 19th. At sunrise fired the cannon once. My horse was saddled. I rode until late. Scouted to the mission valley. Found nothing but the tracks of a large hog, that led to the lower ground where the animal defecated. In the evening fired the cannon again. Baur returned from San Antonio where he was sent early Friday. The shoemaker Vogel remarked on the way: "The past fades away in the Lethe ("river of forgetfulness") and we become a part of mythology." Ed Brun confessed to the theft of the whisky.[29]

Sunday, [April] the 20th. Rained all night; the same during the day, therefore no sermon. It cleared up in the evening and I went horseback riding.

Monday, [April] the 21st. I rode with Zink into the woods. Had him worried. The investigation about the theft continues.

Tuesday, [April] the 22nd. The weather cleared up; finally there is sunshine again; but it is still rather wet. In the evening the usual ride.

Wednesday, [April] the 23rd. I rode to the crossing of the Guadalupe. Zink works his way through the thicket. The workers fire at the passing riders.

Thursday, [April] the 24th. Chief Johnson of the Tonkawa tribe arrived in the morning, swam the Guadalupe.

Friday, [April] the 25th. Hays returned from Austin in the morning, bringing with him four Tonkaway Indians. They departed after breakfast, others stayed behind.

Saturday, [April] the 26th. Mail from Europe dated 4 April. Arrangements for the cornerstone laying are not completed. For this reason the ceremony is postponed until Monday. Wrede killed three deer.

Sunday, [April] the 27th. The pastor's sermon was tolerable. Punch at Zink's in the evening.

Monday, [April] the 28th. Balloting was scheduled for 9 A.M., but it did not take place until afternoon. The cornerstone laying was at 1 o'clock. A short speech by me, then a speech and blessing by the pastor. All this during a thunderstorm. Cannon salute and raising of flag. At 3:30 P.M. dinner under the improvised tent. Thirty settings. Toast to Sophie's health, then mine. For the first, a 21 gun salute. In the evening Anton made a scene with Fritsch and was run off.[30]

Tuesday, [April] the 29th. Slept poorly during the night. In the morning Anton turned over his things. I talked to him. At noon he sent a challenge to Fritsch. In the evening scene with him. Letter to Herding.[31]

Wednesday, [April] the 30th. Rain and wind during the night. I did correspondence during the day. Major Neighbours arrived with Indians.[32]

Thursday, May 1st. Ascension Day. No church service because of the rain. I didn't do much correspondence.

Friday, May 2nd. Finished my correspondence. Every day there are many Indians in the camp.

Saturday, May 3rd. Colonel Leutenegger and von Wrede Sr. rode to Galveston, Cloudt to Carlshafen and I went to the Indian encampment. Beautiful wife, but otherwise a real devil's disciple. Returned in the afternoon.[33]

Sunday, [May] the 4th. Church service, many Indians present. They claim to have eaten a Wakor. The Catholic priest left for Austin. (Köpp from New Orleans.)[34]

Monday, [May] the 5th. Rahm left for San Antonio. At noon Wedemeier (he is a fuddy-duddy scribe). In the evening all-out effort to find shingles.[35]

Tuesday, [May] the 6th. The fat madam cooks a meal for the first time and it is superb. In the evening, before retiring, Rahm arrived with the news of the purchase.[36]

Wednesday, [May] the 7th. After a bad and sleepless night off to San Antonio, made it in three and one-half hours. Began immediately with the unpleasant affairs. Walked to Mr. Camble (ship of the desert). Checked in at Ant. Lochmar's, horrible lodging.[37]

Thursday, [May] the 8th. Went to Addicks several times. Major Howard came with Voss in the evening regarding the business of Voss. Talked with him in Guilbeau's presence.[38]

Friday, [May] the 9th. Business matters until 11 o'clock. Got away finally at 1:30; at Sophienburg by 4 o'clock. Talked with Wrede Jr. Slept finally that night; a cover was not necessary.

Saturday, [May] the 10th. General Campo[s] (Tonka) was present at breakfast. (Gave him beefsteaks, no Wacos.) New problems with Zink. He sold whisky. I called on Wedemeyer. Reminiscences from last year! How happy I was in Kyrburgum Dhaun.[39]

Sunday, [May] the 11th. Church service in the morning, good sermon. I wrote down information for Meusebach. In the afternoon at Wedemeier's. I heard new scandal about Zink (The cabinetmaker Zirus in Nürnberg is a fictitious person, the old Russerian wrote the bill as well as the receipt). Zink did not want to turn over the whisky. He admitted so. At noon the entire family is drunk. Later when the group went riding, Miss Zink fell off the horse once and then Thomae twice.[40]

Monday, [May] the 12th. A year ago I received Holy Communion in the church at *Kreuznach*; afterward [?] to my Sophie May flowers and thunderstorm. In the evening went to Bingen!!! Whit Monday the communion service. I, too, received communion. Indians (Racidor). I visited with Wedemeier in the evening. (Such memories!)[41]

Tuesday, [May] the 13th. I did a lot of correspondence. Afterward meeting of the Colonial Council. Zink's "Peranda." In the evening the scene with Rahm who called him a dog.[42]

Wednesday, [May] the 14th. Everything was put in order and sealed. In the evening I gave a farewell speech to the immigrants.[43]

---

[1] *Olive Branch*: reference could be to the sloop *Orange Branch* on the Sabine River (*The Civilian and Galveston Gazette*, 16 November 1844, p. 1, col. 2). Eberhardt: identity unknown. San Louis: San Luis (see Chapter IV, note 22). Main channel: between Galveston Island and the mainland of Brazoria County. Oister Creek: Oyster Creek, in Brazoria County. Velasco: see Chapter IV, note 20. Cavalcade: a dramatic sequence of events. Solms's party rode west on Galveston Island, crossed over at San Luis Pass, and staying close to the coast, reached Velasco. Other writers of this period comment that traveling overland, even in a light wagon or buggy, from Galveston to Matagorda along the coast was not such an uncommon occurrence (Mary Austin Holley, "The Texas Diary, 1835–38," *Texas Quarterly*, Austin: The University of Texas, Vol. VIII, No.2 (1965), p. 56; Hollon and Butler, *Bollaert's Texas*, pp. 84–88).

[2] Brazos River, San Bernard River, and Cedar Lake Creek: see Chapter IV, note 20. Caney Creek, Matagorda County, empties into the Gulf of Mexico. Jeman's: Jospeh Yeamans, Sr. (? –1897). He married Margaret Schmidt of Germany in 1833 (*Historic Matagorda County*, Vol. II, p. 573). Dittlingen near Bingen, Germany. After crossing the Brazos River the party continued west along the coast.

[3] Yeomans: Yeamans. Town of Matagorda, Matagorda County, on Matagorda Bay. When Solms traveled through this area Matagorda Bay was still one body, not divided into two distinct bodies of water, East Matagorda Bay and West Matagorda Bay, created by the silt from the Colorado River.

[4] Minnesänger: medieval minstrel singer.

[5] Mr. Poland: probably John Polan, an early settler in the area south of Victoria where Winn Traylor was developing his extensive holdings (Roy Grimes, *300 Years in Victoria County*, Victoria, Texas: The Victoria Advocate Publishing Co., 1968, p. 176). Solms must have traveled the same trail mentioned in Chapter IV, note 51.

[6] The camp referred to here was on Spring Creek about three miles north of the town of Victoria in Victoria County.

[7] Solms's mother was the former Duchess Friederike of Mecklenburg-Strelitz (2 March 1778–29 June 1841). Her first marriage (26 December 1793) was to Prince Ludwig of Prussia (? –28 December 1796); the sec-

ond marriage (1 January 1798) to Prince Friedrich Wilhelm of Solms-Braunfels (22 October 1770–13 April 1814), the father of Prince Carl; and the third marriage (29 August 1815) to the English Duke of Cumberland (? –11 November 1851), an uncle of Queen Victoria and who became King Ernst August of Hanover in 1844 (Ehrenkrook, *Genealogisches Handbuch der fürstlichen Häuser*, Vol. VI, p. 303; Adams, "British Diplomatic Correspondence" in *Southwestern Historical Quarterly*, Vol. XIX, p. 286). The camp was established on McCoy's Creek in DeWitt County. Hermann von Assel arrived in Texas in November 1844. Renner: apparently Julius Rennert whose arrival in Texas is undocumented.

[8] This was the Fourth Colonial Council; for particulars see Fey, *New Braunfels*, Vol. I, p. 75, as well as Chapter IV, note 44.

[9] Writing activity corresponds with the *Ninth Report* dated "Encampment at McCoy Creek, 5 March 1845" (Geue and Geue, *A New Land Beckoned*, p. 63).

[10] Louis: identity unknown. Cloudt: see Chapter IV, note 38.

[11] The Society's militia or "company": Solms organized two companies of militia to help keep order on the trek to the interior as well as to offer protection should Indians attack. Besides the militia, Solms had his own entourage. Heidtmeyer: Johann F. Heidemeyer; see Chapter III, note 13.

[12] John G. King: located west of Gonzales; see Chapter II, note 21. The trail paralleled the Guadalupe River on the east side.

[13] San Jeronimo: Geronimo Creek, Guadalupe County. Antonio Navarro: see Chapter II, note 23 and Chapter IV, note 62. "March to Santa Fe" refers to the Texan Santa Fe Expedition. Following its independence from Mexico, the Republic of Texas both felt entitled to the area of Santa Fe and coveted the lucrative trade carried over the Santa Fe Trail. A plan evolved to bring this area and the trade under the Republic's jurisdiction. In June 1841 a military force left Austin, among them Jose Antonio Navarro. After a harrowing journey of three months they reached Santa Fe only to be taken prisoners for trespassing upon Mexican land. The men were marched 2,000 miles to Mexico City to be imprisoned. Most of the prisoners were released in 1842; Navarro was detained, escaped in 1845, and returned to Texas (Noel M. Loomis, *The Texan-Santa Fe Pioneers*, Norman, Oklahoma: University of Oklahoma Press, 1958). Passo del Norte: El Paso, Texas. Jose Marcos Antonio Veramendi, son of Juan Martin Veramendi (1778–1833) who was given his land grant in Texas in 1825. The trail to San Antonio followed approximately present-day Interstate Highway 10.

[14] Pluto: identity unknown. Canyon Viejo: location unknown. McCamel: McCampbell.

[15] Signor Calvo: Father Miguel Calvo. Mrs. Jaques: Jacques. Signor Garza: Rafael de la Garza, husband of Antonia Veramendi. DeVine: probably Thomas Jefferson Devine (1820–1890), later a district judge in San Antonio. Riddle & Robinson: merchants in San Antonio (see Chapter II, note 53).

[16] Signor Meadjake: possibly Menchaca. Alexander: see Chapter 4, note 28. Mons. Mauris: probably M. Maris (see Chapter IV, note 68).

[17] San Pedro Springs: in San Pedro Park, San Antonio.

[18] Fink: identity unknown. "Camp": refers to location on McCoy's Creek in DeWitt County. (The creek empties into the Guadalupe River north of the town of Cuero.) Signor Rodriguez: identity unknown. Maria Antonea Veramendi-Garza: sister of Jose Marcos Antonio Veramendi and wife of Rafael de la Garza. Mission La Concepcion: see Chapter II, note 27.

[19] Signing of the document by Solms, Rafael de la Garza and his wife, Antonia Veramendi-Garza signified the purchase of the "Comal Tract" (1,265 acres) by the Society for $1,111 (Biesele, *German Settlements in Texas,* p. 118; Haas, *History of New Braunfels and Comal County, Texas,* p. 173). Morgan: Judge David Morgan.

[20] Comal tract located north of the San Antonio-Nacogdoches Road and east of the Guadalupe River, Comal Creek as well as Comal Springs.

[21] Lindheimer's Peak: location unknown.

[22] Heinrich the butcher: identity unknown.

[23] Writing coincides with *Tenth Report* dated Comal Creek, 27 March 1845 (Geue and Geue, *A New Land Beckoned,* p. 66).

[24] Mrs. Campbell: identity unknown.

[25] Addicks: identity unknown. Veramendi, Jr.: probably Jose Marcos Antonio Veramendi. Verron: identity unknown; see "Mr. Vernos" in Fey, *New Braunfels, Vol. I,* p. 577; see also Solms's entry for 16 April 1845.

[26] Sophienburg: named for Solms's betrothed Princess Sophie; headquarters of Solms and the Society. Solms indicates that two individuals, Anton and Louis, had constructed the building, another source offers the information that "he [Solms] resided in a hut, woven of branches roofed over with straw, until the double block-houses were finished which he had delegated to the Smith brothers of Seguin to erect" (Haas, *History of New Braunfels and Comal County, Texas,* pp. 24 and 27).

[27] Phillippi: identity unknown; see also entry for 17 September 1844. Loma de la Mission: identity unknown; however, Mission Nuestra Senora de Guadalupe was established on the Guadalupe River at or near present-day New Braunfels in 1756 and abandoned two years later fearing possible destruction by Indians (*The New Handbook of Texas,* Vol. II, p. 293).

[28] The "plot": according to Hermann Seele was caused by dissatisfaction among the settlers. They were unhappy over the smaller land allotments they were given in the Comal Tract compared to the promise made in Germany of 320 acres to a family and 160 acres to a single male. The settlers also disliked the Society's directives, wanting from it only material support (Seele, *The Diary of Hermann Seele*, p. 260). Eduard von Hartz: arrived in Texas in December 1844. George Friedrich Holekamp: arrived in Texas in November 1844. Moret: Adolph Mouret was hired by the Society as a drover. Carl Bellmer: arrived in Texas in November 1844. Verron: see note 25 this chapter.

[29] Louis (or Ludwig) Vogel, Sr. (1808–1880): arrived in Texas in November 1844. Ed Brun: not clear if this is Eduard Brun, brother of Georg Christian Brun.

[30] Election: presumable election of Oscar von Claren as commandant of the company organized for the protection of the settlement against Indians (Biesele, *German Settlement in Texas*, p. 122).

[31] Herding: identity unknown; see also entry for 18 May 1844.

[32] Date coincides with *Eleventh Report* written at the Sophienburg 30 April 1845. Major Neighbours: should be Neighbors (see Solms's entry for 7 October 1844 and Chapter III, note 26).

[33] Colonel [possibly Lieutenant Colonel] Leutenegger: identity unknown. Richard von Cloudt, at times also spelled Kloudt (see Chapter IV, note 38).

[34] Wakor: Waco, a subtribe of the Wichita Indians (W. W. Newcomb, *Indians of Texas*, Austin, Texas: The University of Texas Press, 1961, p. 247). Hermann Seele also reports this incident. He states that the Tonkawa Indians had a bloody orgy in the Guadalupe bottoms. They cooked, roasted, and ate one of their enemies, a slain Waco (Seele, *The Cypress and Other Writings*, p. 67). Köpp: possibly a misspelling of the name Köpf, see Chapter VI, note 19.

[35] Adolph von Wedemeier (1822– ?): see Chapter IV, note 42. Shingles were in great need for the building of cabins.

[36] The "fat madam's" culinary skills were still undiminished when Roemer visited New Braunfels in 1846 (Roemer, *Texas*, p. 98). The meaning of the statement that "Rahm arrived [from San Antonio] with the news of the purchase" is unknown. The same holds true for the remark entered the following day "[In San Antonio] began immediately with the unpleasant business."

[37] Camble: Campbell. Camble is the phonetic transcription by Solms. The word is close to the German word "Camel," hence the pun, "ship of the desert." Anton Lochmar: local innkeeper.

[38] Addicks: see previous spelling, note 25 this chapter. Voss: identity unknown.

[39] General Campos: Tonkawa Indian chief. Solms jokingly said that at breakfast he served the Indian beef rather than a Wakors (a Waco Indian). Kyrburgum Dhaun: see Chapter I, note 14.

[40] Baron Otfried Hans von Meusebach (1812–1897): born Baron Otfried Hans Freiherr von Meusebach and schooled at prestigious universities in Germany, he was appointed the Society's commissioner-general in Texas to succeed Solms. Soon after his arrival in Texas he dropped the title and anglicized his name to John O. Meusebach. He held the Society's office for two years in which time he not only labored to serve the needs of the new immigrants but also helped found Fredericksburg (1846), and made a peace treaty with the Comanche Indians in which they agreed not to molest the settlers (1847). In 1851 Meusebach was elected to the Texas State Senate and in 1854 appointed commissioner with the authority to issue land certificates to the immigrants who had come in 1845 and 1846 and had been promised land by the Society. In 1867 he laid out on his own land in Mason County, the town of Loyal Valley, where he and his family retired in 1869 (*The New Handbook of Texas,* Vol. IV, pp. 469–50; Irene M. King, *John O. Meusebach,* Austin, Texas: The University of Texas Press, 1967). It is not clear if the comment "Rußer" refers to Alois Russer who arrived in Texas in December 1844 and apparently was an acquaintance of Nicholas Zink. The reference to Miss Zink poses the question who this individual was. The Society's emigrant list shows a W. Zink arriving with Nicolas Zink and his wife while another source reports that Zink had no issue (*Secretary of State, Record Group 307,* ARIS-TSL; Fey, *New Braunfels,* Vol. I, pp. 506 and 621).

[41] The remark about Indians may refer to the Tonkawas; see note 39 this chapter.

[42] Zink's "Peranda": meaning unknown.

[43] Solms's preparations for his departure from Texas.

Chapter Six

Thursday, [May] 15th. Sophie's Day. The flag was hoisted. I rode off at 6 o'clock—cannon salvo. Zink caught up; he overslept again. Racidor brought the news that the Wacos had shot and killed a woman (*squaw*). Five miles from Sophienburg said good-bye to Coll, Lindheimer and the other people. It was Heidemeier's company. At 10:30 at Flores's place, rested there and ate. On the way again at 2 o'clock. At Erkins's at 3:30; he is not at home, it is near Capote. The old white horse was forced to the ground and examined, a terrible illness. Beautiful acreage, oats, rye, wheat. A good bed but the supper left something to be desired.[1]

Friday, [May] the 16th. Up at 5 o'clock but didn't get away until 7 o'clock. Minder gave me his sorrel horse. At King's at 10 o'clock where we learned that von Meusebach had passed through. Wrede left for New Braunfels and I went to Gonzales where we arrived at 1 o'clock. Wilke arrived in the afternoon. He had been waiting here for three days.[2]

Saturday, [May] the 17th. I didn't sleep a wink during the night on account of fleas. At 10 o'clock off to Mathews who has plenty of livestock (married old King's daughter). Had lunch there. Returned in the afternoon. Waited in vain. Spent the night on the porch. Uncomfortable but fewer fleas there because I didn't undress.

Sunday, [May] the 18th. Rahm off at 6 A.M. Boredom! A Negress with Mathews's children arrived from King with the news that Germans were there. Rode to the San Marcos, at 5 o'clock with von

Meusebach and returned with him to Gonzales. Long conversation with him. Early to bed. Mail from 4 April.

Monday, [May] the 19th. Business matters with him [Meuesebach] in the morning, lunch, afterward goodbye to Wilke. Reached Brockhaus in the evening. Meusebach & Wrede followed. I find Meusebach capable, though slightly absent-minded and at first hard to become acquainted with.

Tuesday, [May] the 20th. Early on the way. 30 miles to Christwell, six and one-half hours in the saddle, rested 2 hours, then 12 miles to LaGrange. Rohde handed me a letter from Ernst containing a report of the discussion at Nassau. LaGrange. Hotel is run by a parasite, a former German. The two stragglers arrived late in the evening.[3]

Wednesday, [May] the 21st. Slept on the upper porch, got up early, before sunrise in the saddle and on the way to Nassau. The overseer was not there. His sister had him fetched. Jim talked about him, Fordtran & Denman. Lots of business matters. Both stragglers arrived at suppertime. The rye looks all right, the cotton not particularly so, many weeds between the plants. The hoeing was hard on the Negroes. In the afternoon off to Industry with the overseer catching up to me. For once Father Ernst did not sing, he favors annexation, his son and wife (Mad. Brey). Good supper (he must get something from Germany.)[4]

Thursday, [May] the 22nd. I had a wonderful night's rest. At sunrise we were on our way, 22 miles to San Felipe. Rested there for an hour and a half. The owner of the hotel has mammoth bones from the Brazos River. Head, i.e., the neck of a mammoth or tapir with horns (half), deer skull, etc. In the evening made it to Pine Island.[5]

Friday, [May] the 23rd. At sunrise everyone was on the way to Habermacher's. We rested there for two hours. In the evening reached Houston; turned in at the Alabama House; found Anton & company there.[6]

Saturday, [May] the 24th. Got up late; thorough washing up and shaving. Visited by Robson, he dined with me. Mitchell's death certificate. Went riding in the evening.[7]

Sunday, [May] the 25th. Slept poorly on account of the bugs. Stayed at home all day because of the heat. In the evening at Schrimpf's, ate sausage there. The steamer arrived.[8]

Monday, [May] the 26th. Count von Meusebach conducted business with Fischer. I also saw Fischer because of matters pertaining to Baron Meusebach. At 4 o'clock on board the *Col. Woods*, departed at 6 o'clock. The company was terrible as well as numerous.[9]

Tuesday, [May] the 27th. From 6 until 9 o'clock stuck on Clopper's Bar, arrived in Galveston at 4 o'clock. Checked in at Matossy's where Arcieri welcomed me. The Baron of Fremont, Wrede to Beissner. Excellent supper. Champagne toast to George's health.[10]

Wednesday, [May] the 28th. Slept heavenly in Elliot's room and bed. Called on Klaener whose wife is sick, Kennedy, Rebecka. My entire wardrobe sent off to be repaired and cleaned. At noon an outstanding dinner. In the morning worked with M[eusebach], took a walk in the afternoon. Early to bed. The *McKim* departed. Visit from the alleged Count Sandoszy (Doczky).[11]

Thursday, [May] the 29th. Terrible heat. Business with Rainer. After dinner a buggy ride on the beach. In the evening I attended a meeting where Col. Love spoke. The man is a pig! He presents himself as a democrat.[12]

Friday, [May] the 30th. Called on several people in the morning. After lunch Elliot arrived with Col. da Brezle (commander of the corvette *La Perouse*) from Mexico. He carries a tract. In the evening at Klaener's, afterward at Kennedy's. Wrede had supper at my place.[13]

Saturday, [May] the 31st. Conversation with Elliot who had learned the day before of his sister's death. Riding a coach between Vera

Cruz and Mexico City he was robbed by six masked men. He praises the Mexican cavalry and their horses. Dinner without him because he is suffering. The physician from the La Perouse came ashore. I took a stroll with M[eusebach] and Wrede. The *New York* arrived, without Saligny.

Sunday, June 1st. Departure of Elliot and Wrede, Sr., on the *Col. Woods*. In the morning at Kennedy's. Supper for six. Took a stroll with the Frenchmen. Talked politics during the meal. Offshore at anchor is the corvette *La Perouse*, 16 cannons. The U.S. has four ships among them the *Princeton* (Commodore Stockton) and the *Porpoise* (Captain Hunt). Very tired in the evening as I was all day.[14]

Monday, [June] the 2nd. Throughout the night and day strong wind from the east. In the afternoon took a stroll with the French. Meeting in the Tremont Hotel. Col. Love states he may have had a grandfather, maybe this is so. Dinner and evening as usual.[15]

Tuesday, [June] the 3rd. Dinner at Kennedy's. Captain Hunt, the mayor of Galveston, Major Allen, a ship's builder from Nova Scotia. It lasted from 2 until 6 o'clock. Many boring speeches. Another meeting in the evening.[16]

Wednesday, [June] the 4th. Business matters with Klaener, the North German Baron can not get finished. Departed Galveston on the *New York* at 11:45; we bring the American officers on board. I stretched out on my overcoat outside the salon. High seas; very boring. When night arrived, you couldn't read any longer.[17]

Thursday, [June] the 5th. Again boring, slept rather well.

Friday, [June] the 6th. Passed the Ballise between 3 and 4 A.M. Shaved and washed, slept after breakfast because I hadn't slept during the night. Arrived in New Orleans at 4:30 P.M. Checked in at the St. Louis Hotel. I went immediately to Lanfear where Sophie's letter from Dülmen awaited me, what joy. I made the acquaintance of Mr. Noessel, daguerrist, had to sit immediately, the results were poor. Supper and then to bed.[18]

Saturday, [June] the 7th. Called on von Werthern, Köpf, Simmons and others. Bathed. Mons. Vogel. Afterward walked to Lanfear and Vogel. Called on Saligny. At 3 o'clock Armand Geyerl in regard to Simmons. Ward arrived and the matter was arranged. Dinner in the St. Louis, a tolerable lady. In the afternoon to Lac Pontchartrain. (Three lighthouses, a long wharf; three steamers ready to leave for various points, Biloxi, Pass Christian and for Mobile, Bay St. Louis, etc.) In the evening visited by Lanfear & Ward. Invitation to dinner on Monday. Went to sleep while the piano played across the way.[19]

Sunday, [June] the 8th. Called on Mrs. Vogel. Dr. Labatut and Rod. Urquhart. Otherwise it rained all day. Eggers called on me; in the afternoon at Noessel's.[20]

Monday, [June] the 9th. In the morning visit from Ward and Briggs (lawyer). Dinner at Lanfear's (Col. Greyms) at 4:30. At 9 o'clock to Mrs. Vogel, piano played by Dam. Choppard. Returned home at midnight.[21]

Tuesday, [June] the 10th. Lots of rain, received the news from Lanfear of little Mary's death. Took a walk in the evening, got soaking wet. Didn't find Saligny though I called on him twice.

Wednesday, [June] the 11th. I got up early. Called on Vogel and Lanfear. Discussion with Briggs; afterward with Ward to the club, read in the *Times* briefly about my poor little Mary's death!!!—At 2:45 departed by railroad for Lake Pontchartrain; there said goodbye to Wrede, his handshake. On board the *Creole*; a narrow boat, fairly elegant, considering the circumstances, a good dinner. Four beautiful women on board, one truly a Venus-figure, nice profile, full; one striking, resembled Rosa Carviani. A gentleman, who wants to establish settlements in Florida. In the afternoon on the top deck. From Lake Pontchartrain through a natural channel to Lake Borgne. This channel is nothing more than mud and water, reeds wherever there is water. To the right of the channel, or inland water, not far from the exit from Lake Pontchartrain lies Fort Pique; built in a swamp, in a half-circle, brick wall with casements (twelve embrasures for cannons), wet moat and covered walkway with a short *glacis* [slope]; an unprotected guard post on the earthen embankment, the buildings and barracks of wood, water stands under the barracks which are located on a small island and are connected by a bridge with the round tower (hollow bastion with no separation between the face and flank because it is a modified plan). On the rampart, without any breastwork, is the commander's house with a guard post in front. Thus we traveled on Lake Borgne on a north-north-easterly course. We entered finally the Bay of St. Louis where we stopped at the summer resort of Bay St. Louis; a low-lying, bare area, from there to Pass Christian, more wooded but also of a very low elevation, each community has about 1,000–1,500 inhabitants, more during the summer, when the well-to-do from New Orleans come here, as well as from Biloxi and Parskagola. The ladies disembark, among them the Venus figure who has a monster with blue glasses for a husband, a dirty devil; so does Wrede's earlier acquaintance with husband as well as her sister and her sister's gentleman friend. To bed at 10.[22]

Thursday, [June] the 12th. Up at 6 o'clock and had my coffee. The landscape remained unchanged, low and wooded shore. We arrived in the Bay of Mobile at 8:30. The larger ships in the bay were being unloaded. At the Alabama River, which here forms the harbor, were many large barges at the numerous docks. Mobile is a town built in the American style. Went on board the *Marquette* which will take me upriver; afterward to the Mansion [?]. Rested and cleaned up. Dinner was bad; company even worse. I am so alone. On board again at 5 o'clock, departed at 7 o'clock. Broad river, first the Mobile, then the Alabama; very bad supper, and even a worse and dirty bed. (Mobile has a population of 15–18,000, New Orleans supposedly 130–150,000.)[23]

Friday, [June] the 13th. The river banks are wooded, here and there a farm or a small settlement; partially loam, partially rock, a few beautiful sights. In the evening discussion about religion. The captain, a Catholic, converted out of conviction.

Saturday, [June] the 14th. The landscape remains unchanged. Every day a reading of "Les Mysteres de Paris."[24]

Sunday, [June] the 15th. Arrived in Montgomery at 1:45 A.M. By coach to Montgomery Hall; what a room, what filth! To bed nevertheless, slept until 9 o'clock. Since this place has only one street it can be viewed easily. The entire day . . . Dinner poor, the company is much more vulgar. In the afternoon thunderstorm and rain. The silly American woman from the ship is also in the hotel. To bed by 10 o'clock; because of the heat it was impossible to sleep. Got up at 11:30 and walked until 12:30. Afterward by coach to the railroad.

Monday, [June] the 16th. Departed at 1:10 o'clock. A very bumpy ride; arrived in Chehard at 4 o'clock, 40 miles. Had breakfast there (the town is comprised of two houses). From there by stagecoach, I rode <u>outside</u>, 42 miles to Opelika. Constantly forests, narrow trails, awful heat! Gesseta a miserable place, dinner, then 27 miles to LaGrange, always the same rolling, wooded terrain. From LaGrange to Grantsville 21 miles. Ate at Mr. Border's late in the evening then slept the rest of the night. Grantsville to Griffin 40 miles, a terrible careless driver, the moon went down, complete darkness, a bad, rocky road. This man let the horses run whenever possible, uphill, downhill. It was so dark the first pair of horses in the team couldn't be seen. Arrived in Griffin at 6 A.M. [25]

Tuesday, [June] the 17th. 7 A.M., after breakfast, 42 miles to Covington, still the same area (Georgia), a good driver. Arrived in Covington at 2 o'clock. Dinner, then on the railroad, sofa where I gently fell asleep.[26]

Wednesday, [June] the 18th. Arrived in Augusta at 2 A.M.; U.S. Hotel; slept until 5 o'clock; I cleaned up and was at the station at 6 o'clock. A coach with a team of six. In Charleston by 3 o'clock too late for the steamer; Charleston Hotel; dinner, afterward a stroll; early to bed.[27]

Thursday, [June] the 19th. Visit from Mr. Trapmann, Prussian Consul. Bathed. Ate; at 3 o'clock on board the steamer on the way to

Wilmington; poor service on board. Slept quite a bit, beautiful moonlight.[28]

Friday, [June] the 20th. In Wilmington at 8 o'clock, on the train at 9 o'clock (but what a train!!!) to Weldon; heat, rain, thunderstorm, uncomfortable; 140 miles to Weldon where we arrived at 10 o'clock. On a new train to Petersburg.[29]

Saturday, [June] the 21st. Rode through the night. Arrived in Petersburg at 6 A.M. where I had breakfast. Mr. Baldouin with the green glasses did not let up. At 7 o'clock continued via Richmond (Va.), wonderful location, to Fredericksburg and the Potomac. On board the *Augusta*; made the acquaintance with Gen. Maj. Scott, Commander in Chief of the Army, 6' 10" tall, courteous, had been to Europe, familiar with Germany, that is the Rhine. Landed in Washington at 4 o'clock. To Coleman's Hotel. Cleaned up. Called on von Gerold (absent); de Pontoze, Gen. Scott, letter from him to Capt. Thomas at West Point. Took a stroll with Mr. Baldouin and Mr. Polk to the Capitol, beautiful building, mottled style, the dome is rather tasteless, nice location. Statue of Columbus, not much imagination put into it. He is posed in armor with a naked Indian girl next to him![30]

Sunday, [June] the 22nd. Visit from von Korponay (Quartermaster)! then from von der Stratten-Pontkoye, who is being transferred to Brazil, finally by Baldouin who picked me up for church. Called on Peckenham, at first [?], later a lively luncheon at his place. At noon ate at Pontkoye's. Baron von Stoeckl, secretary to the Russian ambassador. To bed at 11 o'clock.[31]

Monday, [June] the 23rd. In the morning with Pontkoye to the museum which is a horrible mausoleum, then to the Capitol, hall under the dome has historical scenes. Called on Fr. von Corponay, née von Werner and on Mad. Fleischmann at the institute. Pontoye had lunch at my place, at 5 o'clock on the train. In Baltimore at 7:30 P.M. A beautiful area with the most wonderful views into the distance, good train. To the E [?] Hotel, in a coach to Bolton. It is a lie, the house belongs to Mother Urquhart; both sons and Mad. Urquhart who is very beautiful. Home by 9:30 o'clock and to bed.[32]

Tuesday, [June]the 24th. On the train at 8 o'clock, rather crowded but only <u>one</u> drunk. Heat, in Philadelphia at 3 o'clock. I ate at the Manier House, afterward strolled through the beautiful town. In bed at 9 o'clock.

Wednesday, [June] the 25th. At 8 o'clock on the way by steamer. Found Mr. Rose; 26 miles to Bristol, then by train to Trenton, and New Brunswick. In New York at 2 o'clock, beautiful view of the city and the North River. To the Globe Hotel. Called on Primer, Ward & King. Ward speaks German, told me of Carl Maltzahn's trip to the Rocky Mountains. Dinner a la carte. Serurier came by. In the evening the French Opera: *The Favorite*, unfortunately it was bad.[33]

Thursday, [June] the 26th. Picked up the pistols, to Serurier. Parade of the National Guard before the Secretary of War. What a farce! First I went to Castle Garden, next to the floating Battery. Serurier joined me at dinner, afterward took a walk. In the evening at Theater Vaudeville, *de Vicomte de l'Etoriere*, quite nice.[34]

Friday, [June] the 27th. Tested the pistols in Hoboken, in the company of [?] born in Holstein. After dinner visited by Ward, tickets to the opera. His wife, very beautiful, then the old Mad. Greyms, very common. Invitation to Sunday dinner. Made acquaintance with Chev. Gevers.[35]

Saturday, [June] the 28th. At 7 A.M. on a steamer to West Point, nice banks of the Hudson, 55 miles, arrived at 10:30 A.M. Buildings in the gothic style. Capt. Swift in the absence of Capt. Thomas. Academy class rooms, drawing room, lights from above, library, chapel, both gothic style with plenty of wood carving; everything is first-class. [?] living room. A new [?] under construction (estimated cost of $120,000—annual budget of $100,000). Two men per, [?] then a new course. Models, mixing of physical [?] as well as steam engine and new invention, even electro-magnetic. Knowledge of the young officers. The laboratory is well planned. View from the hotel; dinner; departed at 2 o'clock. Boredom, disgust, rain. Arrived in New York at 5:30 o'clock, thoroughly soaked. Dinner in the room, in bed at 9 o'clock.[36]

Sunday, [June] the 29th. Started with bad colic yesterday, the night was horrible. In spite of that at 8:30 A.M. with Gevers to the Staten Island Ferry. Middleton, H. Ward. Beautiful location of Mad. Greyms' farm on Staten Island. Well built, small gothic Swiss houses. Dinner, Ole. Bull arrived; exceptional beautiful view, unfortunately gloomy weather. The old Greyms talked about [?] and had herself served. At 1:30 o'clock with Gevers and Middleton to New Brighton, then to New York. Took a walk with Gevers. Indian things. Dinner at 6 o'clock. Serurier came at 8 o'clock. To bed at 10:30.[37]

Monday, [June] the 30th. Got up four times during the night. Bad weather.[38]

---

[1] Sophie's Day: meaning not clear, unless that starting with this day he will be getting closer to her. Solms departed New Braunfels for Seguin where he crossed the Guadalupe River. After resting at Flores's place, he stopped overnight at Erskine's, twelve miles southeast of Seguin.

[2] Minder: identity unknown. The trip continued south of the Guadalupe River to Gonzales where the river was crossed.

[3] Christwell: L. V. Criswell (see Chapter II, note 54). Rohde: presumably H[enry] Rhode (see Chapter II, note 16). From Gonzales the party traveled east on the Gonzales-Columbus Road. In the vicinity of present-day Moulton Solms took the La Bahia Road to LaGrange and Nassau Farm.

[4] Jim: Solms spelled the name also "Gim" (see Chapter II, note 56 and Chapter IV, note 3). Madam Brey (1816–1889): Johann Friedrich Ernst married Marie Ann Brey (née Krumm) at Industry, Texas, on 18 May 1845. She was the widow of Ferdinand Brey who died in February 1843 on the Mier Expedition (York, *Friedrich Ernst*, p. 141). Presumably Solms traveled the Gotcher Trace which passed through Industry.

[5] There are other references to fossil remains along the Brazos River. A. J. Sowell recounts some finds below the town of Richmond in Fort Bend County (A. J. Sowell, *History of Fort Bend County*, Houston, Texas: W. H. Coyle & Co., Stationers and Printers, 1904, reprint, 1964, p. 346; Goyne, *A Life Among the Texas Flora*, p. 85). Pine Island: Solms must have unintentionally misnamed this locality. Considering that he traveled in an easterly direction from San Felipe to Habermacher's place, he passed in the vicinity of present-day Katy which was first known as Cane Island (*The New*

Handbook of Texas, Vol. III, p. 1039). After an overnight stay in Industry the party continued to San Felipe where it crossed the Brazos River and spent the night in the vicinity of present-day Katy.

[6] Alabama House: presumably a boarding house. Coming from the west, Buffalo Bayou was crossed about where today it is bridged by Highway 6.

[7] Robson: probably Robert Robson. Bollaert records that Robson owned, in addition, an estate called "Scotch Hermitage" two miles from Montgomery, Montgomery County, Texas (Hollon and Butler, *Bollaert's Texas*, pp. 242n and 266; see also Chapter IV, notes 9 and 54). Mitchell: identity unknown.

[8] The arriving steamer must have been the *Colonel Woods*; see entry for the following day. Johann Wilhelm Schrimpf: a resident of Houston, 40 years old, butcher by profession, born in Germany (*1850 U.S. Census, Harris County, Texas*, p. 019, National Archives Microfilm M432, Roll 911).

[9] *Colonel Wood*, James W. Wood, master: possibly a side-wheeler of 134 tons (Puryear & Winfield, Jr., p. 79). It took the steamer *Colonel Woods* twenty-four hours to get to Galveston which normally was an overnight trip. Leaving the afternoon before, it became stuck on Clopper's Bar in the morning hours and may have had to wait for the tide to be refloated.

[10] Matossy, Jacob: in 1839 he sought a divorce from his wife Caroline on the ground of infidelity (Hays, *Galveston*, p. 389); on 15 January 1844 he married Mary A. Boullan (*Galveston County Marriage Records 1838–1850*, Book A, p. 6). Baron of Fremont: meaning unclear. Bissner: Charles L. Beissner (1810– ?) arrived in Galveston from Bremen on the brig *Ferdinand* in the fall of 1842. Trained in the hotel business, he leased the old Planter's House and turned it into one of the most popular hostelries in Galveston (Hays, *Galveston*, p. 911). "toast to George": meaning unclear.

[11] Elliot's room: presumably Charles Elliot's, British chargé d'affaires in Galveston. Count Sandoszy (Doczky): possibly the Hungarian Count Zondogi who was accompanied by G. W. Kendall to Texas ([*New Orleans*] *Daily Picayune*, 15 April 1845, p. 1, col. 6).

[12] James Love, Galveston merchant; anti-Houstonian as well as opponent to the annexation of Texas. Rainer: accountant with the firm E. Kauffman & Co., Galveston (see entry for 12 October 1844 and Chapter III, note 31).

[13] Elliot: Charles Elliot, see note 11 this chapter. Elliott embarked on a secret mission to arrange an armistice between Mexico and Texas which in his mind would preclude the annexation of Texas by the Untied States. He departed from Galveston to Vera Cruz in early April, and continued from there by coach to Mexico City. Returning to Galveston on the French corvette *La Perouse*, Elliot wrote his superiors in England "I proceed [to

Washington-on-the-Brazos] tomorrow in company with M. le Commandant Dubremil, who has a letter from the Baron Alleye de Cypress to His Excellency [President Anson Jones]" (Adams, "British Diplomatic Correspondence" in *The Southwestern Historical Quarterly*, Vol. XX, no. 2; p. 173).

[14] The four U.S. naval ships under the command of Commodore Robert Field Stockton were the frigate *Princeton* (thirteen guns), Lt. E. R. Thompson; brig *Porpoise* (twelve guns), Lt. W. E. Hunt; ship *St. Mary's* (22 guns), Capt. Saunders; and ship *Saratoga* (twenty-two guns), Capt. Shubrick ([*New Orleans*] *Daily Picayune*, 13 May 1845, p. 2, col. 3; and 25 May 1845, p. 2, col. 2).

[15] The meaning of Love's statement is not clear.

[16] Captain Hunt: presumably of the U.S. naval ship *Porpoise*. Mayor of Galveston: identity unknown. Major Allen: insufficient information to ascertain if this is Ebenezer Allen, Secretary of State (1844–45) of the Republic of Texas.

[17] North German Baron: Meusebach.

[18] Ballise: see Chapter I, note 36. Dülmen: town southwest of Münster in the state of North Rhine-Westphalia. Solms's arrival on the *New York* in New Orleans is noted on the passenger list submitted to the District of Mississippi, Port of New Orleans (*Passenger Lists of Vessels Arriving at New Orleans, LA., 1820–1902*, National Archives Microfilm M259, Roll 24, Document 88).

[19] von Werthern: identity unknown. Köpf: identity unknown, see also Chapter V, note 34. Simmons and Armand Geyerl: identities unknown. Lac: Lake Pontchartrain.

[20] Rod. Urquhart or Robert Urquhart: identity unknown. Eggers: see Chapter IV, note 24.

[21] Briggs (lawyer), Col. Greyms, and Dam. Choppard: identities unknown.

[22] "little Mary's death": meaning unclear. The train mentioned here was the Pontchartrain Railroad built in 1832, the third oldest railroad in the nation. Steamer *Creole*, Capt. Hiern: side-wheeler, 306 tons, built in New York, NY, first port New York, NY, in 1841, sold in 1853 (Lytle, *Merchant Steam Vessels*, p. 42). This ship went to Pensacola by way of Mobile (*[New Orleans] Daily Picayune*, 20 July 1844, p. 2, col. 1). Lake Borgne: provides access to Lake Pontchartrain from the Gulf of Mexico and vice-versa. Fort Pique: or correctly Fort Pike, named in honor of Zebulon M. Pike (1779–1813). Was begun in 1819 in the aftermath of the War of 1812 to protect the entry into Lake Pontchartrain as well as prevent an attack by land on New Orleans (Bertram H. Groene, *Pike: A Fortress in The Wetlands*, Hammond, Louisiana: Southeastern Louisiana University Press,

1988). Bay St. Louis, Pass Christian, and Biloxi are all located in the state of Mississippi. Parskagola: Pascagoula, Mississippi.

[23] Ship *Marquette*: side-wheeler, 126 tons, built in Pittsburgh, Pennsylvania, in 1842, first port Pittsburgh, Pennsylvania, lost in 1845 (Lytle, *Merchant Steam Vessels*, p. 121).

[24] *Les Mysteres de Paris* (*The Mysteries of Paris*), 1842–43 by French novelist Eugène Sue (1804–1857). His books were also popular in North America. The J. M. Jones Stationary in Galveston placed ads in the newspaper announcing the arrival of this title (*The Civilian and Galveston Gazette*, 12 June 1844, p. 1, col. 2; *Telegraph and Texas Register*, 8 June 1845, p. 4, col. 4).

[25] Chehard, Alabama: Chehaw, Alabama. Gesseta, Alabama: Cusseta, Alabama. LaGrange, Georgia. Griffin, Georgia.

[26] Covington, Georgia.

[27] Augusta, Georgia. Charleston, South Carolina.

[28] Wilmington, North Carolina.

[29] Weldon, North Carolina. Petersburg, Virginia.

[30] Baldouin, Gerold, von der Stratten-Pontkoze, and Polk: identities unknown. Van der Straten-Ponthoz, see Chapter 1, note 9. Richmond, Virginia. Ship *Augusta*: several possibilities, see Lytle, *Merchant Steam Vessels*, p.14. Major General Winfield Scott (1786–1866).

[31] Peckenham and von Korponay: identities unknown.

[32] "institute": identity unknown. Bolton: identity unknown. Mad. Urquhart: not enough information to establish a relationship with the Urquharts in New Orleans.

[33] Bristol, Trenton and New Brunswick: all located in New Jersey. Mr. Rose: identity unknown. Primer, Ward & King: identities unknown. Carl Maltzahn: identity unknown. *The Favorite* (French opera): identity unknown.

[34] U. S. Secretary of War: William L. Marcy (1786–1857) served as Secretary of War in the Cabinet of President James K. Polk. He assumed his duties on 5 March 1845, and served until 8 March 1849. Castle Garden: a few years later became the first landing place in New York for immigrants from Europe. "floating" Battery: not clear what Solms meant by "floating;" however, the Battery was built over a landfill and the name refers to a line of cannons once mounted here to defend the shoreline. *de Vicomte de l'Etoriere*: identity unknown.

[35] Hoboken: New Jersey. Mad. Greymes and Chev. Gevers: their identities unknown.

[36] Portions of the entry for this day are illegible. West Point: the proper designation is United States Military Academy, located at West Point, New York. Capt. Alexander Joseph Swift (ca. 1810–1847), Class of 1833, Corps

of Engineers, in addition to being an instructor of practical engineering at the Academy, was also from 1844 to 1846 the construction engineer for the cadet barracks (Central Barracks). Solms observed some of this construction. It was completed in 1851. Capt. John Addison Thomas (ca. 1811–1858), Class of 1833, Artillery, was an instructor of tactics and, from 1842 to 1845, the Commandant of Cadets (Letter dated 13 October 1995, from the United States Military Academy, West Point, New York, to W. M. Von-Maszewski).

[37] Staten Island, New York, located in New York Bay, off the New Jersey shore. Mr. Middleton and Mr. H. Ward: identities unknown. On the eastern half of Staten Island there is an area that today is still referred to as Grymes Hill. New Brighton: community located in the northeastern corner of Staten Island.

[38] Solms missed his self-imposed departure date because he remarked in the *Eleventh Report*: "I have arranged for my departure on Thursday the 15th of May. I hope to arrive in Boston in a month so that I can depart from America by steam boat on the 15th of June."

APPENDIX

Britannia, sister ship of the *Caledonia*
Charles Dickens, *American Notes*, London: Illustrated Library Edition, 1862

Steamship *Caledonia* of Glasgow
Edward G. Lott, master
from Liverpool to Halifax and Boston
19 May–1 June 1844

NAME	AGE	GENDER	OCCUPATION	PLACE OF RESIDENCE	DESTINATION
Hamerkoch, Wm.	32	m	merchant	New York	New York
Phipps, Wm.	44	m	merchant	Boston	US
E. C. [Mrs.]	?	f	-	"	"
M. E. [daughter]	?	f	-	"	"
Marshall, Wm.	31	m	merchant	Virginia	"
G. V. [Mrs.]	?	f	-	"	"
Thorn, H.	60	m	gent.	New York	"
Boyer, L.	32	m	doctor	Canada	Canada
Wilson, P. J.	34	m	painter	US	US
Collins, Henry	27	m	gent.	England	"
McKintosh, Neil	43	m	merchant	Scotland	Canada
Lane, E. W.	20	m	gent.	Canada	"
Gunning, W. H.	49	m	clergyman	Ireland	"
Denny, W. H.	47	m	cashier	Penn.	Penn.
W. G.	21	m	farmer	"	"
Norris, Th. P.	43	m	gent.	New Jersey	US
Gossed, Richard	25	m	manufacturer	Penn.	"
Conrad, Celt	37	m	lawyer	New Orleans	"
Cromwell, Chas. F.	35	m	lawyer	New York	"
H. F. [Mrs.]	27	f		"	"
Hook, J. Z. N.	33	m	merchant	"	"
Patterson, J. W.	32	m	merchant	"	Boston
Mrs.	25	f		"	"
child	1	f		England	"
Felton, Ann	37	f		"	"
Fletcher, J. H.	31	m	gent.	"	"
Torrance, F. W.	20	m	"	Canada	Canada

NAME	AGE	GENDER	OCCUPATION	PLACE OF RESIDENCE	DESTINATION
Harris, G. W.	31	m	merchant	Penn.	US
Goodall, Isaac	23	m	merchant	England	"
Harwood, George	26	m	?	"	"
Solms, Prince Chas. de	32	m	officer of cavalry	Austria	Texas
Orvanne, Bourgeois de	38	m	gent.	Paris	"
Hamilton, J.	34	m	soldier	Ireland	Unknown
Armstrong, D.	25	m	servant	"	"
Torcsinsky	40	m	[Solms's] servant	Austria	Texas
Rilti	19	m	"	Germany	"
Ruck	23	m	"	"	"
Brockhald	23	m	[Orvanne's] servant	France	"
St. Georges, Quelton de	24	m	proprietor	France	Canada
Babut, A.	21	m	"	Belgium	US
Razim, Carl	23	m	merchant	Austria	"
Serurier, Viscount	27	m	Sec. of Legation	France	"
Carter, John	38	m	gent.	England	Canada
Graham, A.	68	m	manufacturer	New York	US
Harris, R. W.	65	m	merchant	Ireland	Canada
Call, A. W.	25	m	"	England	US
Hartwig, C. F.	44	m	Captain	Prussia	"
Kruge, C.	24	m	Mate	"	"
Sturgis, Miss	25	f	-	Canada	Canada
Vassas, Mr.	40	m	merchant	Germany	US
Mrs.	34	f	-	"	"
Miss	24	f	-	"	"
Hillern, Mr.	46	m	merchant	"	"
Gray, John	43	m	gent.	Scotland	Canada
Johnson, Lt. Col.	40	m	"	England	"

NAME	AGE	GENDER	OCCUPATION	PLACE OF RESIDENCE	DESTINATION
Maitland, Henry	34	m	merchant	"	"
Castro, H.	29	m	"	Prussia	US
Pontz, Baron V. T. S.	25	m	gent.	"	"
Montrave, Count F. de	31	m	"	Austria	Canada
Thomson, B.	27	m	merchant	US	US
Perry, Mr.	34	m	"	"	"
Hill, T. W.	33	m	"	"	"
Scissors, John	15	m	servant	Norfolk	"
Kellogg, Mr.	37	m	farmer	Illinois	US

(*Passenger Lists of Vessels Arriving at Boston, MA., 1820–1891,* National Archives Microfilm M277, Roll #17, Document #76; *Passenger Lists, 1840–1853,* Record Group GM22, Cunard Archives, Liverpool University Archives, United Kingdom)

Diary of the Colonial Director of the Society for the Protection of German Immigrants in Texas[1] [by Bourgeois d'Orvanne]

San Antonio de Bexar, August 1, 1844.[2]

Traveling on horse, the Society's Commissioners[3] did not have the opportunity until today to maintain a diary of the things that they saw and did. The Colonial Director will here attempt to outline briefly his observations since the arrival in Texas.

June 1, 1844. After landing in Galveston on June 1, the Commissioners desired to meet the government officials as soon as possible. The first available steamer took them up the Buffalo Bayou to Houston. No difficulties were encountered going through customs, however, we were not able to take with us the items bought in New Orleans for the Society's use. They should have come in duty free. Moreover, the original plan to travel directly from New Orleans to the port of Lavaca had been changed.

Important notice. If at all possible, merchandise should not be sent to Texas, except on immigrant ships. Otherwise it is subject to custom duty. During their stay in Galveston the Commissioners made the best possible arrangements for an expeditious delivery of letters, packages, and goods. French Vice-Consul Cobb[4] in Galveston, has been designated the Society's temporary agent there. His instructions are to forward everything addressed to the Commissioners to French Consul Guillebeau[5] in San Antonio de Bexar. In turn, Cobb will forward to the offices of Schmidt & Co.[6] everything that the Commissioners address to the United States and Europe.

The people of Galveston are sympathetic with the Society's goals. Former Secretary of War Colonel Hinkley,[7] Congress member Dr. Jones[8], Colonel Williams,[9] Sheriff Smith[10] and many others expressed a deep interest and assured us that Congress would quickly renew the colonization land grant.

British Consul Kennedy,[11] acting in the absence of General-Consul Captain Elliott,[12] as well as on instruction from his government, extended his services to these Commissioners. This good and friendly gesture by the cabinet at Buckingham[13] is due to the royal goodwill of His Regal Highness Prince Albert.[14] The Colonial Director intends to mail a letter of thanks to his Highness. In a similar manner, the Society can depend on the assistance from the French representative.

The absence of England's and France's diplomatic representatives at the time when the annexation was proposed, had much to do with the unwise decision by the head of state. It would be prudent, if both governments could be influenced, so that they force their representatives to stay at their posts. This is of the greatest political as well as general importance.

The government of Texas, without any actual strength, left to its own devices, can make major mistakes. With the assistance of the diplomatic corps, Texas gains an important influence and can withstand the oftentimes dangerous interests of individuals.

The Society's Commissioners are convinced that the presence of diplomatic representatives of the President would have itself averted the ill-fated step. We have the assurances of that. The Commissioners left Galveston at 10 A.M. on the 3rd and arrived in Houston at 7 P.M. There they found similar sympathy on the part of the town's people. Everyone perceives the Society's importance and its goals. A 21-canon salute greeted Prince Solms at his arrival.

The necessity of going to the Nassau Plantation,[15] naturally diverted the Commissioners from the major purpose of their trip. The Commissioners, however, recognized the importance of meeting with the government representatives. The two of them decided to go to Washington[16] and they sent their subordinates directly to Nassau.

This required the procurement of horses and a wagon to carry the baggage. An American horse for the Prince cost $100 and three Mexican mustangs were bought for a total of $75. The sellers profited from this transaction and they got more for the animals than they were worth. The fact that one of the Commissioners has the title of prince makes it necessary for us to pay a dear price for the things we buy. In addition, a wagon with a horse was leased for $20 to transport the luggage and servants. On account of these preparations the Commissioners did not leave until 5 or 6 P.M. of the following day. While they traveled to Washington, the rest of their party, under the care of Ducos,[17] left for Nassau.

July 5. At 9 P.M. the Commissioners stopped at Turkeim's,[18] nine miles from Houston. Here began the harsh lessons in Texas with the terrible suppers and terrible beds.

July 6. We left Turkeim at 5 A.M. and reached Hamblin's[19] farm, 12 miles distance, at 9:30 A.M. The atmospheric observations made here were: 90°[F] at 10 A.M., 93°[F] at noon, 98°[F] at 3 P.M. and 95°[F] at 4 P.M. The dwelling is by a creek. The water that we drank from it was 80°[F]. At 10:30 P.M. we had traveled 19 miles and stayed at Stevenson's on Bond Fish Creek.[20] Here we found several individuals who had left Houston a day ahead of us. Poor trail conditions prevented them from traveling faster.

July 7. The Commissioners continued at 5 A.M. and after 19 miles of poor trail through the Brazos Bottom arrived at Washington at 10:30 A.M. This year's floodings are responsible for the poor conditions of the trail. We called on the Secretary of State.[21] The reception was very cordial and he left a good impression with the party. He assured them that Congress has a friendly disposition toward the Society and that he had the same feeling for the Colonial Director. The next meeting was set for noon the following day.

July 8. Drafted and handed to the Secretary of State:

1. Report about the loan of $1,000,000.
2. Report about the land grant.
3. Letter of introduction.
4. Translation from German to French of the [Society's] program.
5. The Society's membership list.

During our meeting the Secretary of State regretted that our grant on the Medina River could not be renewed without the approval of Congress. He assured us, however, that he had no doubt that Congress would consent to the Society's wish. In the meantime, the Commissioners should proceed with prudence, waste no time and travel to the area, purchase land bordering the grant, in order to make there the necessary preparations for the immigrants' arrival. The President[22] who was sick at the Trinity River was expected to return any day. The heat in the valley in which Washington is situated, its unhealthy location caused the Commissioners to leave the seat of government. They asked the Secretary of State to inform them of the President's return should it happen in the near future.

After inviting Anson Jones to have supper with us, we left Washington at 7 P.M. During our conversation the topic turned to Castro's land grant. Contrary to the decision by the government, and thereby ignoring it, the Secretary of State declared that Castro[23] would keep his grant without needing to renew it. The justification was that he had already brought immigrants into the country. This part of the discussion became rather lively; fortunately, it did not stay on the subject for long. This conversation can be considered to be confidential, as well as the frank remarks of the Texas government. At 9:30 P.M. the Commissioners arrived at Foster's plantation,[24] 3 miles from Washington. Atmospheric observations for the day: 85 degrees at 8 A.M., 92 degrees at noon, 99 degrees at 3 P.M.; 96 degrees at 5 P.M.

9 July. At 8:30 in the evening, after a journey of 42 miles, the representatives arrived at Nassau Farm after a stopover in Mandeville [Mount Vernon?].[25] The people and the luggage sent directly from Houston had not yet arrived. It was too late to inspect the property. The [head]quarters under the care of Mr. Lessely[26] seemed to be in good order. Later inspected the land around the headquarters which appears to be rich and fertile; there is a good forest, water, hills, prairie. The land was well chosen.

10 July. At 9 A.M. Fordtran[27] brought our small expedition. The group was forced to stay overnight at his place. It was two days late arriving on account of the awful trail through the Brazos Bottom.

The Colonial Director gave the guide who led us from Washington a letter to take back to the Secretary of State and the President. It was in reference to the land grant and he asked for a speedy answer on the subject.

At this time Congress cannot renew the grant. But as a result of the above-mentioned discussions, until a decision is reached by Congress, no settlements can be established on this land.—Visits by various Germans from the local area. A young physician, Dr. Mayer,[28] who is Swiss, who had served in the Dutch army, and who was a recent arrival in Texas was temporarily hired by the Prince without the Commissioners knowing the exact reason of his arrival in this land. Although he appears to be intelligent and well educated, before he is permanently employed, the Commissioners should inquire about his past.

Inspected Nassau Farm. It is poorly planned and managed and the work in the fields is poorly organized. The Negro quarters are wretched. Not a high recommendation for a plantation owner. This year's expected harvest of corn will only be half or less from the previous year and only with luck will there be 15 to 20 bales of cotton harvested. Half of the ninety acres is corn, half cotton.

11 July. An inventory[29] was started at Nassau Farm. What mismanagement of money with nothing to show for it! This plantation needs a skillful and frugal manager. With 25,000 Gulden an experienced individual would have accomplished more and brought in a harvest equal to that of the first year.

12 July. Visited the areas around Cummings Creek and Mill Creek where many Germans live.[30] They may be rich in land but are poor in hope. Among the Germans lives a botanist. His name is Lindheimer.[31] Appears to be a scholar who is wrapped up in his work. He can be of use to us by informing us about the flora on our grant.

The land between Nassau Farm and the settlements on Mill Creek is generally good. Within 2 to 3 miles there are not many trees. Fordtran lives 9 miles from here and Ernst 12 miles.[32]

13–14 July. Stayed at Nassau Farm. No word from General Houston. Worked on the inventory. Wrote the Directorate regarding the colony and the farm.[33] Mailed the inventory. Denmann, manager of Nassau Farm, requested $500 for certain expenses.[34] It was agreed that he remain on the plantation until December under the same stipulations as his predecessor. Matters will not improve until an individual takes charge of the plantation who has a financial stake in it. A salaried manager or director does not fill the bill.

Wrote to the President and the Secretary of State expressing our regret that the Commissioners could no longer wait because their instructions demanded that they resume their journey and inspect the Society's lands.[35]

Wrote to de Saligny,[36] French chargé d'affaires, and asked him that he get in touch with [Secretary of State] Anson Jones and keep alive the favorable opinion that the latter has of the Society.

The Commissioners intended to leave this evening but with the disappearance of the mules the plans fell through.

16 July. Completed preparations for the departure. The Commissioners left Nassau Farm at 4 P.M., accompanied by Ducos, Dr. Mayer, Fordtran, Abbe Auger[37] and four servants. The plantation provided for the trip a wagon with two mules, an American horse, a mustang and a pony. The members of the caravan were armed. Two servants rode with the wagon, the rest was mounted on horses.

In the evening a creek had to be forded and Dr. Manly of Rutersville offered his assistance.[38] At 10 P.M. a pair of his oxen arrived. The caravan spent the night in front of his house, 10 miles from Nassau. One of our men, the cook, became sick during our arrival.

17 July. The wagon, damaged crossing the creek, required repair. This delayed our departure until 8 A.M. Everyone's health was excellent. We arrived in LaGrange on the Colorado [River] at 10:30 A.M. Purchased provisions. The town is ideally located, at the center of the actual population of Texas. There are several businesses that carry a poor choice of merchandise at a very steep price. Terrible heat. Departed at 4 o'clock, crossed over the Colorado. The trail through the bottoms was difficult for our mules. The scenery changed. A splendid view, a magnificent valley at our feet ringed by neighboring hills. Looked for the home of Brookfield who is Fordtran's stepfather.[39] Arrived there at 8 o'clock and for the night camped in front of his house. Great hospitality. Today the caravan covered only 14 miles.

18 July. Departed at 5 A.M. Crossed the small Navidad River at 10 A.M. It has good water and is not deep during the summer.

Steep embankments, oaks of various kinds, different kinds of nut trees. Only a few fruit trees, however, the late frost destroyed what little there was. Difficulties in crossing over but the mules managed it. Since the morning we have put behind us 18 miles. Continued on the trail at 3 P.M. The Commissioners wanted to buy a draft horse but the asking price horrified them. Reached Mixon Creek. The wagon got stuck in mud so that it was unable to be pulled out. Earlier, it had turned over in another creek. The guide was sent off to find a pair of oxen. When Indians let themselves be seen in the valley, concern arose over an ambush by them. Camp was made next to the creek. The night was peaceful, interrupted only by the howling of the wolves. The guide did not return.

19 July. No help arrived. At 5 A.M. the wagon was unloaded, lifted out of the mud, reloaded, and the journey continued. Men were posted in the lead, the rear and to the sides. The rear guard noted the Indians inspecting our last camp site. Two miles down the trail we met our guide with an American who led two oxen. Now the mules became mounts for the two men who rode in the wagon. In this fashion we arrived at Clark's place at 11 A.M. He is a Catholic priest serving the settlements along the Lavaca River.[40] We crossed this river without any problem. During the summer, this river, as is the case with many others in Texas, carries little water; however, when it rains, it rises swiftly. The riverbed was rocky and sandy. We met the Reverend Bishop Claudiopolis, Apostolic head of Texas.[41] Damage to the wagon forced us to take a two-day rest here. The springs were tightened and the wagon put back together. An additional mule was acquired to help pull the wagon. The guide from Nassau is sent back and the American Smith hired to drive the wagon to San Antonio.

Along the Lavaca are 20 to 25 small settlements. Almost all are inhabited by American Catholics from Missouri. The Catholic priest appears to have a strong as well as beneficial influence upon them. It seems that Catholics are easy to lead. It would be nice, if in the beginning the Society could send only Catholics to settle this land.

The good Bishop will accompany our expedition to San Antonio. Since he knows everybody, he can be of great assistance to us as well as help us in reaching agreements with land owners. We purchased provisions for the trip. The style in which we travel and the manner of our fellow travelers only raises our expenses.

21 July. Departed Clark's farm at 8:30 A.M. Rode through an expansive prairie that had numbers of turkeys and wild horses; there were hills of a good height between the Lavaca and the Guadalupe River. We covered 20 miles without any serious incidents. Camped on Becker's Farm.[42]

22 July. Left at 6 A.M. The mules had disappeared but the guide found them. Traveled 15 miles. Gonzales, a small town on the San Marcos River, looks run-down. It was ravaged by the [Texas] war of independence. Bought a few provisions at rather high prices. It was impossible for our mules to pull the wagon across the San Marcos. Thanks to the bishop's intervention a pair of oxen belonging to Johnston[43] were hitched to the wagon—and we were across the river. Spent the night at King's place[44] on the Guadalupe, 6 miles from Gonzales. We still pay dearly because of our prince's title. Room without board cost us 8 dollars.

23 July. Departed at 6 A.M. Crossed the Natchez, Mill and Geronimo Creeks. The conditions of the creeks are all the same. Not much water during the summer, steep embankments, difficult crossing for a wagon pulled by mules. After 27 miles arrived in Seguin at 4 P.M. A rest was needed by men as well as beast. Forded the Guadalupe; a fourth of the party camped at Flores' place.[45]

The doctor took care of the sick during the journey. The Guadalupe River is one of the prettiest rivers in Texas. The water is deep enough to mirror the blue sky. Major Auphin,[46] a landowner along the Guadalupe, drifted on a raft loaded with cotton the length of the river to Lavaca Bay. The navigation of the Guadalupe is a great discovery for this region. If it is really possible, it offers a great transportation opportunity.

Looked around Seguin. A small town of 5 or 6 homes, it is spread out, has a beautiful location. Water is obtained from the Guadalupe River and numerous springs which flow strongly. Fresh water abounds. The Mexican language prevails in Seguin. Garcia's[47] land is 3 miles from Seguin. Flores and Navarro,[48] who are important landowners here, remarked that this is one of the prettiest areas.

Atmospheric observations: 90 degrees at 10 A.M., 92 degrees at noon, 94 degrees at 3 P.M. The Mexican people are preferable to Americans; they are honest, polite, hard-working, and hospitable.

Hired a Mexican guide from Flores.

25 July. At 5 A.M. said good-bye to Señor Flores. It was 33 miles to San Antonio. Rumors went around that Indians had been seen. Everyone was armed and prepared. The pace is increased on the trail. The Colonial Director and the Bishop did not share the others' fear. Our party crossed the Cibolo, Santa Clara, and the San Antonio without incident. In, at times, suffocating heat, we arrived in town at 2:30 P.M.

Hot wind, like the Sirocco,[49] blew across the burned-over prairie and carried with it hot ashes. Not a single Indian was spotted. Wild game. Splendid farms. A well-constructed irrigation system around the town. The Commissioners decided to rent a house in San Antonio and make it their headquarters. From here they will travel throughout the country, looking for the best areas and making contracts for the lands. Castro arrived in San Antonio 8 hours ahead of us. From Washington to Gonzales he was accompanied by just one person, from there to San Antonio there were five. Mexicans travel this road without any fear from danger. Without protesting about this, seven individuals accompanied Castro to his land grant. His immigrants are in the worst shape possible and for this reason do not want to follow him to his grant.

26 July. The Commissioners visited the County Surveyor to have a look at the county map. This map is inaccurate and poor. Colonel Hayes[50] promised us all the necessary information. He expects momentarily the return of his assistant James[51] along with Castro.

The Bishop is busy calling on the landowners along the Medina River, encouraging them to cede some of their land to the Society.

Castro's immigrants who are mostly French from the Alsace, want to join the German colony [Society]. Many are sick and complain bitterly about their predicament.

Dr. Mayer looks after all the sick. In their gratitude the Alsatians are becoming Germans and look upon the Society as their own.

27 July. The Bishop joined the Commissioners on the ride and showed them the land surrounding San Antonio. The area around Mission San Jose[52] is magnificent and if it were not new, the Commissioners would have tried to situate their first settlement there. Buildings and the mission church are already established which could form the center of the colony. It would give the [colonization] a timely as well as nice sparkle.

28 July. Business cannot be discussed on Sundays. Catholics spent the day praying while the rest drink. The Colonial Director visited with Senator Smith[53] to get his opinion regarding the establishment of our first settlement on our land, that is before Congress extends our land grant. A sensible and intelligent man, he is of the opinion that we should wait until the concession is renewed before we undertake anything on that land. On the basis of this sensible advice the commissioners decided to talk to the various landowners. The Society has to be sure that it can have ready a settlement for the first group of immigrants. Wrote to the Committee.[54]

29 July. The Commissioners had planned to leave and inspect the land assigned to them but were delayed for two reasons. First, it was necessary to have the surveyor along who presently is traveling with Castro and second, they wanted to complete the contracts with the landowners. The Colonial Director considers Cassiano's lands[55] located between the San Antonio [River] and Cibolo [Creek] as important to the Society. This land is also irrigated by both streams. Here the settlers can establish themselves to their advantage as well as that of the Society. Roughly 80 miles from the Gulf of Mexico and 40 miles from San Antonio, this settlement would be an ideal stopping place for the expeditions. It would no longer be necessary to store large amounts of provisions at the harbor. Should something happen during a trip, whether above or below the confluence of the rivers, the settlement on the Cibolo could come quickly to give assistance. From the commercial point of view also, this place would become of importance in the future. Traveling from Laredo, the Mexicans will have a shorter trip to this place than to San Antonio.

The Commissioner-General does not share this view. He thinks it imperative that the immigrants be brought as quickly as possible to the nearest section of the land grant. The Colonial Director and the Bishop continue their negotiations with Cassiano.

McMullen,[56] another landowner on the Medina [River], is in a hurry. He owns 22 miles of land adjoining our property, some is surrounded by ours. He seems ready to negotiate but has some obligations. The Bishop is kind enough to take care of these negotiations. McMullen authorized the Bishop to offer his land to the Society with the stipulation that it will advance him a loan of $1,000, using the property as security.

30 July. The commissioners met with McMullen at the Bishop's residence. They are willing to loan him the requested sum providing the Society approves of it. An investigation of the land deed revealed that the property is in litigation but at the same time all indications as well as legal aspects point in McMullen's favor. The Colonial Director determined to close a deal with Cassiano and McMullen before Castro returns.

31 July. Additional investigation of McMullen's situation convinces us that success is around the corner; however, closing of these contracts is such a slow process that Castro has had time to return. He inspected McMullen's land and found it to be beautiful, very fertile, and well situated. It is located 18 miles from San Antonio, on the Medina River with excellent bottom soil on both sides of the river.

After his return, Castro's first call was on McMullen; he wants the land. As a result of this visit, McMullen has second thoughts. He demands from us $2,000 and requests that our immigrants settle on a portion of his land. This new development demands good and proper steps and not hesitation and then action.

Because of differing opinions among the Commissioners this wonderful and great opportunity was lost. We could have secured 10 to 12 miles of the best land, most of it located within our grant.

We could have used the land as were our intentions. Now we have to avoid McMullen's new demands. Still, it has to be mentioned that McMullen apparently is hesitating over a contract with Castro. Perhaps he will approach us again. In the meantime the Commissioners decided to continue their negotiations with Cassiano and they will meet with him tomorrow.

We were visited by the chief of the Lipan Indians. This tribe lives in the vicinity of San Antonio. He left us, with an invitation directed to his highest chief, to visit us. In situations like this one, the Prince's title is advantageous to the Society. Eventually the Prince will have stature among these tribes.

1 August. Visited with Cassiano. He agreed to negotiate with the Society. This Mexican can be trusted. He can offer only 3 miles of land but is busy pulling together the other sections of his land which would bring it to a total of 7 to 8 miles. He asked time until the 5th so he can pull it together. McMullen, on his visit to the Bishop, reported that Castro is ready to accept his demands but that he still preferred negotiating with the Society.

In this matter the Commissioners have no authority. Besides, it seems unwise to buy land at a time when large quantities of land can be gotten for practically nothing. We simply let Castro do what he wants to do and hope that McMullen will come back to us.

Today we started on our first inspection trip. The Prince's head and body ache. A rest will put him back in better shape.

2 August. This morning the chief of the Lipan Indians visited us. We invited the Indians to breakfast. If their promises can be trusted, we have become their friends. We gave this reception all the glamour possible. The Prince wore his medals; the weapons were artistically hung. The Bishop wore his violet vestment and served as our translator. The Prince was introduced as a great chief from across the great ocean where a large tribe follows his commands, that we desired to live in friendship and peace with the Indians and were ready to fight along side them or fight against them, depending on their attitude toward us.

The Bishop's speech had its effect. The Indians looked upon the Prince as a great chief. Soon we will visit them in their camp.

They want to send some of their chiefs to the Comanche and invite them for a treaty making. Although one hears their promises of friendship, one should keep the rifle at hand. They were given cheap presents which made them happy.

Castro had another conference with McMullen this morning. The outcome is not known to us.

The baggage and other items that we left behind in Galveston still have not arrived. In regard to our messages and the arrival and the posting of our letters, we expect to have certain difficulties and delays.

This evening our guide had bilious fever. He was immediately attended to by our physician and the crisis passed.

3 August. We are still in San Antonio and lose precious time. Castro, in the meantime, travels about, reaches agreements with his neighbors, buys oxen, cows, etc., and makes preparations to move to his grant in eight days. The willpower of one is better than that of two. By now we should have inspected our land grant as well as that of Cassiano's. At the present time, our surroundings are detrimental to our cause. The Colonial Director is opposed to making contracts with Castro's immigrants until Castro has gone to his grant and we know who will follow him. Several reasons support this opinion. First, it avoids giving our competitor grounds to complain about us and to depreciate us in the opinion of the Congress. Second, having exhausted all their own means, these immigrants would require advances for the next 18 months. Third, it would require giving them land set aside for new immigrants coming from Europe. Also they would have to be paid for their work. Fourth, until we are certain which portion of the land we wanted to settle, we could not stop them from buying livestock, which right now is an unnecessary expense.

4 August. The Commissioners left San Antonio at 4 P.M. to inspect their land grant. Rather than take us directly to our land grant, the guides took a circuitous route. It was not the right trail for us. After covering a distance of 10 miles we camped overnight on Leon Creek. We traveled through beautiful prairie land, magnificent country. Continued on the same trail, inspected the less desirable portion of McMullen's land. The character of land on which mesquites and abundant grass grow, is chalky, the soil is deep and of black color, ideal for cotton. The bottom lands of the Medina that we passed through are shallow, have good stands of trees and the water is clear and flowing and more shallow than deep. During the raining season the river rises 10 to 12 feet. The embankments are steep and rocky and covered with various kinds of growths, a type of soil that is difficult for cultivation but excellent for grazing land.

6 August. Since we traveled to inspect the grant land, the Colonial Director wanted to see the area around the Arroyo Seco as well as the other side of the Quihi. Rather than angling off to the right, the guide continued along the course of the Medina. This left us on the McMullen land. At 11 A.M., we were only 2 miles from Quihi Creek, when the Prince decided to go no further but to return to the Medina. Our guides reported that the Quihi Creek was dry. This contradicted the surveyor's statement who reported that this arroyo had rather extensive water surfaces. Again, we crossed the Medina by boat. Here the river is open, there are not many trees; however, upstream and downstream it is forested. This was still land belonging to McMullen.

7 August. We were on the trail and upon the Colonial Director's request crossed McMullen's land in a straight line to Potranca Creek, the first boundary of our land. The land between this creek and the Medina is generally very good. There are a few hills, rocky but with a growth of mesquite grass. There are rocks to build with and good land for farming. The Potranca is a small creek that is presently without water. Arrived in San Antonio at 6 P.M. This first and ill-planned trip gave the Commissioners no information about the worth of their land.

The Colonial Director made this brief comment: the land along the Medina is wonderful, very fertile on both sides of the river. There is sufficient wood for the planned buildings and for firewood. Trees in the hills are insufficient but some of them can be useful. Mills can be constructed at certain spots on the Medina River. The area that we inspected is owned by McMullen. The Society would be pleased with it. Settlements built there at certain distances from each other would complement the whole.

The temperature between 5 A.M. and 4 P.M. ranged from 82 to 96 degrees.

8 August 1844. At today's conference the Commissioners discussed the advantage of buying land outright over making contracts with the individual landowners. The opportunity for the Society to obtain free land gives it certainly a higher value, depending on the land owners. On the other hand, the special relationship with the landowners aids in the development of the colony's property as it also raises the value of the land that the owner retains. In this case the Society has a tremendous outlay, its activity is isolated and the sale of this land brings a lesser profit in comparison with the first, the "redemption plan."[57] No decision was reached one way or the other. The rumors about a Mexican invasion[58] brought our activity to a stop and the Commissioners were forced to postpone until Monday the 12th their trip to the Cibolo where they plan to establish the first colony.

Castro has not yet closed a deal with McMullen who constantly makes new demands, a situation created by the competition between the two colonies. The Commissioners will not act on this matter until their return by which time Castro should have departed. Maybe then it will be easier to come to an agreement with McMullen. Castro suggested that we send our first group of immigrants to his land. This is a clever way to give his colony more credence but the commissioners did not fall for it.

9 Aug. 1844. Castro complained that persons from the Prince's party were swaying his immigrants to come over to our camp. He bases this on an incident, especially regretful to us, because it gives validity to his complaint. This happened on Princess Sophie's birthday. Our Prince wished to celebrate this day properly. A cannon salute was fired and money distributed among Castro's people. Naturally, these people's enthusiasm was great. When Castro heard the cheers, he interpreted that situation differently and hurriedly wrote a statement, which was endorsed by six other persons, in which he claimed that the Society was luring away his immigrants with money. This letter was mailed to Washington [on-the-Brazos]. When this development came to the Colonial Director's attention, he wrote immediately to the Secretary of State to defuse any unfavorable impressions upon the Society. The Prince's behavior and generosity I consider to be in error.

The unanimity which at first existed between the Commissioner-General and the Colonial Director is slowly dissolving. The Prince and I do not share similar views. Bad advice can put us in a dangerous situation.

10 Aug. 1844. Rumors about a [Mexican] invasion increase. Many Americans are leaving. One, a Mr. Ridel, offered us his home which we accepted.

As requested by the Colonial Director, the two Society representatives would adhere strictly to the [Society's] instructions which they had received. He is of the opinion that if we fail to abide by them the advancement of the Society's goal would only be hampered. The Commissioner-General appeared to concur with this observation.

11 August. Received a polite letter from the President with good news and for the Society most welcome arrangements. It refers to information which will come to us from the Secretary of State in response to the letter of 10 July mailed by the Colonial Director to the government. Included with the President's letter was a newspaper article which talks about the Society's program [in Texas]. The newspaper, dated 22 June, is from Liverpool. The representatives did not receive a copy of this paper because for some unknown reason they failed to receive any mail from Europe.

12 August. The Colonial Director wrote the President and the Secretary of State. The former he congratulated for having regained his health and to express our appreciation for his favorable view [toward the Society] and the latter he asked to let us know as soon as possible of the President's decision [regarding the Society matter].

Castro wrote Congress again today regarding certain promises made that would give his immigrants work. We will not leave for Cassiano's land today. Tomorrow Colonel Hays will place at our disposal two or three of his men. The rumors of an invasion have dissipated. A group of 16 Mexicans arrived this morning to make purchases. A messenger was sent to Lavaca regarding our luggage and provisions.

A man from Colorado whose republican views apparently affected his mind said yesterday this about the Society: "Why are these strangers here? These princes come here only to enslave us as they do in Europe. To hell with them." We need to avoid everything that would offend them which should be easy for us. This man's opinion when shared by many other like-minded individuals could be the beginning of an angry opposition.

13 August. Finished preparations to visit Cassiano's land. It is located between Cibolo Creek and the San Antonio River. Made sure that this time it would be a successful inspection trip. We agreed to start with Carameal's [?][59] land and follow the Cibolo to the confluence with the San Antonio River. There are too many individuals in our party who are really unnecessary.

14 August. We left San Antonio at 6 A.M. and reached Seguin's[60] ranch, a distance of 36 miles. We rode through magnificent land and visited many settlements along the San Antonio River. They are totally isolated. There is not much corn and the cotton is fair. The cattle look healthy and are of a large type. Everything is lifeless, without organization. The war of 1832[61] ruined the landowners.

15 August. Left at 6 A.M. and arrived on Carament's [?] land at 11 A.M. The road from San Antonio to this point is good with the exception of two crossings over creeks. During the winter it's supposed to be a difficult task. Oxen overcome this difficulty regularly. A coach with one or two horses could carry the mail, etc., as it is done in Europe, also without any problems. Visited magnificent country sites. Caravat's [?] land has a large quantity of stone suitable for building material, mesquite wood, many weeds which are not as good as mesquite grass. Plot No. 7 on Cassiano's map[62] is of much better quality. Mesquite grass, mesquite wood, several types of oaks which are good for fencing and as fire wood as well as many Mexican dwellings. It is a beautiful plateau of about 1500 acres of grass land that includes Cibolo Creek with a good crossing.

At noon we stopped to rest the horses and let them graze. Used this opportunity to investigate the arroyo on both sides. Water is everywhere, at some places it undercuts the bank and at other places the gravel is two feet deep. The embankment is high but not high enough in the rainy season to prevent overflow and flooding, however, there is no fear of that on Cassiano's land. As I mentioned earlier, it is situated on a kind of high plateau. The river flows strongly, is full of mussels and rich with mother-of-pearl. Along the embankments grow trees of various kinds like cottonwood or Carolina poplar, pecans, hickory, mulberry, etc.—These trees are not in abundance everywhere. They would be sufficient only for a moderate number of settlers. On the other side of the arroyo, about 3 miles distance, grow plenty of oak trees.

At 3:30 we were on the trail again. The Prince, Cassiano, my servant and I were five minutes ahead of the rest. Under normal circumstances we should have followed the trail; however, the Prince, perhaps tired or listening to the advice of his companions, completely changed directions. He asked us to go on while he would wait for the rest of the group. Cassiano and I continued into the country and woods. About an hour later we looked for the group. We noticed that they proceeded to the southwest, rather than the south, without a doubt to take a short cut to the San Antonio River to reach the place called Capote. We followed the trail to meet up with them. This was an unnecessary effort. The group had stopped during my absence and decided that further inspection of the land was unnecessary because with part of the land seen, everything about the property was known. For this reason the decision was made to proceed directly to Capote. The responsibility given me by the Society was to inspect these lands and I found myself bound to remind the Prince of this and attempt to change his mind. My justified remarks were received with haughtiness. After a spirited exchange of words the Prince said to me: "Our horses are tired and so are we. We cannot continue like this, we will march to Capote."

[Here the diary skips to page 121. Remark on the margin: "The rest is missing, Cappes."][63]

"Once we get there, we will continue riding and see where the Cibolo joins the San Antonio River." To my remark that it is impossible to inspect the land in such a manner and that it would be better to go to Capote, the Prince shouted: "Gentlemen, to Capote!" He gave the spurs to his horse and disappeared with the doctor and one of his men without knowing where he was going. In the belief that Cassiano knew his way around I let him take charge. An hour later our small group, that is Cassiano, my servant and I, arrived at a large and magnificent area of rich land with beautiful surroundings. "This is Capote," informed us Cassiano. In vain did we shout and fire our rifles. There was only deep silence. We tried unsuccessfully to find the other two [groups]. Cassiano lost his head, we were without provisions. The childish fear of Indians terrified my companions. We had to find the main trail. I will not relate of our riding back and forth, of the natural obstacles, the arroyos that we had to cross, to the west, east and north. In addition, we were surrounded by a large prairie fire that we had to pass through. At 10 in the evening we stopped at a dry arroyo so we and the animals could rest. Without food and water, tired and concerned over our predicament, we spent a very bad night.

16 August. After we became oriented in the morning, we found the San Antonio River and reached Seguin's ranch, close where we had spent the night of the 14th. It was 5 o'clock, we were dead-tired, starved and had only warm water in our bellies. During our entire time on the trail the temperature was between 92 and 96 degrees. No one had arrived, although an hour earlier we met our group. Nobody had seen the Prince. They had looked for him without any luck. A group of 8 or 10 of us were in the process of going in search for him when, to our joy, he showed up. Of course, he was lost. He looked right and left for the Capote and finally found his way to Seguin's ranch. There he arrived very tired and starved, the same as I. All that we accomplished was a leisurely ride but not much in regard to inspecting the land. As long as we continue in this manner, the Society's business is in poor hands. Instead of handling ourselves business-like and acting like local people, we move around like children. We travel about the way in which Europeans take their leisurely walks. At one time we ride in a walk, then we change to a gait, and more often ride in gallop. As a conscientious person I understand the importance of our mission and therefore deplore the two unsuccessful trips, to the Medina River and to the San Antonio River. I imagine that all future trips will be similar and our trips will be a waste. I deplore this situation but there is nothing that I can do. The Prince accepts all responsibilities and appears to acknowledge my advice but then, the financial means are at his disposal and not mine. I cannot give orders if I am not the man with the money.

17 August. The next day we started back for San Antonio, that is, today at 5 o'clock.

18 August. There was no news from Europe in today's mail. The contact between New Orleans and Galveston is temporarily severed. The two steamers that normally provide this service left for New York. In the meantime sailing vessels travel between these two cities. I acknowledged the offer by the representative from General Mercer, general manager of Peters & Co.,[64] who is willing to let us have some of his land. It is located in the Cross Timbers on the Red River; however, it is too far from our lands for us to accept the offer.

19 August. The lack of outside news gave the Prince an idea which I vainly try to discourage. He wants to send a special messenger from San Antonio to Galveston to see if any mail had arrived for us. The doctor may be this special messenger. I opposed this idea that for the sake of the Society is needless, groundless, burdensome as well as a silly expense.

Needless, because of the arrangements made the mail will reach San Antonio faster than by special messenger; groundless because if any letters arrived in Galveston our representative there would forward them immediately. Every Sunday we receive mail from that port. Burdensome because such a venture will cost the Society 6 Piaster (300 Flourins)[65] and almost silly because any letters expected from Europe, if they are really there, will be dated no later than July 4, and therefore will not contain much of importance to us.

If my judgment is right, and based on the rumors going around town, this messenger, should he find no letters in Galveston, is to proceed by any means and at any cost to New Orleans. When this plan was brought to my attention I fought strongly against it. The outlay of 1,000 Flourins for one letter is a serious mistake, especially when there is no justifiable need. If the Society's funds cannot be handled any better, then the combined expenses will not only exceed my estimate but also the Society's resources.

Although I did not have the opportunity to inspect Cassiano's land, as he had asked, we did agree to send our first group of immigrants that way. For this reason I completed a few transactions today which will allow us finally to begin with our task. I purchased 8 pair of oxen but rather than pay $50 as per my estimate I obtained them for $16. I have no doubts that my calculations are correct but I did not include any unnecessary expenditures and housekeeping cost. I no longer want to stick my nose in that matter, after I indicated what I considered to be the correct course. My suggestions are ignored. The daily housekeeping costs must run 12 to 15 dollars. I asked, without results, for the expenses so I could add them to the ledger and report them to the Committee. The Prince responded that it was unnecessary to make any accounting before the credit was gone.

20 August. I considered it as my duty to prevent, if possible, the departure of the messenger. The Prince told me that he anticipated this and that he would assume all responsibilities for his action.

At this time I am busy closing a contract with Cassiano. He will turn over to us half of his land with the stipulation that we settle thirty or so families there. I looked at the deed and it appears to be in order. The land is well situated. He and I will discuss certain points tomorrow and I hope to bring this matter to a conclusion. My desire is to depart soon from here and get to work. The Prince suggests that we send off workers to prepare quarters for us and the party.

That is a wrong step which only creates unnecessary expenses and doubles the work. I am against it. Really, we act like children and not like adults. I do not know and do not understand why the

Society chose me to be a companion for our amiable Prince Solms. I myself prefer the Hotel "zum Rhein" (the "Rheinischen Hof") over the town of San Antonio de Bexar. Business has to be conducted in a business-like manner. The Prince was not born to handle such. He is too supercilious and has no experience with the avariciousness of the people that we have to deal with here and he does not understand how to see and look after business with closed eyes. As a representative of the German people his presence here is of interest but as for our work, our expenses, our activities, and our future relations his presence can be detrimental. I really regret that I do not have at hand the Colonial Statutes[66] which contain a great deal of good advice. Here I could find many solutions to my problems. However, I will make a decision and then my peculiar and creative mind will prove at what I have hinted. On the other hand, when the Prince is present I give him precedent out of respect for his person and his rank. What the cost of that is to the Society, we can figure out later.

21 August. For our work, I engaged 2 two-wheeled Mexican carts which cost about $15 each. They will do the job until our wagons arrive. I and two others, we split the expense among us three, sent a messenger to Lavaca to check if our baggage had arrived. He returned this morning, and, indeed, the baggage is at Ewing's[67] in Lavaca but our instruments and provisions have not yet arrived from New Orleans. Without a doubt, we will have to make a few purchases here, so that we will not lose time. I do hope, however, that within 12 days all items will have arrived on our property.

Castro's expedition arrived in Galveston on July 1,[68] with Bexar as its destination but the people are in bad shape. Every immigrant is sick, one died on our land on the Cibolo. Castro hopes to travel to the Quihi in a few days. One person stated, "Only a few people are inclined to go with him." Others say, "Many will follow him." Castro continues his transactions with McMullen.

Tomorrow I will complete this diary, so it can be mailed to the Committee.

22 August. We reached an agreement with Cassiano. I wrote the contract in French, it will be translated into English and signed tomorrow. This contract assures the Society 4,700 acres of land. In accordance with the partition of the land, the Society will introduce 60 families and help establish them as farmers. The land is situated on the [San Antonio?] River and Cibolo Creek. My report will outline the plan, the way it will be carried out as well as give the Committee an insight to make its judgment.[69] That way it will know that the land in question extends 12,500 meters on each side from both rivers. When this land is divided into 120 lots of 100 feet by 500 ft, each of the 120 families receives 15 acres of land to build their house on. In this partition Cassiano keeps for himself 60 lots where he can settle families. His land encompasses a total of 9,400 rather than 4,700 acres [in places illegible]. Each immigrant will receive 75 acres which totals to 9,000 acres and added to that are 400 acres reserved for the town. Among the immigrants there will certainly be artisans who will prefer to live in town, so that approximately 80 immigrant [families] will settle on the land. I am in the process of arranging for provisions at reasonable prices. I was offered 600 male sheep at 60 cents a head. Tomorrow I will make the purchase.

Certain land owners offered their land for the same price as Cassiano. Once work begins I will have at my disposal 12 to 15 miles of land, most of it bordering our land. A great deal of this success I owe to the support from the Bishop. Our first settlement will cause a move to the Cibolo. Fifteen Mexican families want to leave for their lands at the same time as we do. This will lend strength to our settlement and give our work a stamp of sincerity. Although our settlement on the Cibolo is limited, it will be advantageous to the Society beginning with the first year, actually from the moment that the first house is constructed and the first provisions have arrived.

The announced construction of a flour mill and a cotton gin will cause a large number of Mexicans in San Antonio, Seguin, Victoria, and Goliad to plant corn and cotton.

By the next harvest the mills will be in operation and the Society can expect an income between 6,000 to 7,000 dollars the first year.

This beginning I consider to be a good omen.

I want to reiterate to the Committee: The rules for colonization based on my experience show clearly that for our business affairs to be guided correctly a firm and clever mind is needed.

Two heads with two different minds will not accomplish our goals. As Colonial Director I am obligated to act accordingly, or the Society will later criticize me. In any event, I want to act in its behalf.

San Antonio, August 22, 1844

Al. Bourgeois d'Orvanne
Colonial Director

---

[1] Solms's and d'Orvanne's diaries complement each other as well as share information in common. Whenever the latter situation is the case, the reader is referred to the endnote in the Solms's diary, in an effort to avoid duplication of similar information.

This translation by the editor is published with permission by the Center of American History, The University of Texas. The German text is found in the *Solms-Braunfels-Archives* (Vol. VIIILa, pp. 150–192).

[2] The diary leaves open to question if d'Orvanne wrote it during his travels with Solms or if he rewrote it in August, after being dismissed as Colonial Director, as a means to plead his case before the Society's directors in Germany.

[3] The Commissioners referred to here are the Commissioner-General Prince Solms and the Colonial Director Bourgeois d'Orvanne.

[4] French Vice-Consul (Henry Adolph) Cobb: see Chapter II, note 1.

[5] French Consul (Francois Guilbeau) Guillebeau in San Antonio: see Chapter II, note 24.

[6] Schmidt & Co. (of New Orleans): see Chapter I, note 29.

[7] Colonel (George Washington Hockley) Hinkley: see Chapter II, note 2.

[8] Dr. Levi Jones: see Chapter I, note 35.

[9] Colonel Williams: not certain if this was Samuel May Williams.

[10] Sheriff Smith: probably Henry M. Smythe (Hays, *Galveston*, p. 449).

[11] Consul (William) Kennedy: see Chapter, II, note 2.

[12] General-Consul Captain (Charles Elliot) Elliott: see Chapter IV, note 61.

[13] Buckingham (Palace, London). Although a constitutional monarchy, Queen Victoria took an active part in the government's affairs and her ministers consulted with her.

[14] Prince Albert, Queen Victoria's consort.

[15] Nassau [Farm] Plantation: see Chapter II, note 9.

[16] Washington-on-the-Brazos: see Chapter II, note 7.

[17] (Armand) Ducos: see Chapter I, note 28.

[18] Turkeim: identity unknown.

[19] (William K.) Hamblin: see Chapter II, note 6.

[20] Stevenson's on Bond Fish Creek: see Chapter II, note 6.

[21] Secretary of State: Anson Jones: see Chapter II, note 7.

[22] President Sam Houston: see Chapter II, note 7.

[23] Henry Castro: see Chapter I, note 33.

[24] Foster's plantation: probably James L. Farquhar; see Chapter II, note 8.

[25] Mandeville: probably Mount Vernon, see Chapter II, note 9.

[26] Mr. Lessely: identity unknown

[27] (Charles) Fordtran: see Chapter II, note 10.

[28] Dr. Mayer: probably Dr. Emil Meyer; see Chapter II, note 10.

[29] Bourgeois d'Orvanne's inventory: see section in Solms's diary on pages 45–51.

[30] Cummings Creek and Mill Creek: see Chapter III, note 8.

[31] (Ferdinand) Lindheimer: see Chapter II, note 12

[32] (Friedrich)Ernst: see Chapter II, note 12.

[33] Directorate: Society's directors in Germany.

[34] Denmann: see Chapter II, note 55.

[35] Society's land: this must be the Burgeois-Ducos land grant; see Chapter II, note 5.

[36] (Alphonse) de Saligny: see Chapter IV, note 54.

[37] Abbe Auger: probably Abbe Ogé; see Chapter II, note 3.

[38] Dr. (A. P.) Manly of Rutersville: see Chapter II, note 13.

[39] Actually Brookfield was Fordtran's father-in-law.

[40] Clark's settlement: Father Edward A. Clarke was the spiritual leader of this settlement of Catholics. Most of the families were of Maryland origin. After the Revolutionary War, as new lands opened in the West, Catholics from Maryland moved to Kentucky and some to Spanish Missouri. In the 1830s these groups began moving to Mexican Texas. See also Chapter II, note 18.

[41] Bishop Claudiopolis: Bishop Odin; see Chapter II, note 3.

[42] Becker's Farm: probably Charles Braches's Farm; see Chapter II, end-note 20.

[43] Johnston: identity unknown.

[44] (John G.) King: see Chapter II, note 21.

[45] (Manuel) Flores' place: Chapter II, note 22.

[46] Major Auphin: identity unknown.

[47] Garcia: identity unknown.

[48] (Jose Luciano) Navarro: see Chapter II, note 23.

[49] Sirocco: the terminology comes from the Mediterranean area. It denotes a hot oppressive wind from the Libyan deserts that blows chiefly in Italy and Sicily.

[50] Colonel (John Coffee "Jack" Hays) Hayes: see Chapter II, note 24.

[51] County Surveyor: probably John James; see Chapter II, note 34.

[52] Mission San José: see Chapter II, note 27.

[53] Senator Smith: probably John William Smith who represented Bexar County at the Seventh, Eighth and Ninth Congresses, 1842–1845 (*Biographical Directory of the Texan Conventions and Congresses*, Austin: Book Exchange, Inc., 1941 [?], p. 173).

[54] Committee: he may be referring to the Society's directors.

[55] (Jose) Cassiano: see Chapter II, note 24.

[56] (John) McMullen: see Chapter II, note 30.

[57] Redemption plan: whereby the Society would furnish the emigrant with money and provisions for the voyage and, as agreed upon, these individuals would repay this advance either in cash or in services within three years (Biesele, *German Settlements in Texas*, p. 97).

[58] After Mexico lost the Texas province to the Texians in 1836, it constantly threatened to invade the former province. In 1842 it made good the threat. It invaded San Antonio and carried as prisoners Anglo citizens of that city back to Mexico.

[59] Carameal: identity unknown.

[60] (Erasmo) Seguin; see Chapter II, note 42

[61] The war of 1832: the date should be 1836.

[62] Cassiano's map: In addition to his diary, Bourgeois d'Orvanne sent a report to the Society's directors in Germany. This report contains a map that shows landownership between Cibolo Creek and the San Antonio River. It is not clear whether or not this map is based on Cassiano's map (*Solms-Braunfels Archives*, Vol. VIIIa, p. 197).

[63] (Philip) Cappes: Society official in Germany.

[64] Charles Fenton Mercer (1778–1858) would by now be disassociated from the Peters Colony having received his own empresario contract in January 1844 for a colony located east of the Peters Colony (*New Handbook of Texas*, Vol. IV, p. 628).

[65] Piaster and Flourins: former European coins.

[66] Colonial Statues: "Constitution of the Society," adopted in March 1844, was published (pp. 29–37) with other Society documents in *Gesammelte Aktenstücke des Vereins zum Schutz deutscher Einwandere in Texas*

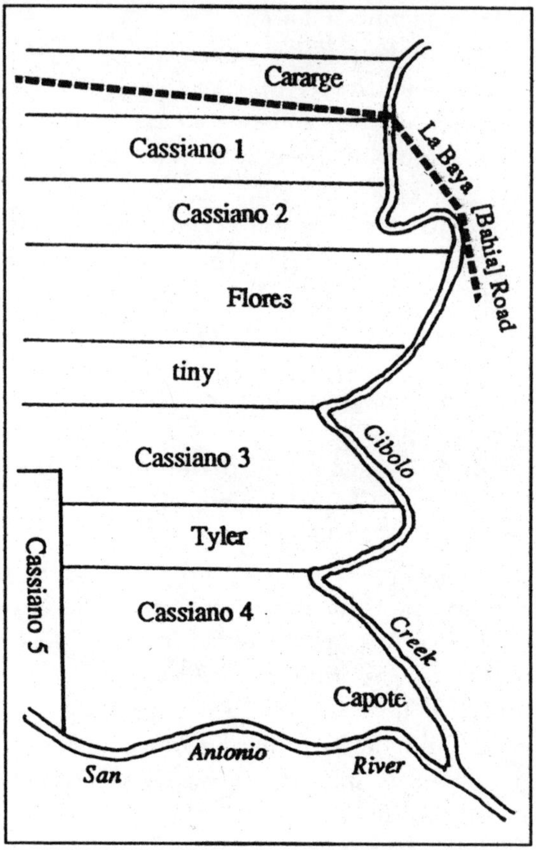

Map redrawn from *Solms-Braunfels Archives*, Vol. VIIILa, p. 197

[*Collected Documents of the Society for the Protection of German Immigrants in Texas*], Mainz, Germany: Verlag von Victor von Zabern, 1845. An English translation appears in Moritz Tiling's *History of The German Element in Texas* (Houston: M. Tiling, 1913), pp. 211–220; for additional information on the topic see Biesele, *German Settlements in Texas*, pp. 86–89.

[67] [William G.] Ewing: see Chapter IV, note 7.

[68] In regard to the fate of Castro's immigrants who arrived in Galveston in July 1844, see Chapter II, notes 29 and 39.

[69] In the report to the directors in Germany, Bourgeois d'Orvanne outlines his idea how the immigrants should be established in Texas (*Solms-Braunfels-Archives*, Vol. VIIILa, pp. 196–204).

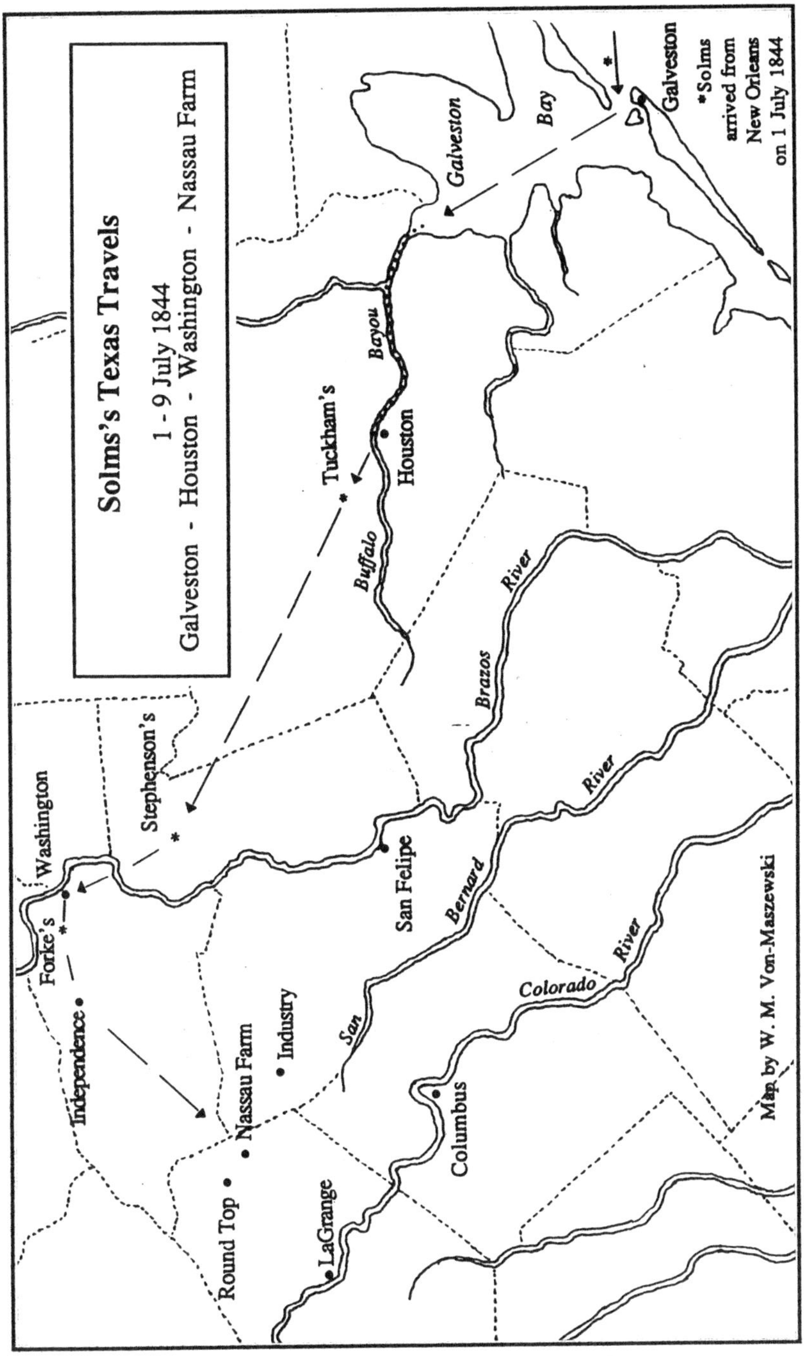
Solms's Texas Travels
1 - 9 July 1844
Galveston - Houston - Washington - Nassau Farm
Galveston Bay
Galveston
*Solms arrived from New Orleans on 1 July 1844
Buffalo Bayou
Tuckham's
Houston
Brazos River
San Bernard River
Colorado River
San Felipe
Stephenson's
Washington
Forke's
Independence
Nassau Farm
Industry
Round Top
LaGrange
Columbus
Map by W. M. Von-Maszewski

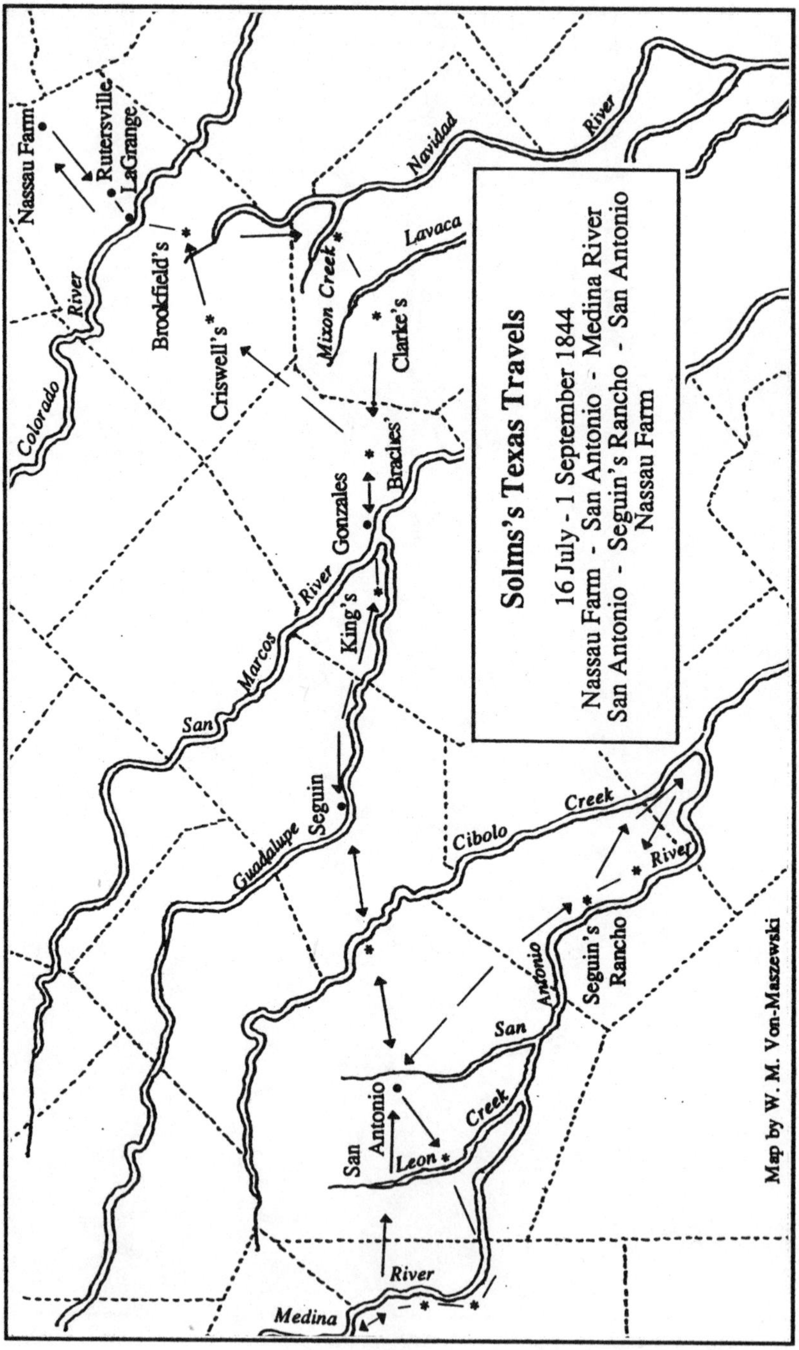

Solms's Texas Travels
16 July - 1 September 1844
Nassau Farm - San Antonio - Medina River
San Antonio - Seguin's Rancho - San Antonio
Nassau Farm
Nassau Farm
Rutersville
LaGrange
Colorado
River
Brookfield's
Criswell's
Navidad
River
Mixon Creek
Lavaca
Clarke's
Bracles'
Gonzales
San
Marcos
River
King's
Seguin
Guadalupe
Cibolo
Creek
River
Seguin's
Rancho
San
Antonio
San
Antonio
Creek
Leon
Medina
River
Map by W. M. Von-Maszewski

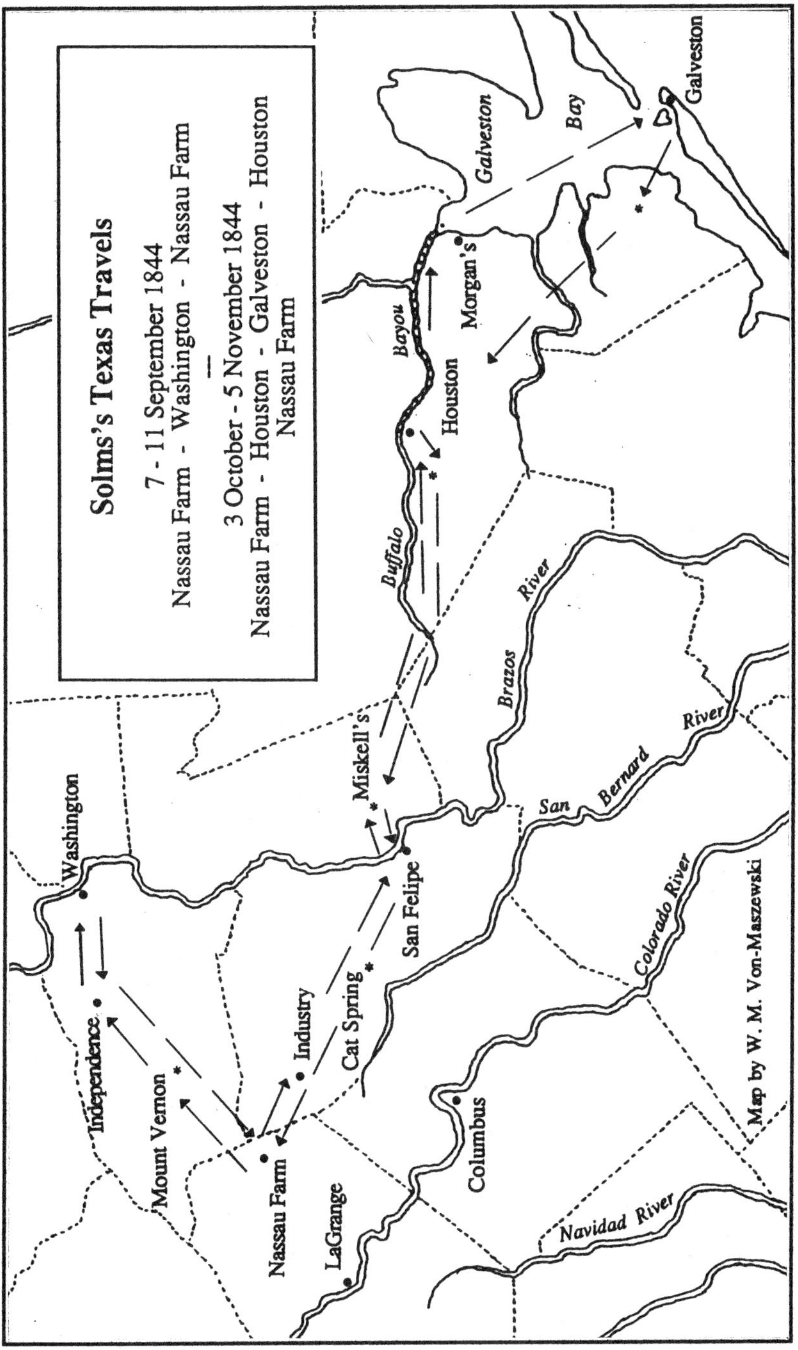
Solms's Texas Travels
7 - 11 September 1844
Nassau Farm - Washington - Nassau Farm
—
3 October - 5 November 1844
Nassau Farm - Houston - Galveston - Houston
Nassau Farm
Washington
Independence
Mount Vernon
Nassau Farm
LaGrange
Industry
Cat Spring
San Felipe
Miskell's
Columbus
Buffalo Bayou
Houston
Morgan's
Galveston Bay
Galveston
Brazos River
San Bernard River
Colorado River
Navidad River
Map by W. M. Von-Maszewski

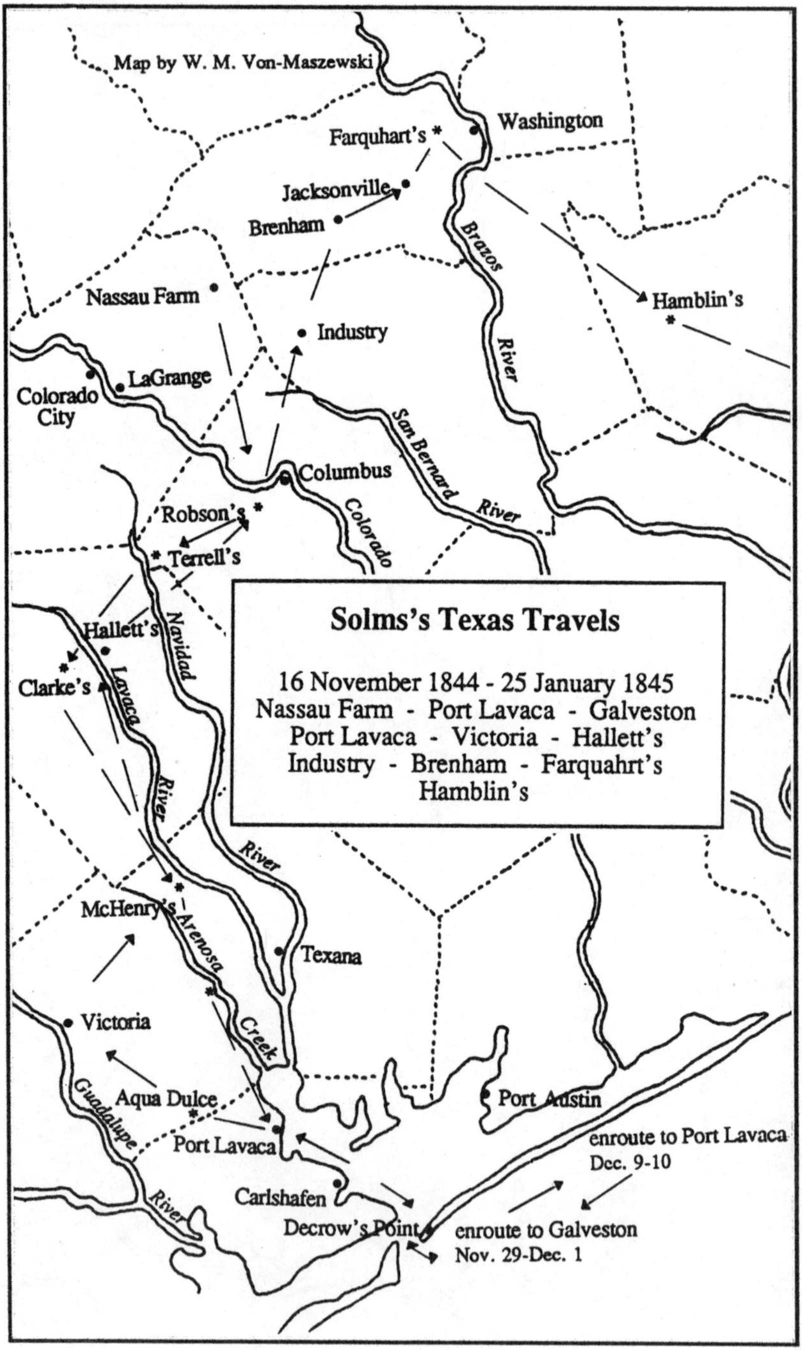
Map by W. M. Von-Maszewski
Washington
Farquhart's
Jacksonville
Brenham
Brazos
River
Hamblin's
Nassau Farm
Industry
Colorado City
LaGrange
San Bernard
River
Columbus
Colorado
Robson's
Terrell's
Hallett's
Navidad
Clarke's
Lavaca
River
River
McHenry's
Arenosa
Creek
Texana
Victoria
Guadalupe
River
Aqua Dulce
Port Lavaca
Carlshafen
Decrow's Point
Port Austin
enroute to Port Lavaca
Dec. 9-10
enroute to Galveston
Nov. 29-Dec. 1
Solms's Texas Travels
16 November 1844 - 25 January 1845
Nassau Farm - Port Lavaca - Galveston
Port Lavaca - Victoria - Hallett's
Industry - Brenham - Farquahrt's
Hamblin's

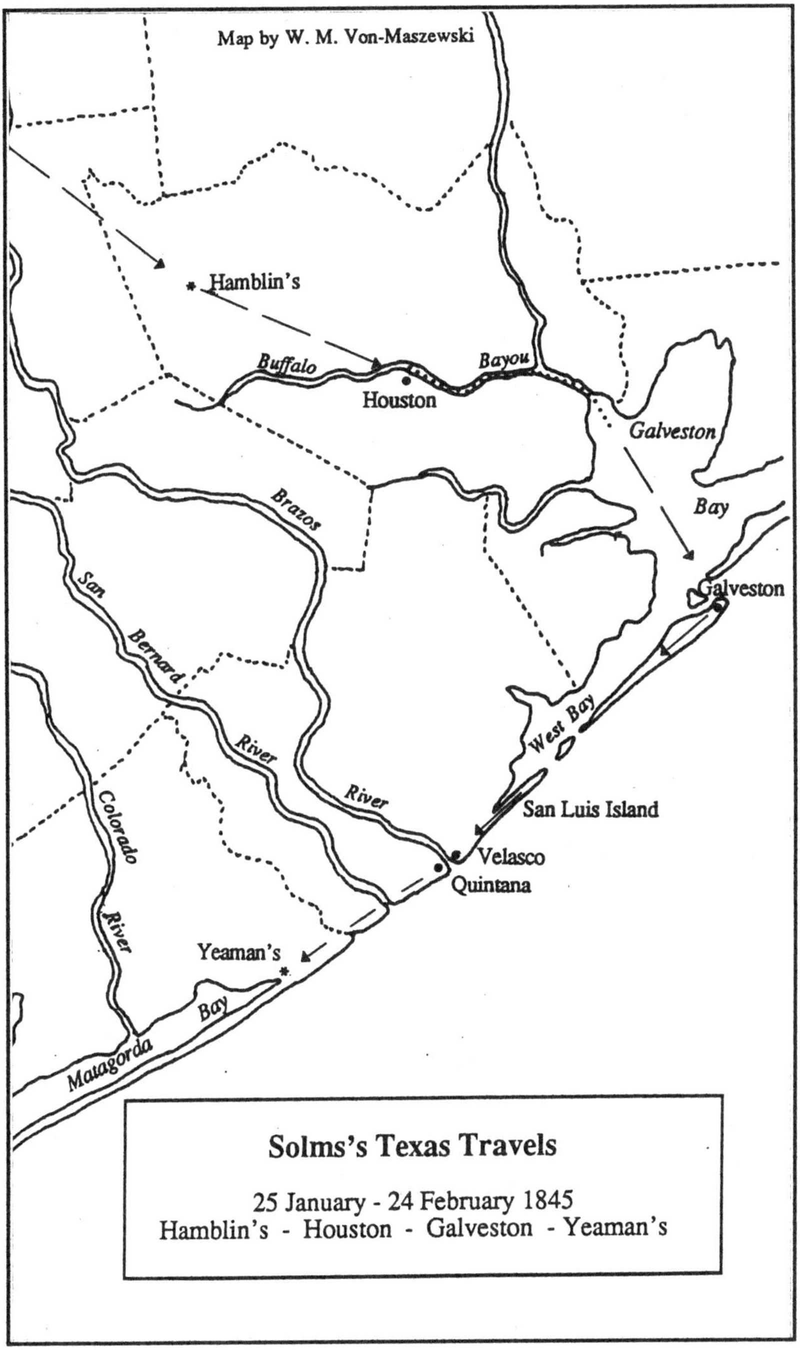
Map by W. M. Von-Maszewski
Hamblin's
Buffalo
Bayou
Houston
Galveston
Bay
Brazos
Galveston
San
Bernard
River
River
West Bay
San Luis Island
Velasco
Quintana
Colorado
River
Yeaman's
Bay
Matagorda
Solms's Texas Travels
25 January - 24 February 1845
Hamblin's - Houston - Galveston - Yeaman's

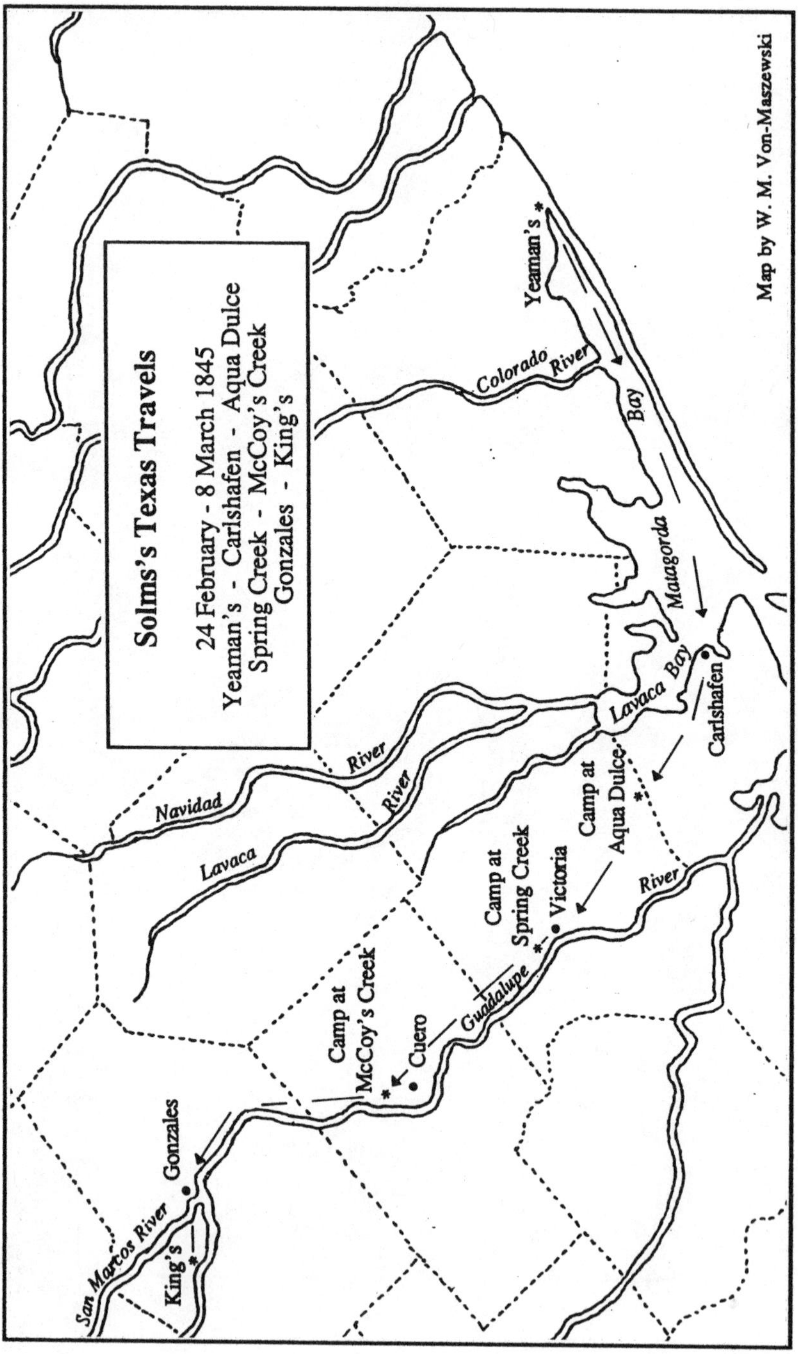
Solms's Texas Travels
24 February - 8 March 1845
Yeaman's - Carlshafen - Aqua Dulce
Spring Creek - McCoy's Creek
Gonzales - King's
Yeaman's
Colorado River
Matagorda Bay
Lavaca Bay
Carlshafen
Navidad River
Lavaca River
Camp at Aqua Dulce
Camp at Spring Creek
Victoria
Guadalupe River
Cuero
Camp at McCoy's Creek
Gonzales
San Marcos River
King's
Map by W. M. Von-Maszewski

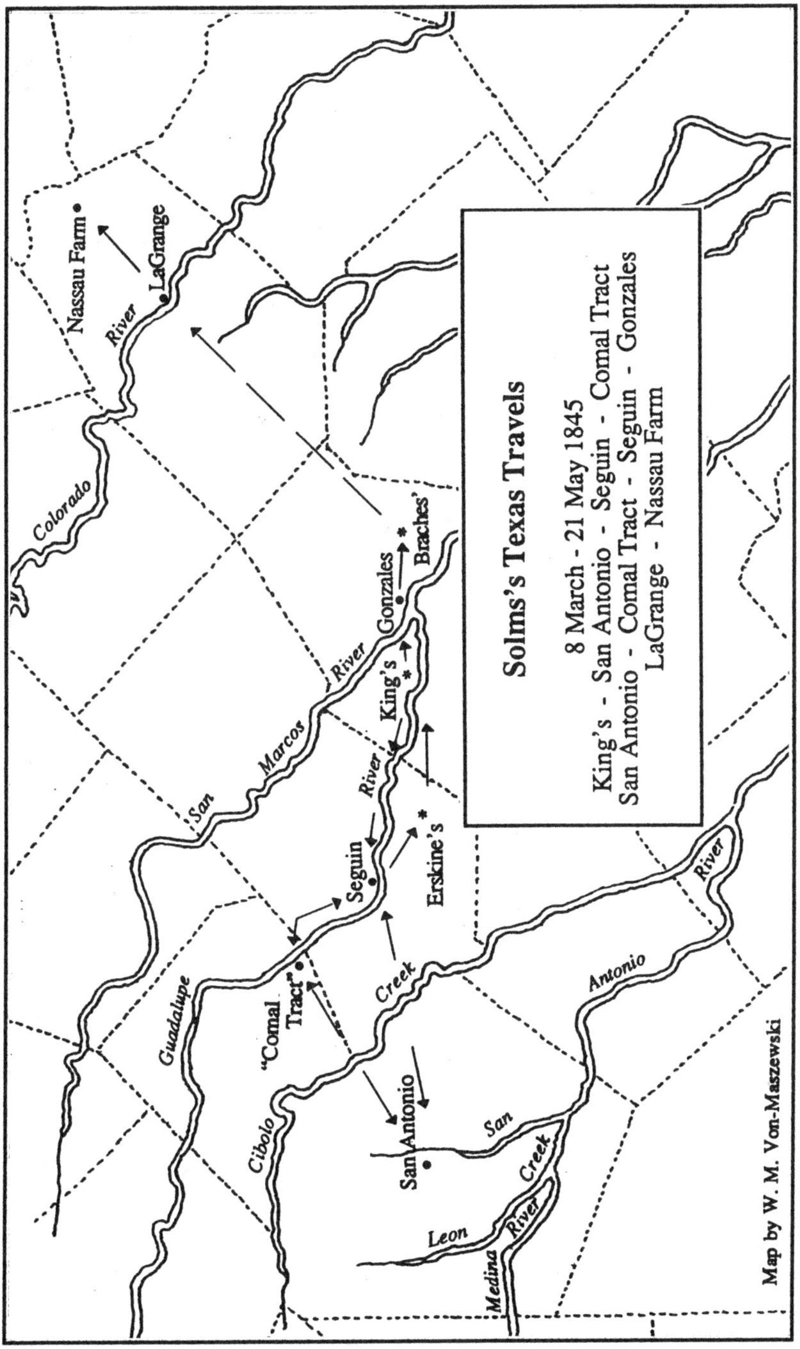
Solms's Texas Travels
8 March - 21 May 1845
King's - San Antonio - Seguin - Comal Tract
San Antonio - Comal Tract - Seguin - Gonzales
LaGrange - Nassau Farm
Nassau Farm
LaGrange
Colorado
River
Gonzales
Braches'
King's
San
Marcos
River
Seguin
Erskine's
"Comal
Tract"
Guadalupe
Cibolo
Creek
San Antonio
San
Antonio
River
Creek
Leon
Medina
River
Map by W. M. Von-Maszewski

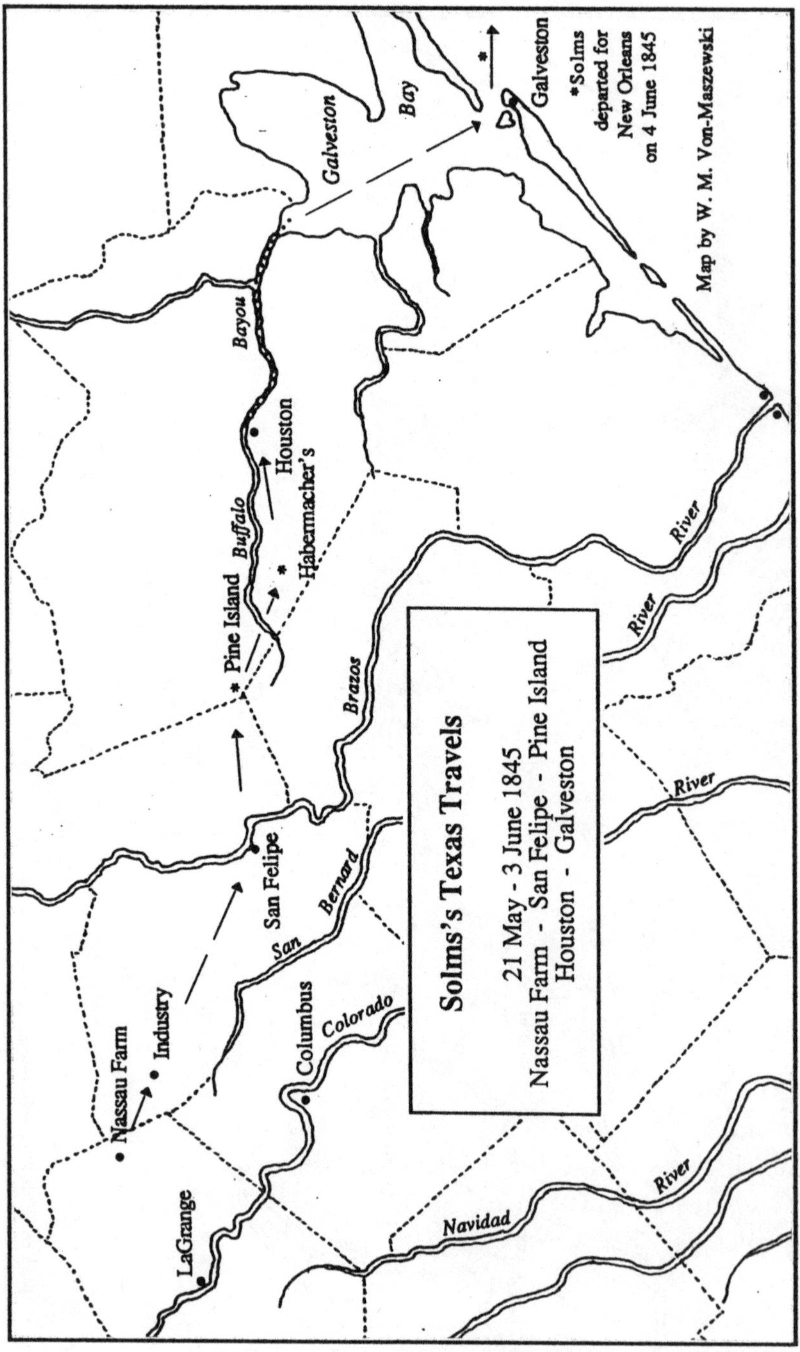
Solms's Texas Travels
21 May - 3 June 1845
Nassau Farm - San Felipe - Pine Island
Houston - Galveston
*Solms
departed for
New Orleans
on 4 June 1845
Map by W. M. Von-Maszewski
LaGrange
Nassau Farm
Industry
Columbus
Colorado
San Bernard
San Felipe
Brazos
Pine Island
Habermacher's
Buffalo
Bayou
Houston
Galveston
Bay
Galveston
Navidad
River
River
River
River

Memoir on American Affairs Written at Rheingrafenstein in December 1845 and Delivered to Her Majesty Queen Victoria by Count Leiningen [Prince Carl of Solms] in January 1846

When two powerful nations have differing opinions over one or another matter and these issues are also debated in newspapers as well as in the law-making chambers, such articles and debates arouse the interest of intelligent individuals.

The results of such differences of opinion can evoke a very special interest in the matter under discussion. And this is true not only for those who are immediately involved in it. For their influence can be extended to events and affairs which at the moment seem to be far removed from the situation. Cause and effect can be unpredictable, sometimes even strange, both in a person's life as well as in the life of a people and of a nation. He who reads history carefully and whose intellect reaches deeply will be satisfied and not settle for simple events and outcomes.

But for the correct understanding of the events of history it is absolutely necessary to have the thorough knowledge of the character of those persons involved in it, to the extent that it can be derived from the histories of great individuals. Understanding the present and making conjectures about the near, as well as distant, future requires not only a comprehension of the event that for the moment holds our attention but also a knowledge of a person's or people's character as well as that of the nation that determines the course to war or to peace.

The citizen acquires this expertise and, based on it, makes hypotheses and reaches conclusions because of his interest in the politics of the nation. The regent, the official called to the helm of the state, must intuitively have this knowledge. He must make similar deductions and reach similar conclusions. If he judges the events correctly, his deductions and conclusions are correct. He renders his country an invaluable service, even if, at present, the world is not yet able to judge these great consequences. Later generations, however, will place his name among the great of the nation.

Wrong decisions, inadequate knowledge and understanding of the situation as well as of the character of a nation, wrong conjectures and conclusions are counter-productive. Even if they are not noticeable at the time, they become twice as damaging in the future.

World history becomes the world's court of justice.

For some time now the eyes of the world have been directed at the mutual interests of England and the United States. Newspapers talk about it and exhaust themselves with conjectures. In Great Britain's Parliament as well as the United States Congress there has been talk. Many consider themselves well informed and judge the matter in accordance with the ideas on the subject that are prevalent in Europe. In my opinion, only a person who has lived with Americans for a while, studied their character, traveled through the country, become well acquainted with their various institutions, estimated their resources, followed their politics, is, I feel, in the position to make an appropriate judgment about the current situation and offer the appropriate deductions about the future.

In a monarchy the opinion of the regent and his government, more or less, predominate, especially in such important decisions as war and peace. In a constitutional nation the opinion of men leading this or that party dominate. These individuals are distinguished by their high position as well as by their intellect. Together they influence the nation's representatives but to some degree are also independent of them. Their position precludes vying for the people's favor. This explains why in Europe we are accustomed to consider an event from every aspect and give consideration to all possible consequences. Even intense debates in Parliament are conducted with decorum, something that a great nation owes itself. How different from our own are the conditions in the United States.

The executive, the highest post, is filled by the party who wins the election on the basis of cheap flattery and promises to the public. The president's backers make up the government. Every senator and representative is elected in a similar fashion. They make promises to the electorate, agree with their views, flatter the rabble in the most ordinary ways and with the help of alcoholic drinks make liberal statements. What is then the basis of power in a republic in general and the United States in particular? Popularity. On account of it, the elected officials' judgment is bought or sold before they reach Congress. And what is the goal of every citizen in the United States? Whether rich or poor, he wants to become a member of Congress, to improve his financial standing with the salary paid him during his attendance in Congress. This fetish of advancement, or money, is one of the chief traits deeply ingrained in the Americans' character and says something about the elected officials and the electorate. In no other country has an individual as much influence on the machinery, be it in internal or external relationships, as in the United States; in no other country do the masses influence the leaders so strongly. They are not independent acting, but like the president who is the highest official in the nation, they are the obedient whores of the masses. And the kind of people who go to the polls! It becomes a scam when more individuals of the lowest class can vote than the law already permits.

How do we learn of a people's or nation's character? A person who resides in a country for an extended period and observes all classes of people and not just socializes with the upper class and looks at the lower class in amusement, needs to conduct business with all classes of people in different parts of the nation. In this way they are observed in their customary activity, their opinions and views are heard, and the government's policies as well as those of the opposition are followed. Some of this information is found in newspapers, and some other comes from experts on the constitution who voice their views. Finally, all this information is compared and a conclusion drawn.

By the trust bestowed upon me by my peers, I was placed for a time at the head of a private undertaking that put me in touch with people of different countries in the New World. It also made it my duty to follow the policies of these countries and that of their leaders because events, that is, the outcome of influences, can and will affect such an undertaking that I was leading.

Here then is the result of my objective and calm observations on the present situation in the United States, its plans and its means to carry them out.

As previously stated, the influence of the masses on an individual and his, in turn, on the administration of the country is nowhere as clear and obvious as it is in the United States. If its politics are to be understood it is important to take a closer look at the American's character.

The so-called American nation is composed of the worst element of all European nations, from the north to the south, from Sweden to Russia, down to Sicily, Spain and Portugal. Immigrants from all of these nations have passed on part of their makeup to their descendants, so that it can easily be said that the United States possesses the vices of all of the European nations without having inherited any of their good qualities.

The American is cold and calculating. From his father who immigrated to the promised land in the New World to become rich, he inherited the characteristic of needing to accrue, of needing to make money. To achieve this, nothing is forbidden. When he cheats a stranger who arrived in this country as a guest or an experienced merchant, he consoles himself with the thought, "why did he let me cheat him." Likewise, he will sell anything if he believes that he can make a profit. As long as he can make money, he gives up, without any qualms, his parents' home, every pet animal, and naturally the slave, who has served him well and loyally for years and with whom in Europe a bond would be forged. Family ties are also much looser, less binding than in Europe. A twelve- or thirteen-year-old boy leaves the parents' house to make a livelihood and start his own life. The parents show no emotion at his parting.

In passing I will mention how deeply the ownership of slaves and the trade in these unfortunate ones who are looked on and treated as animals corrupts a person's character. Avarice turns the American into a speculator, by extension frequently into a swindler. So when he turns to politics, his desire being to become a member of Congress, he paves the road to a government position by courting the electorate's favor. He criss-crosses the country on horseback, cleverly hears out the people's opinion and then tells them what they want to hear. Here he learns about slippery roads and quicksand which later will stand him well when he is a statesman and politician.

It would appear that the ambition to be influential would satisfy a republican. This is not the case. There is also the mania for a title. A few Americans are addressed by the title of general, colonel, or major but for sure many by captain, doctor, or judge, even if it is only a courtesy. If there is a bad side to the American, there certainly are good aspects that cannot be overlooked. These are his courage, keen perception and determination. Starting from early youth he depends on himself, is accustomed to travel through wild and uninhabited areas that are frequented by Indians, and is used to hardship. Many a time he is forced to make a quick and correct decision as well as take decisive action to withdraw from a life-threatening situation. These traits mark his personality and his political philosophy. This, however, does not make the American politician superior to our diplomats. When the opportunity arises, he certainly challenges the latter. It is cunning against cunning (and here the American tips the scale) or it is honesty against cunning and deceit. Furthermore, when foreign diplomats complain about such behavior, the President and the Secretary of State offer the standard excuse: "We are not responsible for this; we tried our best but it is not according to the wishes of Congress and the Nation." These are not the things, I tell you, that makes the American dangerous to us. The American's superiority is not in words but in action. In Europe we are accustomed to our diplomats having meetings, resolving issues, writing protocols and issuing statements. Everything follows a calm and rational course and only after all avenues have been tried does it come to the decision of *ultima ration regis* [the final decision of the king]. On this side of the Atlantic we have followed this approach for centuries. We are so accustomed to it that we cannot believe in a different approach. And yet that is the way it is. While our statesmen debate and exchange communiqués, the Americans act and the deed is done. For proof of that I don't have to look far. It comes from recent times. I just mention the annexation and occupation of Texas and the incorporation of the Oregon Territory to the United States.

What does it matter whether a beautiful but thinly populated land like Texas or a desolate, unpopulated, and supposedly not very fertile area visited only by Indians, like the Oregon Territory, falls into the hands of the United States or not?

Both areas must be of some importance to the United States, or it would not have used every means available to gain control of them. Here is the answer to the riddle. For years now it has been the policy of the United States to extend its control over the North American continent. This is based on the belief that no European nation has a right to get involved in the affairs of the New World. Although this belief has no basis in our thinking, it suits the American purpose very well. Not only do the events prove to us the presence of this political philosophy, but it is also openly discussed in Congress. I am reminded here, for example, of the speeches made this last winter about the annexation of Texas and the justifications offered for doing so. Even President Polk in his inaugural speech took the position which described in broadest terms the western boundary. The United States already controls commerce on the eastern coast and part of the Gulf of Mexico. It became important to expand its hold in the Gulf and for this reason Texas had to be dragged into the United States. When I arrived in the United States in May, 1844, the annexation question had just been defeated. Even in Texas the government and the people strongly opposed annexation and were in favor of retaining their independence and their sovereignty at <u>any price</u>. In the summer of the same year emissaries from the United States arrived in Texas; some were land speculators, others immigrants. Their leader was General Duff Green. They criss-crossed the country in every direction in pursuit of their various businesses. During session of Congress in 1845 the annexation issue was again brought up. A sum of one to two hundred thousand dollars was appropriated by Congress for negotiation expenditures. In 1845 the Texas Legislature in Austin approved the annexation. United States troops crossed the Sabine River and landed as well in Corpus Christi and Brazos de San Jago (Rio Grande River). A fleet of three warships, each armed with 74 cannons, and a steamer outfitted with a propeller (the infamous *Princeton*) also armed with 74 cannons under the command of Commodore Stockton cruised in the Gulf of Mexico, and Texas became a state in the union.

Just as it had been said about Texas in Congress the year before *"We must have it, we don't care how,"* so did the United States act in a similar fashion with Oregon. The time regarding the question of the administration of Oregon had past. Great Britain and the United States provisionally had joint possession of the area since the Peace of Geneva. When the compromise was presented over free navigation on the Columbia River, which flows into the Pacific Ocean and is the only important river on the west coast between the Straits of Magellan and the Bering Strait, the United States rejected it. Great Britain was assigned an unimportant strip of land of limited productivity between the 49th and 54th latitudes where the western possessions begin. It was readily understood that this could not be accepted. For the problem to be resolved quickly, hundreds of those bold adventurers gathered. They consider hardship and a fight with the elements and Indian tribes as a pleasure and joy. On the upper Missouri they are called squatters, backwoodsmen, as well as pioneers of the war. In June 1845 they crossed over the White and Rocky Mountains into the Oregon Territory. They are a kind all to their own, these squatters, rough, almost wild and shy; they and their families always live isolated, at least two to three miles from the next family. They only come together when they pursue Indians. Nothing is too difficult for them; there is no obstacle in the terrain that cannot be overcome. A love of enterprise, boldness, courage, energy and consistency are their chief characteristics. It flatters their vanity to constantly expand the boundaries of the United States. Why do they go beyond when there is still so much uninhabited land within the recognized borders of the United States? Why does the government encourage them? What is there about the Oregon Territory which has such little fertility?

Texas makes the United States a neighbor of Mexico, the weak Mexico that consists of immense sparsely populated areas and a land for years torn apart by internal strife. It consequently becomes an easy prey for the United States which finally can dominate the entire commerce also in the Gulf of Mexico. In a similar way the Oregon Territory with its Columbia River brings the United States to the coast of the Pacific Ocean and on its way to California. With the steady advance of its population, the United States can grab California away from Mexico without a fight. Even at the present Mexico cannot show resistance to the annexation of Texas. Were it so inclined, then perhaps there would happen today what we will experience in a few years when an army crosses the Rio Grande and invades Mexico, while its fleet clears the Gulf of Mexican ships and blockade its ports. Should Mexico show any opposition to the occupation of California, it would offer the United States the suitable pretext to take these steps. During last year's Congressional session, to which I will return, the treaty was discussed that had been negotiated with China. It was considered much more advantageous than the one England had forced upon the Heavenly Emperor. Mr. Calhoun said on that occasion that "Today's generation will enjoy the knowledge that New York is in touch with the Pacific Ocean by railroad and steamer, and with that trade with China is established." The implication is that complete control had been achieved over commerce on the Atlantic coast, the Gulf of Mexico and the trade with China and East India, in other words, world trade. This is the objective of the United States' striving and its means are the constant pushes to the south and west. Whether these things are only figments of my imagination or already part of history, there is no doubt about that.

Of course it has been maintained that Great Britain would not declare war on the United States simply on account of the incorporation of Texas as well as that of the Oregon Territory, the latter a land of limited fertility and only visited by trappers and Indians. If the problem were limited to just these two areas of land, there would be no reason or excuse for a war over them. But Texas is the road to Mexico and the Oregon territory is the road to California and the Pacific Ocean. And through both lies the road to world trade.

If we show a good deal of concern over the speeches in Congress at Washington as well as the newspaper accounts based on them, then more than half of it can be attributed to the Americans' excessive vanity and the inherent hate <u>against</u> us by everyone individually and the nation in general and a contempt based on enormous vanity <u>for</u> everything that pertains to Europe. What remains is still sufficient to justify our concern.

A person needs only to read the congressional speeches and newspaper articles, and the heart of every intelligent and well-educated individual will be indignant over the harsh and obscene tone that the dirty American democracy breathes toward Europe in general but especially against Great Britain. This tone arises from the overestimation of one's own methods and the disregard and low opinion of foreign methods.

Even if England looks indifferently upon Texas and the Oregon

Territory, can it also look indifferently at the control of the oceans? The Atlantic Ocean, the Gulf of Mexico—but especially the Pacific Ocean and the trade with China and East India are questions that intimately affect England. It cannot look at this situation with indifference; it needs to assert its right with all its power.

Not only is world trade and the control of the oceans in danger, so is England's industry as well as that of the entire continent endangered. In the United States, that is in the north, factories have been on the rise and they demand protection against the import of foreign goods and manufactured articles. An extremely high tariff is already in place in the United States and is a chief source of income for the country.

How would it be when the Union after enlarging and fortifying its hold in Texas, and in few years maybe even in Mexico, suddenly raised the tariff on foreign goods and manufactured articles or by law would forbid the import of such goods? What would then be the fate of the English factories, what misery would face the thousands of unfortunate factory workers who, robbed of a livelihood, either die of hunger with their families or beg from their well-to-do neighbors and brothers and not from rapacity but from sheer need would become robbers and murderers?

Does not a large part of the English factories' output, as that of the continent, go to America? If the United States is permitted to continue its course unhindered, the ruin of Great Britain's commerce and the factories is certain, maybe not today, not tomorrow, but in a short time, not in the far distance. That no nation will give up its trade and its inner welfare—together they make up its prosperity—without a fight demands no explanation. But a person can retort: "All that is in the future. Why should we fight now for something that will be of concern to our sons?" For this reason, let us look at the population numbers in the United States derived from formal sources. We will see where it stood fifty years ago and where it stood five years ago in the last census.

The following table on the population comes from the official *American Almanac* for 1845.[1]

[The next two pages show statistics about the United States' population in the years 1790, 1800, 1810, 1820, 1830, and 1840 as well as statistics on the slave holdings.]

This information illustrates that since 1790 the population has almost tripled every twenty years. Where in an European nation is there anything similar? Since 1840 emigration has increased in a startling progression. The lists from European ports, especially those in Germany and France provide a picture. I consider just as telling a fact which I personally experienced. During my last stay in New York June 27–29, in these three days three thousand German emigrants passed through the custom house. These are three days out of a year and this is only one port in the country. Unfortunately the reasons to emigrate (which this is not the place to discuss) have increased during the past ten years so that it has become a necessary evil of our time. If from 1790 to 1840 it took only twenty years to double the population of the United States, it can be assumed that with the increase of immigrants since 1840 it may take fifteen or only twelve years to repeat this feat. Each day adds to the Union new immigrants, new blood, new strong hands, new money. It is not only the poor who emigrate, on the contrary. More well-to-do individuals leave their birth country for various reasons. By this means the United States gains in strength day-by day. Therefore, I boldly make the well-founded assertion, based on the preceding, that when it comes to the questions of livelihood like the control of the oceans, trade with China and East India, the preservation of industry, and with it tranquillity and peace in one's own country, and if then one is inclined to fight for them, then every day of a prolonged peace is a loss for us and a clear gain for the United States.—The same *American Almanac* gives the strength of the navy.

9 ships of the line with	74 guns
1 ship of the line with	120 guns
1 frigate with	54 guns
12 frigates with	44 guns
2 frigates with	36 guns
17 sloops with	20 guns
1 sloop with	18 guns
5 sloops with	16 guns
7 brigs with	10 guns
3 schooners with	10 guns

1 schooner with	4 guns
4 schooners	not armed
8 steamships with	10 to 44 guns
2 supply ships with	8 guns
1 supply ship with	6 guns
1 supply ship	not armed

The strength of the army is given as follows:

2 regiments of dragoons
4 regiments of artillery
8 regiments of infantry[2]

[The supplement has a detailed table taken from the *American Almanac.*]

By law every man is obligated to militia duty. That comes to a strength of 1,749,082 men. Even if only half, or just a third are found fit for duty, the militia can only serve within the district where it lives. The men are obligated and called upon to uphold order, public peace, and safety. How they discharge these duties at times is offered by the example in Philadelphia in June 1844 when the burned churches, and the ransacked homes of the clergy offered the picture of a plundered town. In fact, the militia is more for show than for military duty.

In case of a war, a call would go out for volunteers and they would be brought up on par with the regular troops. Every town and district would have sufficient men. The militia and the under strength army would become the cadre to these volunteers. These troops would not lack courage and resolve, but they would certainly lack discipline, subordination and training, while the low and high-ranking officers would lack know-how and experience. Even though the militia is undisciplined and lacks military esprit de corps, the troops stationed partly in harbor fortifications and the individual forts along the western border show a manly bearing. The garrisons in the latter areas are constantly in training since they are constantly having to deal with Indians or having to keep an eye on them. The Indian War in Florida, however, does not speak in favor of the troops. But one has to consider the impenetrable and marshy terrain that worked in favor of the Indians and to the disadvantage of the soldiers. (The army's annual budget lists the position of purchaser of large dogs from the island of Cuba to be used in the war in Florida but the use of the animals is frowned upon.) For the most part the officers of the standing army are well trained for their task. The officers' academy at West Point on the Hudson is one of the best military educational institutions that I have ever encountered. It takes no second place to any European academy. In fact, I am of the opinion that in the variety of the different disciplines of knowledge and the thoroughness of each, it surpasses most of them. Annually it graduates between thirty to fifty well-trained officers accustomed to discipline and subordination.

Soldiers are recruited and serve for a specified period. They can reenlist as many times as they desire. They come from a class of shiftless people without any means. When an opportunity arises, they desert before the expiration of their enlistment. Among the soldiers are many European immigrants. The cavalry is well-equipped but lacks knowledge of movements and tactics as a group of riders. They are more a mounted infantry, as it has to be in the kind of climate, the type of soil and the speed needed to cover immense stretches of land.

The commanding general is Major General Winfield Scott in command of the army and militia as well as all military posts and institutions. He is sixty plus years old. In the War of 1812, he already had a high command in the army and earned his laurels. Since that time he has taken several tours through Europe, seen many of Europe's armies and assessed all our institutions with knowledge and a clear mind. He is sprightly and reminds one immediately of the departed and just as distinguished General of the Infantry Von Grolmann, well-known to all of the armies. In case of a war Scott would certainly be able to lead the army. Not much praiseworthy can be said about the other general officers, except one. General Gaines was trusted the most and given command over the troops already gathered on the Red River in the summer of 1844 for the purpose of invading Texas, as well as over the stockpiled stores of ammunitions and other essential materials to equip volunteers. I met General Gaines, seventy-four years of age, in New Orleans. He did not strike me as suited for the job, in particular since the volunteers destined to march into Texas, in case of a conflict with Mexico, are not a body of easily controlled men. They have to see a lot of activity and spend a great deal of energy to please the man and not the office.

About the fleet that I saw in the Gulf of Mexico, I have no expertise with which to form a judgment. It is assumed that this will be the first engagement for the United States—but the sailors have been brought together from all nations of the known world—a large number supposedly are Europeans and Irish men who deserted from the English merchantmen.

In case of a war the government will freely issue privateering letters with the result that in every port many small and large boats would be outfitted for this purpose by Americans who are always ready for adventure and profit-making.

Even though this would substantially increase the fleet, as boastful as the American nation is presently and ready to go to war, herein lies the reason that they would soon ask for peace; even Congress would force the executive to do so, if it were necessary. It is well known that the American privateer attacks any ship, regardless of nationality, and if possible will capture it. American ships mean the same to him as those of a foreign nation. These privateers will consequently assist the British navy by removing American ships from all waters. In short, they will assist in the destruction of United States trade.

A word about the military posts in the United States.

Some are individual barracks close to town, like those near New Orleans, Baton Rouge, and elsewhere, which are posts lacking any military importance and serve only as garrisons for a small detail of soldiers. There are also scattered forts guarding (and patrolling) rivers and the access to the various supply bases. In the northern part they are located at the Great Lakes. Examples [in the South] are Fort Bend and Fort Philip, the first on the right, the other on the left side of the Mississippi River between New Orleans and the so-called Balize (a series of channel markers and lighthouses that mark the mouth of the Mississippi River below New Orleans). Both forts are located in rather marshy terrain and have low earthwork. The inside, in both cases, is also very small. Fort Pique on the channel that leads from Lake Pontchartrain to Lake

Borgne and into the Bay of St. Louis was also built in a marsh and water. The fort consists of casemated work with embrasures for twelve canons. It can be called a hollow bastion. Furthermore, there are no faces and flanks. With all angles deleted, they merge into each other. The wooden barracks, located on a so-called island, stand year-around in water and are protected from the channel by only a short and low earthen wall without any breastwork.

The three named forts which I have mentioned protect the access to New Orleans, the first two on the Mississippi River, the last through the lakes.

The third type of forts is structures built for the protection of harbors. The fortifications at Boston harbor appear to me best suited for this purpose; those in New York are more for show and beautification of the magnificent bay and its enchanting shore than of any practical use. Fort Moultrie and Castle Pickney at Charleston are of minor importance. Fort Mifflin near Philadelphia on the Delaware River is a four-cornered redoubt of earthen walls with very little space inside. None of the buildings is bombproof. Fort Morgan near Mobile is of no significance. It is not armed and has no garrison. This means that these forts serve little or none of their intended purpose, including defense. At Zaida[3] we saw the old walls crumble under the guns of the fleet. The warships tacked before the wind, sailed within firing distance of the walls, fired at them, and withdrew quickly, becoming a vague target. Here then are installations that cover a small area and are most likely without any rooms, or only a few that are bombproof. They cannot be defended because in a short time they can be leveled by canons. The fourth type of forts is those built on the western border against Indians. As a rule they are block houses that serve as barracks and the entire area is enclosed by a palisade.

Based on this, as well as on my personal opinion, and ignoring all other factors, it appears that at this moment Great Britain holds a significant predominance over the United States. I say now—for who can tell what it will be a few years hence considering the rapid population increase.

I am reproached with the fact that a division will occur in the near future between the free and the slave-holding states. It will be even sooner if the United States takes in more land. The annexation of Texas is already a step toward this division between the North and the South. I counter to those who bring this up that they do not know the American's character, otherwise they would not make such statements. The South and the North may separate, be even strained or divided, but they will become one if it comes to a fight against an outside power, especially the deeply hated Great Britain.

Assuming that a confrontation was undertaken, and for Great Britain certainly an advantageous situation, it would be preferable to resolve these important questions now. Leaving these things to the future would give the monster that needs to be fought more time for its growth and the firming up of its power and the development of its strength. Which then is the best course to a fast and favorable peace, which is the object of every war? What approaches are there for Great Britain to take? And, finally, with peace established what rules will permanently safe-guard the advantages fought for and keep the United States within its prescribed boundary? These questions, to be addressed next, appear at first to be quite understandable.

A look at the map shows the immense extent of the United States borders, on land as well as on the water. It follows then that defending these borders against invasion presents not only endless difficulties, but also some impossibilities. The question immediately arises as to what the purposes and consequences of invasions of the United States would have? The invading forces would find desolate stretches of land that were evacuated by its inhabitants. This would make conducting a war difficult. Supplying an army would only be possible through mobile depots. A lack of transportation (wagons and draft animals), roads that are in the most primitive conditions, the destruction of bridges, and the carrying off or destruction of ferries would make matters much more difficult. In spite of the best preparations the soldiers will be exposed to severe shortages. The American, already accustomed to migration, in case of an enemy attack, will load on a wagon his family, his possessions and some basic provisions to survive on, like corn, coffee and salted meat. He will drive his livestock with him and move into an impenetrable forest or swamp. With his ax he will build a cabin similar to the one he left behind. The advancing enemy finds an empty home at the old location or just smoldering timbers. Once the American feels his family is safe, he sets out with his rifle. He gathers with others in groups and on terrain that offers them all the advantages they carry on a kind of war that professional soldiers find very unpleasant. There is constant danger. Every day many become casualties, being shot from ambush and there is little or no glory. And all this for a desolate piece of land. The Americans' riches are primarily the merchant ships that sail the world's oceans and the riches held in the warehouses located in big cities, which in many cases are also ports. They cannot be left and put to the flame like the cheap wooden huts of the country. Here then is where the attention needs to be directed. Confiscation of the merchant ships, destruction of the navy, occupation, and if necessary partial or total bombing of Boston, New York, Baltimore, Philadelphia, Harlington, Charleston, Mobile, New Orleans and Galveston. This is the means of obtaining a quick and favorable peace settlement. Here it would be appropriate for the British navy to assume the dignified role which is in accordance to its fame. That the United States would make reprisals against such measures does not need to be mentioned.

Harbors in the British possessions in North America and the southern border of Canada would be the first exposed to attacks and, therefore, are in need of protection. The Bay and harbor of Halifax (which I had an opportunity to visit twice) have excellent bulwarks and forts. Travel on the bay can only be done during daylight or with the assistance of a pilot familiar with the water. I cannot comment on the harbors of New Brunswick, Nova Scotia, etc., because I did not visit them.

What can be expected before anything else is an attempt to cross the border into British possessions and once there the Americans will spread the principles of democracy, advocate breaking away from Great Britain and offer annexation to the United States, or even force it.

Thus a large land force would be necessary for the protection of the border. I mention here only in passing, the well known principle. An offense is the best defense. Quebec, East and West Canada, Montreal are only sparsely populated areas, and a war carried out there would not be like one fought in Europe. Here there would be mainly the so called small war, e.g., outpost duty and reconnaissance as well as the undertaking of skirmishes between small units.

During the American Revolution, 1775–1783, the British government used mercenaries from Hanover and Hesse. History tells us, and statements by British officers confirm this, that there, as well as later on the Iberian peninsula, the German soldiers did not refuse the old call to war of their country.[4] From the latter there are many who earned the praise of their commander-in-chief, at that time the greatest living general officer of that glorious era, Field Marshal Lord Wellington. Particularly as light cavalry they had occasion to distinguish themselves in small skirmishes.

At the outbreak of a war such a German legion could be organized from the many prospective emigrants that Germany offers. When the desired peace was obtained, these soldiers could be placed in military settlements along the southern border of the British possessions in North America. Populating these areas would make the border secure. Austria's military border, and Russia's military settlements are examples that can be emulated. The German's warlike spirit, being accustomed to law and order, provides good traits for such a colonization. The annual influx of immigrants to the United States would be diverted and the stream directed where it would benefit Great Britain in many ways. Even the immigrants will find it advantageous. They will be assured of a small property instead of falling into the hands of American land speculators and impostors.

This interjected thought deserves closer consideration, and for this reason it should become the subject of closer elucidation.

Just as the northern border of the United States is closed to further expansion, the British government's paternal welfare among the budding German population would stop the further spread of democratic propaganda.

Just as in the north, attention also needs to be given to the southwestern border of the United States.

Mexico's situation is known. The country has a land border with the United States that stretches from the coast of the Pacific Ocean to the mouth of the Rio Grande River at the Gulf of Mexico. It is very doubtful that this nation could put up any resistance to the

United States, or that it could offer the world the assurance of any further encroachment.

The Mexican nation is comprised of Hidalgos who make up a small portion of the population. They are of Spanish ancestry and did not intermix with the indigenous peoples but kept their bloodlines pure. Then among the population there are the mixed blood lines of various degrees between Spaniards and Indians. These mixed bloods again intermingled with the nomadic Indians in the different areas of Mexico and Texas. The missions (we found ruins of these fortified monasteries in southwestern Texas) founded in these parts during the Spanish period encouraged such miscegenation. The Indians, after receiving their instructions in the Christian belief, in farming and other useful trades at the mission, were allowed to choose freely among the daughters of the country. When a priest declared an Indian as mature, he was allotted a piece of land for cultivation. This explains the prevalence of miscegenation found in Mexico and southwestern Texas. In appearance people range from light to dark skin, from a European-looking Hidalgo to a person who cannot be differentiated from an Indian, living in a miserable hut. Today's judgment condemns all these classes. Because of miscegenation all Mexicans are looked upon as an intellectually and physically inferior race. Some aspects may be true; others need to be seen in light of the harsh environment and the poverty in which they live. This is even more true in Texas because of the pressure exerted on them by the haughty Americans who control the land.

On several occasions in Texas a much smaller contingent of Americans has defeated the Mexican army. For this reason the Americans judge them as the most cowardly and poorest soldiers in the world. Facts do not speak in their favor, but it is generally acknowledged that the Mexican surpasses the American when it comes to enduring fatigue and long marches in this climate and through the wide and uninhabited stretches of land (for a European such things are difficult to overcome; only individuals of robust health as well as iron will and determination can perform here). I am of the opinion that the Mexican has more stamina and only modest needs. Like all southern tribes he is easily nourished. The American even acknowledges that the Mexican excels him on horseback, on the hunt, at catching mustangs, at killing buffalo and in the use of weapons.

Didn't we have the example in Europe where troops, formerly with a poor reputation, through reorganization and under new leadership were able to compete with the best of them. I am reminded here of the decline of the Portuguese army after the death of Count Lippe. It lost its former glory but after a complete reorganization by Marshall Beresford in 1808, under the leadership of General Wellington, they earned new laurels.

A certainly appropriate question, although still in the background at this time is, will the introduction of a monarchy in Mexico stop the endless fighting over the executive power (the president's chair) and will it be in the best interest of the European states? Only such a solution can be expected to bring peace to the country.[5] The blood shed for years by the different parties will finally come to an end, and Mexico will again become a counterweight to the United States. The prince chosen by the European powers to head this monarchy must be an individual with extraordinary qualities and must possess great strength and energy as well. That his task will be a most difficult one requires no explanation.

Let us return to the plan of using the military to close the southeastern border of the United States. The task will be Mexico's and to put it into effect there is no other choice but to use British officers. Needing to be fluent in Spanish, they will have to train the Mexican soldiers and provide the leadership. Possibly British auxiliary troops can be landed on the coasts. It is in Europe's interest, but possibly against Mexico's own wish, to offer it the largest force possible. This can be best achieved by directing the immense stream of European immigrants to the northeastern border areas.

For centuries Mexico considered the Rio Frio and the Nueces River as the boundary between the districts (presidios) of Coahuila and Chihuahua on the one side and Texas proper on the other. The Texans, and since the annexation the United States, has arbitrarily shifted the boundary to the Rio Grande del Norte. The justification usually given is that mountains make natural borders but never rivers. This principle is certainly true but every rule has its exception. Such an exception is found in Texas where the Guadalupe River is the boundary between the American and the

Mexican population. On the left side of the river the American language, customs, and architecture dominate. As soon as the river is crossed, beginning right on its shore, a person has the impression of being suddenly transported into a different country. The Mexican people, the dark skin color, Mexican costumes, building style, customs and language are spontaneously noted by the traveler. Even though separated only by a river which they cross daily in both directions to conduct business and in spite of the rule by Americans, the two peoples have retained distinct identities over the years. Thus, the Guadalupe River which rises in the higher mountains of Texas and empties through the Espiritu-Sanctu Bay into the Gulf of Mexico becomes the factual border of Mexico. This river, which I know very well from personal experience, can only be crossed on a ferry at a few places. But with its clear and raging water it offers the beautiful picture of a mountain stream. Boulders in its riverbed make it not navigable for the moment but as soon as sufficient hands and means are available to remove them, the river will be able to be navigated to its upper reaches. On the right side of the upper Guadalupe the lands of the "Society for the Protection of German Immigrants" begin. They extend from here westward into the high mountains and south and southwesterly to the Nueces and Rio Frio and even to the Rio Grande. The Society began its colonization in September 1844 and, as of December 1845, the records show between 5,000 and 6,000 immigrants.

How wonderfully and easily the previously mentioned principle of military colonization could be applied here, either when this land would be returned to the monarchy established in Mexico or if Great Britain should take control of the land strip between the Gulf of Mexico and the high mountains, the Guadalupe River serving as the northeastern border. With the Guadalupe as a demarcation line, fortified forts could be established at appropriate distances on the right side and away from the river. They would be the frontier defense. The right flank would extend to Espiritu Sanctu or Matagorda and Lavaca Bays also permitting communication to the Gulf. The left flank would extend to the mountains. This would provide a defense whose strength against attack at any point could be upheld.

A strong ally in western Texas would be the nomadic Indians, displaced by the Americans and treated with total treachery, a trait that is characteristic of the American. The Indians are well aware of the difference between Americans and the European immigrants. A few numerically small tribes live a nomadic life within the settled areas and on the fringes. They are in fear of the Americans and commit only those acts of thievery for which they believe that they cannot be blamed.

The strongest Indian tribe in western Texas is the Comanche. They will never forget the betrayal that they suffered at San Antonio de Bexar. Their chiefs were lured into the city under the pretense of a peace talk and all of them murdered there. For this reason American settlers will always be their worst enemies. The Comanche are courageous and brave, in spite of what is said about the character of Indians. They show conscientious devotion and faith as well as keep their word to those whom they trust. I speak here from personal experience. They are great warriors and are always ready to fight Americans. In the past when the Mexican armies invaded, they were always accompanied by hundreds of mounted Comanche warriors. These Indians fight only on horseback, are excellent horsemen, and can furnish 10,000 warriors. They make an effective light cavalry. In skirmishes there are hardly any better soldiers than Indians. They will join the British and Mexican armies with joy when it comes to a fight against their hereditary enemy, the United States.

Just as important, but possibly more successful, as the occupation and closing of the northern United States border, is the previously discussed southwest border. The lands of "The Society for the Protection of German Immigrants in Texas" are rather immense. For the past 15 months it has been the destination of a considerable number of German immigrants and their number increases daily. This area should be separated from the United States and made accessible to Great Britain for an important purpose. This certainly deserves careful consideration because it could deprive the United States of its annual increase of new vigor, additional soldiers and new capital.

There remains one other avenue in which Great Britain can give the United States an awful indeed a most terrifying jolt. This would be invading and occupying of the harbors in the slave-holding states, emancipating the slaves, and thereby bringing slavery to an end. The more that a person is acquainted with this institution, the deeper he despises it. It should not be overlooked, however, that with this move the safety of the land and the ownership of these lands will cease in a most dramatic manner.

Only by coordinated planning of the points presented here can the war's end be expedited and the defeated United States shown that she cannot go unpunished for the crimes that she committed against other nations. Since every day of peace permits the Union to gain in strength and capital, it would also be of great benefit for the warring powers to bring the war to an early end because it brings savings in resources as well as human lives. It will compensate for the great expense of resources in the beginning.

A war is too costly to be fought year after year. For this reason, with peace achieved, measures must be implemented to assure its endurance. Great Britain cannot undertake this task without the participation by other European major powers. If they understand their own interest in this matter, they will participate and agree to these measures. The propaganda that is spread all over Europe by the utterly dirty democracy of the United States does not shy away from any means to rock the thrones of Europe. It attempts to convince people that the president of a republic is less costly to feed than the house of a regent which it considers only as a criminal expenditure detrimental to the national treasury. This propaganda has to be stopped. Wherever it appears, efforts need to be made to track down the source, or the time will come when regrets are too late. Closing tightly of the recognized borders and confronting the United States in its hemisphere with a power that is a counterweight are the only means that offer a chance for enduring peace. Mexico could be this power, of course, not in its present condition. Great Britain, together with other European powers must first assist Mexico.

---

[1] *American Almanac and Repository of Useful Knowledge for the Year 1845.* Boston: James Munroes & Company, 1844, p. 200.

[2] Ibid., pp. 120–122.

[3] Zaida: Sayda (Sidon) in present-day Lebanon. Solms alludes to the bombardment of fortifications along the Mediterranean Coast during the Second Turko-Egyptian War (1839–41). Britain, France, and Austria sided with the Turks to defeat the Egyptian armies of occupation in Syria. Lebanon did not become a separate political entity until it was separated from Syria following World War II.

[4] Solms refers to the Peninsular War (1809–14) when the British under Lord Wellington drove Napoleon's army from Portugal and Spain.

[5] After Mexico's independence from Spain (1821) and the subsequent liberal governments, Mexican Royalists lobbied in Europe for a Mexican monarchy. The Austrian court, in particular, seemed to acquiesce to the idea, decades before France set up a puppet monarchy in Mexico City.

Supplement from the *American Almanac for 1845*, pp. 120–122.

NAVY LIST.

1. Commander of Squadrons.

David Conner	*Commodore*	Home Squadron
Daniel Turner	"	Coast of Brazil
Joseph Smith	"	Mediterranean
A. J. Dallas	"	Pacific Ocean
F. A. Parker	"	East Indies
M. C. Perry	"	Coast of Africa

Navy establishments are located in Portsmouth, Boston, New York, Philadelphia, Washington, Norfolk, Baltimore, Charleston.

The Navy asylum [veterans' home] is located in Philadelphia.

Vessels of War of the United States Navy

NAME AND RATE:		WHERE AND WHEN BUILT:		COMMANDED BY:	WHERE EMPLOYED:
		Ships of the line – 10 Guns			
Franklin	74	Philadelphia	1815		Under repairs, Bost.
Columbus	74	Washington	1819		New York
Ohio	74	New York	1820	W. M. Hunter	Rec'g Ship, Boston
North Carolina	74	Philadelphia	1820	B. Dulany	Rec'g Ship, N. York
Delaware	74	Gosport, Va.	1820		Norfolk
Alabama	74				On stocks, Portsm'th
Vermont	74				" Boston
Virginia	74				" "
Pennsylvania	120	Philadelphia	1837	J. P. Zantzinger	Rec'g Ship, Norfolk
New York	74				On stocks, "
		Frigates, 1st Class – 13			
Independence, *Razee,*	54	Boston	1814	Boston	
United States	44	Philadelphia	1797	James Armstrong	Pacific Ocean

NAME AND RATE:		WHERE AND WHEN BUILT:		COMMANDED BY:	WHERE EMPLOYED:
Constitution	44	Boston	1797	J. Percival	East Indies
Potomac	44	Washington	1821	T. M. Newell	Home Squadron
Brandywine	44	"	1825	F. A. Parker	East Indies
Santee	44				On stocks, Portsm'th
Cumberland	44	Boston	1842	Samuel L. Breese	Mediterranean
Sabine	44				On stocks, N. York
Savannah	44	New York	1843	A. J. Dallas	Pacific Ocean
Raritan	44	Philadelphia	1842	F. H. Gregory	Coast of Brazil
Columbia	44	Washington	1836	D. Geisinger	Mediterranean
St. Lawrence	44				On stocks, Norfolk
Congress	44	Portsmouth	1841	Philip F. Voorhees	Coast of Brazil
		Frigates, 2d Class – 2			
Constellation	36	Baltimore	1797		Norfolk
Macedonian	36	Norfolk, *rebuilt*,	1836	Isaac Mayo	Coast of Africa
		Sloops of War – 23			
John Adams	20	Norfolk, *rebuilt*	1820		New York
Boston	20	Boston	1825	G. J. Pendergrast	Coast of Brazil
Vincennes	20	New York	1826	Frank Buchanan	Home Squadron
Warren	20	Boston	1826	J. B. Hull	Pacific Ocean
Falmouth	20	"	1827	J. R. Sands	Home Squadron
Fairfield	20	New York	1828	S. W. Downing	Mediterranean
Vandalia	20	Philadelphia	1828	J. S. Chauncey	Home Squadron
St. Louis	20	Washington	1828	Isaac McKeever	East Indies
Cyane	20	Boston	1837	C. K. Stribling	Pacific Ocean
Levant	20	New York	1837	Hugh N. Page	"
Saratoga	20	Portsmouth	1842	Josiah Tattnall	Coast of Africa
Ontario	18	Baltimore	1813	J. S. Nicholas	Rec'g Ship, Balt.
Marion	16	Boston	1839		In ordinary, Boston
Decatur	16	New York	1839	Joel Abbot	Coast of Africa
Preble	16	Portsmouth	1839	T. W. Freelon	New York
Yorktown	16	Norfolk	1839		"
Dale	16	Philadelphia	1839		Philadelphia
Portsmouth	20	Portsmouth	1843		Preparing for sea
Plymouth	20	Boston	1843	Henry Henry	Mediterranean
Alabany	20	New York			On the stocks
Germantown	20	Philadelphia			"
St. Mary's	20	Washington			"
Jamestown	20	Norfolk			"

NAME AND RATE:		WHERE AND WHEN BUILT:		COMMANDED BY:	WHERE EMPLOYED:
		Brigs – 7			
Dolphin	10	New York	1836		Norfolk
Porpoise	10	Boston	1836	T. T. Craven	Coast of Africa
Bainbridge	10	Boston	1842	W. D. Newman	Coast of Brazil
Perry	10	Norfolk	1843	J. S. Paine	East Indies
Somers	10	New York	1842	J. T. Gerry	Home Squadron
Truxtun	10	Norfolk	1843	Henry Bruce	Coast of Africa
Lawrence	10	Baltimore	1843	W. H. Gardner	Home Squadron
		Schooners – 8			
Shark	10	Washington	1821	N. M. Howison	Pacific Ocean
Enterprise	10	New York	1831		Boston
Boxer	10	Boston	1831		"
Experiment	4	Washington	1831	F. Varnum	Rec'g vessel, Phila.
Flirt		Transferred from		J. A Davis	Home Squadron
Wave		War Department			Norfolk
Phenix		"		A. Sinclair	Packet Service
On-ka-hy-e		Purchased	1843		Norfolk
		Steamers – 8			
Fulton	4	New York	1837		In ordinary, N. York
Pointsett		Trans. War Dep.		R. Semmes	Surveying
Mississippi	10	Philadelphia	1841		In ordinary, Boston
Union		Norfolk	1842	H. H. Bell	Home Squadron
Princeton		Philadelphia	1843	R. F. Stockton	Special Service
Michigan		Erie, Pa	1844	Wm. Inman	Lake Erie
Col. W. S. Harney		Transferred from		E. B. Boutwell	Coast service
Gen. Taylor		War Department		E. Farrand	Coast of Florida
		Store Ships – 4			
Relief	6	Philadelphia	1836	H. K. Hoff	Pacific Ocean
Erie	8	Baltimore	1813	N. W. Duke	"
Lexington	8	New York	1825	W. M. Glendy	Mediterranean
Pioneer		Boston	1836	T. D. Shaw	Coast of Brazil

ARMY LIST

Winfield Scott, *Major General, General-in-Chief*— Head Quarters, Washington City.

Inspectors General of the Amry

Colonel George Croghan

Colonel S. Churchill

First Dragoon Regiment
Second Dragoon Regiment

First Artillery
Second Artillery
Third Artillery
Fourth Artillery

First Infantry Regiment
Second Infantry Regiment
Third Infantry Regiment
Fourth Infantry Regiment
Fifth Infantry Regiment
Sixth Infantry Regiment
Seventh Infantry Regiment
Eighth Infantry Regiment

MILITIA FORCE OF THE UNITED STATES

Abstract of the United States Militia from the Army Register for 1844

Maine	1843	26	95	540	1,659	2,320	42,345	44,665
N. Hampshire	1843	12	30	333	1,244	1,619	28,070	29,689
Massachusetts	1842	9	30	98	464	601	86,010	86,611
Vermont	1843	12	51	224	801	1,088	22,827	23,915
Rhode Island	1842	5	35	99	277	416	14,540	14,956
Connecticut	1843	9	30	311	914	1,364	45,729	46,993
New York	1842	135	863	2,590	6,574	10,162	170,725	180,887
New Jersey	1829	19	58	435	1,476	1,988	37,183	39,171
Pennsylvania	1843	51	188	1,417	6,156	7,812	239,718	247,530
Delaware	1827	4	8	71	364	447	8,782	9,229
Maryland	1838	22	68	544	1,763	2,397	44,467	46,864
Virginia	1843	27	60	1,263	4,882	6232	110,500	116,732
N. Carolina	1841	28	67	723	2,969	3,787	62,524	66,311
S. Carolina	1843	20	135	554	2,041	2,750	50,005	52,755
Georgia	1839	36	98	746	2,212	3,092	54,220	57,312
Alabama	1839	31	187	564	1,382	2,164	42,168	44,332
Louisiana	1829	10	46	183	542	781	14,027	14,808
Mississippi	1838	15	70	392	348	825	35,259	36,084
Tennessee	1840	25	79	859	2,644	3,607	67,645	71,252
Kentucky	1843	43	143	1,074	3,745	5,005	80,510	85,515
Ohio	1841							180,258
Indiana	1832	31	110	566	2,154	2,861	51,052	53,913
Illinois	1841							83,234
Missouri	1841	45	213	658	1,692	2,608	57,081	59,689
Arkansas	1825					157	1,871	2,028
Michigan	1842	6	11	97	1,220	1,334	45,716	47,050
Florida Ter.	1831		1	9	33	43	784	827
Wisconsin T.	1840	1	6	36	126	169	5,054	5,223
D. Columbia	1832	1	3	24	68	96	1,153	1,249
		623	2,685	14,410	47,750	65,625	1,419,965	1,749,082

MILITARY POSTS

POSTS	STATE OR TERRITORY	POST OFFICE	PERMANENT COMMANDERS	REGIMENT AND CORPS
Fort Pickens	Florida	Pensacola	Maj. Jacob Brown	7th infantry
Fort McRee	"	"	"	7th infantry
Fort Morgan	Alabama	Mobile		
Fort Pike	Louisiana	Fort Pike	Capt. Fran. Lee	7th infantry
Fort Wood	"	New Orleans	Bvt. Maj. Rains	7th infantry
N. Orl's Barracks	"	New Orleans	Capt. S. W. Moore	7th infantry
Baton Rouge Bar'ks.	"	Baton Rouge	Lt. Col. Whistler	2d dragoons
Fort Jesup	"	Fort Jesup	Col. D. E. Twiggs	2d dragoons
Fort Towson	Arkansas Ter.	Fort Towson	Bt. Maj. Andrews	6th infantry
Fort Washita	"	"	Bvt. Col. Harney	2d dragoons
Fort Gibson	"	Fort Gibson	Lt. Col. Loomis	6th infantry
Fort Smith	"	Fort Smith	Maj. Hoffman	6th infantry
Fort Scott	Missouri Ter.	Fort Scott	Bt. Maj. Graham	4th infantry
Fort Leavenworth	"	Ft. Leavenworth	Col. S. W. Kearney	1st dragoons
Jefferson Barracks	Missouri	Jefferson Bar'ks.	Col. J. H. Vose	4th infantry
Fort Des Moines	Iowa Ter.	Fairfield	Capt. Jas. Allen	1st dragoons
Fort Atkinson	"	Prairie du Chien	Capt. Summer	1st dragoons
Fort Crawford	Wisconsin T.	"	Col. Davenport	1st infantry
Fort Snelling	Iowa Ter.	Fort Snelling	Lt. Col. Wilson	1st infantry
Fort Winnebago	Wisconsin T.	Ft. Winnebago	Capt. W. R. Jouett	1st infantry

POSTS	STATE OR TERRITORY	POST OFFICE	PERMANENT COMMANDERS	REGIMENT AND CORPS
Fort Brady	Michigan	Sault St. Marie	Capt. A. Johnston	5th infantry
Fort Mackinac	"	Michillimacinac	Capt. M. Scott	5th infantry
Fort Gratiot	"	Fort Gratiot	Lt. Col. McIntosh	5th infantry
Detroit Barracks	"	Detroit	B. B. Gen. Brooke	5th infantry
Buffalo Barracks	New York	Buffalo	Lt. Col. Riley	2d infantry
Fort Niagara	"	Youngstown	Capt. T. Morris	2d infantry
Fort Ontario	"	Oswego	Capt. Barnum	2d infantry
Madison Barracks	"	Sacket's Harbor	Maj. J. Plympton	2d infantry
Plattsburg Barracks	"	Plattsburg	Capt. G. A. Waite	2d infantry
Fort Adams	Rhode Island	Newport	Lt. Col. Pierce	1st artillery
Fort Wolcott	"	"	"	1st artillery
Fort Trumbull	Connecticut	New London	Capt. merchant	2d artillery
West Point	New York	West Point	Maj. R. Delafield	Engineers
Fort Columbus	N. York Harbor	New York	Col. J. Bankhead	2d artillery
Fort Hamilton	"	Fort Hamilton	Maj. John Erving	2d artillery
Fort La Fayette	"	"	Capt. A. Lowd	2d artillery
Fort Mifflin	Pennsylvania	Philadelphia	Capt. G. S. Drane	2d artillery
Carlisle Barracks	"	Carlisle	Capt. Washington	4th artillery
Hancock Barracks	Maine	Houlton	Maj. L. Whiting	1st artillery
Fort Sullivan	"	Eastport	Bt. Maj. Saunders	1st artillery
Fort Preble	"	Portland	Capt. G. Porter	1st artillery
Fort Constitution	N. Hampshire	Portsmouth	Bvt. Maj. Dimick	1st artillery

POSTS	STATE OR TERRITORY	POST OFFICE	PERMANENT COMMANDERS	REGIMENT AND CORPS
Fort Independence	Massachusetts	Boston	Not garrisoned	
Fort McHenry	Maryland	Baltimore	Lt. Col. Payne	4th artillery
Fort Severn	"	Annapolis	Bvt. Maj. Gardner	4th artillery
Fort Washington	"	Ft. Washington	Not garrisoned	
Fort Monroe	Virginia	Old P'nt Comfort	Col. J.B.Walbach	4th artillery
Fort Johnston	N. Carolina	Smithville	Bt. Lt. Col. Childs	3d artillery
Fort Caswell	"	"	"	3d artillery
Fort Macon	"	Beaufort	Capt. w. Wall	3d artillery
Fort Moultrie	Charleston	Charleston	Bvt. Brig. Gen.	3d artillery
Castle Pinckney	Harbor, S. C.	"	Armistead	3d artillery
Oglethorpe Barracks	Georgia	Savannah	Lt. Col. W. Gates	3d artillery
Fort Marion	Florida	St. Augustine	B. B. Gen. Worth	8th infantry
Key West	"	Key West	Bvt. Maj. Wright	8th infantry
Fort Brooke	"	Tampa Bay	B. Lt. Col. Belnap	8th infantry

Index

names in parentheses indicate alternative spellings
editor's notes are in brackets

C

G

H

I

J

K

L

S

T

U

V

W

Y

Z